BAD WEATHER

BAD WEATHER

By William Messner-Loebs

FANTAGRAPHICS BOOKS

FANTAGRAPHICS BOOKS
7563 Lake City Way N.E.
Seattle, WA 98115

Edited by Kim Thompson.
Original editing and additional tonework by Nadine Messner-Loebs.
Design and production by Mark Thompson.
Production assistance by Logan Bender.
Logo by Roberta Gregory.
Color separations by Rayson Films.
Special thanks to Thom Powers.

First Fantagraphics Books edition: November, 1990.
1 3 5 7 9 8 6 4 2

ISBN: 1-56097-029-4

Printed in the U.S.A.

INTRODUCTION

This volume is a joy.

It marks a long overdue return to publication for the adventures of Bill Loebs's most heartfelt alter ego, the gentle survivor, Joshua "Wolverine" Mac-Alistaire. Lord, how the comics industry could use such a pioneer to forge into the uncertain area we are faced with in the 1990s.

What's that?

You say you thought the only Wolverine in comics was a vicious little thug with razors imbedded in his forearms and whose every other word is "bub"?

Guess again, bub.

For those of you casually glancing at this book and who are maybe too young to remember comics of so long ago (those of you who *do* remember have already bought this book are reading this introduction at home, right?), let me just say that in the early '80s comics appeared to be on the verge of a revolution. Small-house publishing was a viable and lucrative reality and the market was suddenly ripe with the products of imaginations unfettered by the restraints of either corporate caution or commercial certainty. This looked to be the utopian ideal for many a young, hopeful cartoonist and even led several exuberant historians to label the '80s the Alternative Age (before they really even happened).

Amongst the people who found publishing havens to develop their off-center talents in those days were the likes of the Hernandez brothers, Steve Rude, myself, and yes, even those multi-million dollar turtles. And one of those leading the pack was Bill Loebs along with his kinder, gentler Wolverine.

When I was still a fledgling art student with grand hopes for a career as a published cartoonist, one of the first independently produced comics I happened upon was the first issue of *Journey*. I remember my amazement at the simplicity of the story's structure (the entire first half of the issue is about an unknown mountain man being tirelessly chased by a bear), and yet not for a moment was my attention any less than enthralled. I didn't know a thing about this character and yet I was soon breathing just as hard as he in his frenzied efforts to shake that damn bear!

Well, that mountain man was soon revealed to be Joshua MacAlistaire, or as he was better known in the Michigan wilderness, Wolverine. Over the next several years, and almost thirty issues, we came to know the ol' scout a little better with every read. Wolverine himself is a contradiction in terms. As mysterious as the very wilderness he inhabits, we soon find Josh to be a unique blend of Popeye,

Daniel Boone, Alistaire Cooke, and even Chuck Jones! Beyond the myriad fun and excitement to be found in his company, we are also treated to a wide range of historical fact, introduced to us so very subtly that we are hardly even aware of our education! This Wolverine was truly a trailblazer.

But what makes Josh and this stage of Bill's career so special? Haven't there been historical comics before? Hasn't the Loebs talent moved on to many other, higher-profile (and better paying) creative endeavors since then? Christ, haven't I seen his name in association with Batman and even the Justice League?! What greater success could a cartoonist ask for?

He could ask for that ideal again. That barren and beautiful gestalt that is his and his alone to do with only and completely what he pleases. Wolverine needs to roam the wilds, for it is with his lanky, buck-skinned buddy that Bill is most truly at home. In the character of Wolverine, Bill has found the vehicle for best expressing himself. Through Wolverine's eyes we are most able to see the world as Bill sees it, a place of indescribable beauty and unmentionable horror; a world that is at the same time demanding, exacting, fulfilling, and sometimes just plain fun. Now which of the big companies, I ask you, would take a chance on something as hard to imagine as that? Isn't life a black-and-white monochrome comprising heroes on one end and villains on the other, with the middle filled in by pubescent sexual fantasies and angst?

No, it isn't.

Bill Loebs knows it isn't.

But, as so often happens in life, we are regularly forced to divide ourselves between that which is necessary to survive physically and that which is necessary to survive both emotionally and spiritually.

Wolverine would know all about that.

So Bill has had to temporarily dig himself under in order to weather the rather blizzardous aftermath of comics in the '80s (remember, I said it *appeared* to be a revolution), and we're the poorer for it. But, as Wolverine could also tell you, no winter lasts forever—even in the wild, wild west—and so, I know that Bill's just waiting for the spring.

We all need that spiritual thaw, Bill.

Hopefully, that sleeping bear will break its hibernation and once again begin to chase ol' Josh across the face of our industry. Such a spirit just refuses to be broken.

Hey. . .here comes the sun.

—MATT WAGNER

EXPLANATIONS
AND APOLOGIES
FROM THE AUTHOR

Those of you encountering this odd frontier world of mine for the first time may be a little off put. This is actually the second volume of collected issues of *Journey*. The first was called *Tall Tales* and is still available from this esteemed publisher. There was very little in that volume which is needed to understand this, except that the year is around 1810 and the place is the Michigan Territories, far beyond the last line of civilization represented by Dearbornville.

It did seem to me that there are a couple of elements in these stories which might be confusing to readers not present when they first appeared in 1983. The first is *Neil the Horse*. Neil was Arn Saba's affectionate tribute to the animated (and surreal) cartoons of the '20s and '30s. He put Neil, his buddy Soapy, and the lovely and romantic puppet, Mam'zelle Poupee, through a number of adventures in his attempt to "Make the World Safe for Musical Comedy." When *Journey* first began, Arn had just started the story *Neil the Horse in New France*, set in the Canada of the 1720s. It struck me that Joshua MacAlistaire, living so close by, might come across some evidence of their passing. And I tried to make the story as romantic, idealistic, wacky, and tune-filled as the book (and the man) that inspired it. Good luck wherever you are, Arn, old pal.

The other confusing element is Ft. Miami, with its little dreaming sentry and cast of unexplained characters. I had originally meant to pull those pages and put them in a later volume, dedicated exclusively to the Ft. Miami storyline, but I realized that there was some interaction with the main plot that made that impossible. So you'll just have to have faith that I won't leave these upstanding citizens stranded in the middle of nowhere. Trust me.

Finally, I'd like to apologize to whatever *Journey* fans remain, for the delays in publishing this volume. Everything that could have gone wrong did, and none of it was the fault of the fine folks at Fantagraphics, who have been rock-solid through all my explanations and delays. Thanks, guys. Here's hoping the next one gets out quicker.

Bread and roses,
BILL

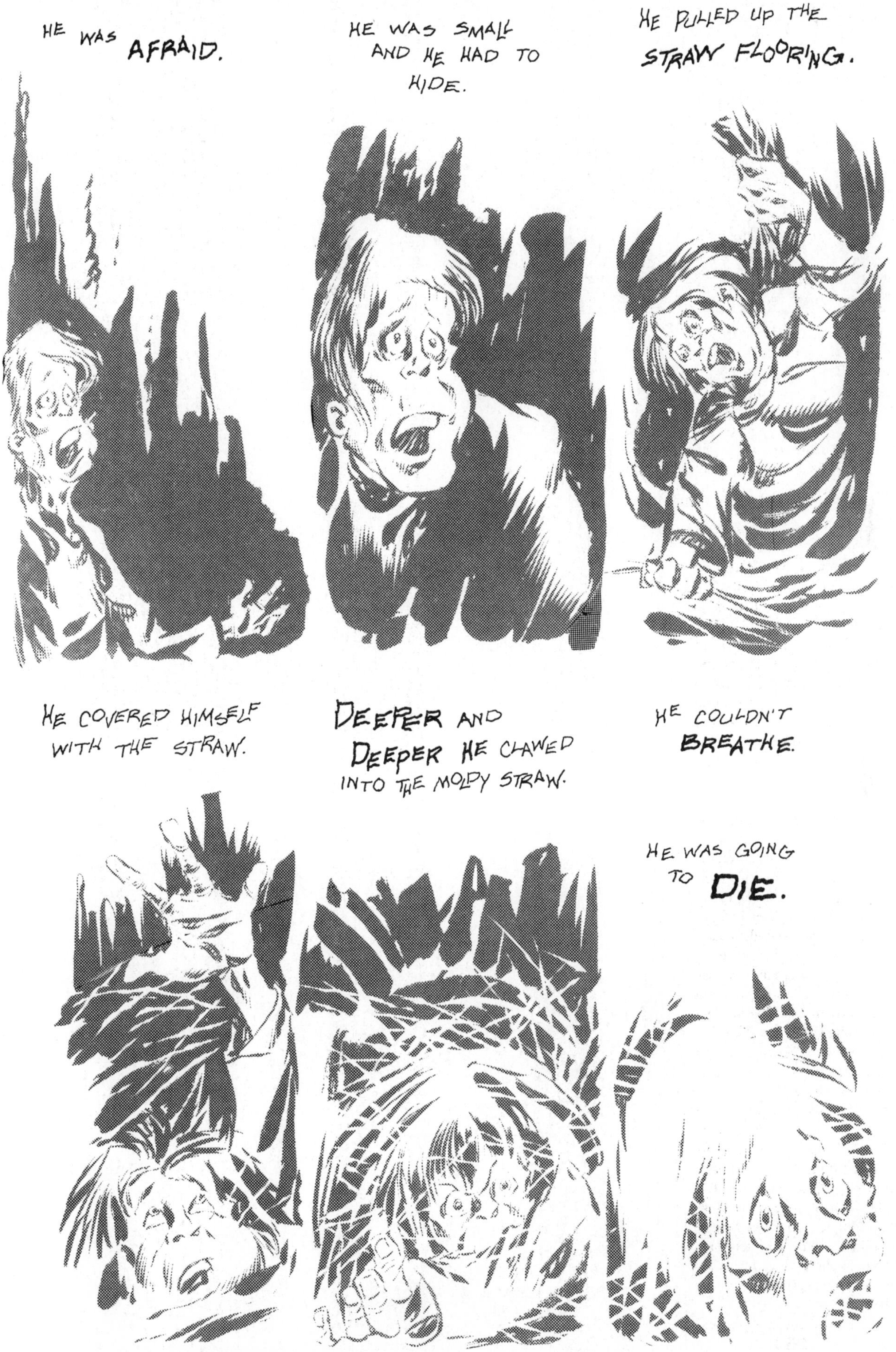
HE WAS AFRAID.
HE WAS SMALL AND HE HAD TO HIDE.
HE PULLED UP THE STRAW FLOORING.
HE COVERED HIMSELF WITH THE STRAW.
DEEPER AND DEEPER HE CLAWED INTO THE MOLDY STRAW.
HE COULDN'T BREATHE.
HE WAS GOING TO DIE.

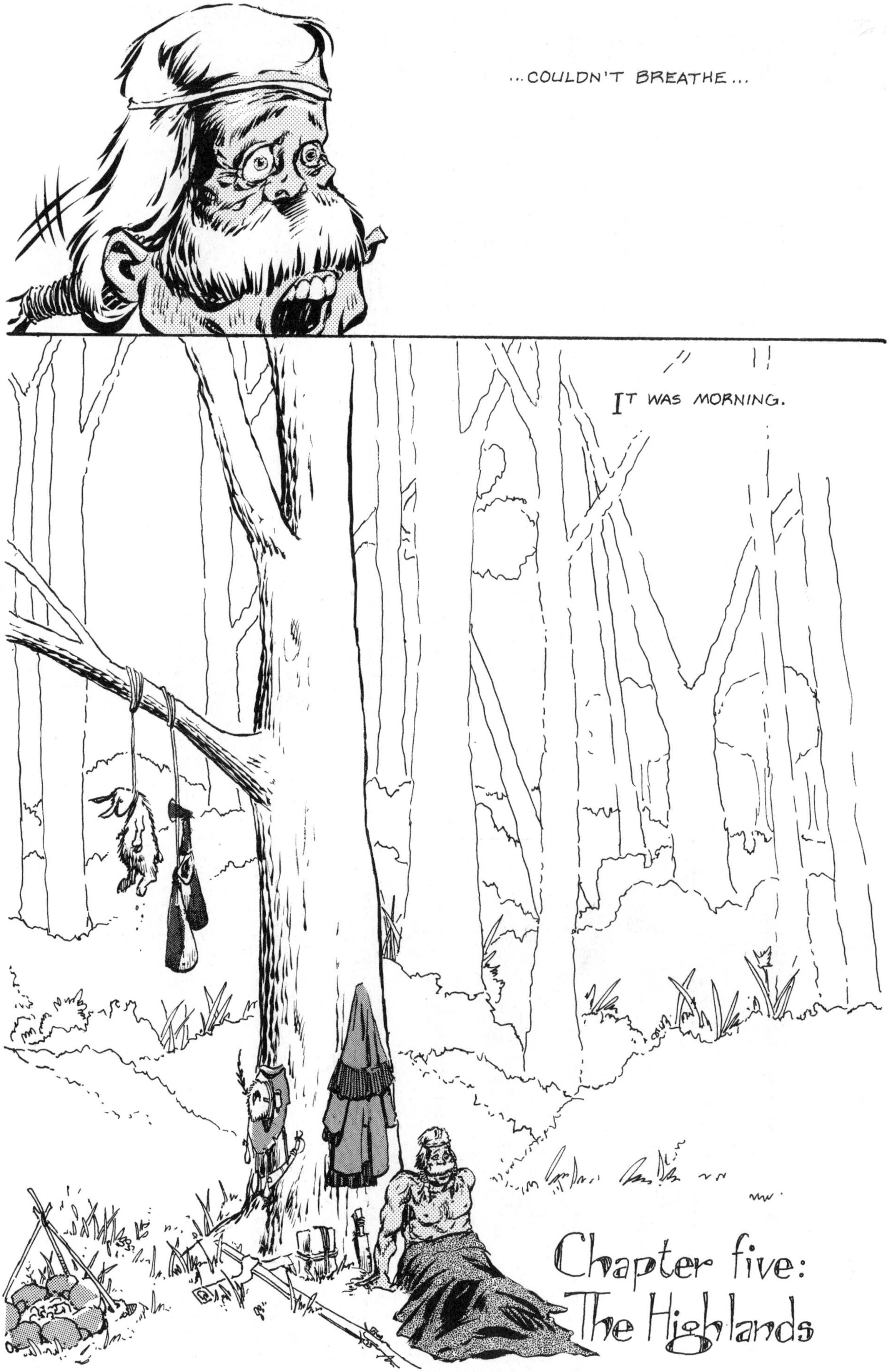
...COULDN'T BREATHE...
IT WAS MORNING.
Chapter five:
The Highlands

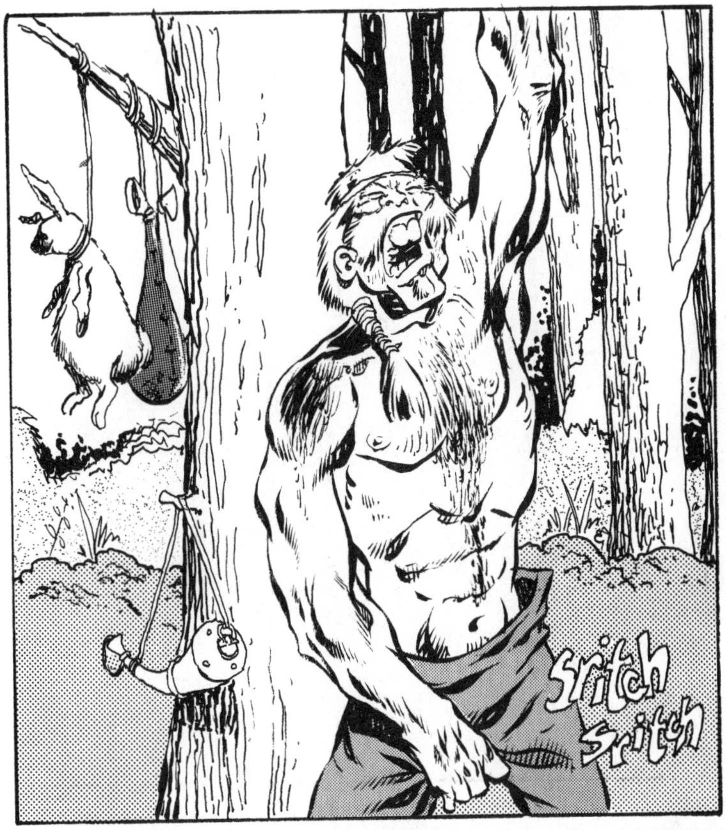
SRITCH
SRITCH

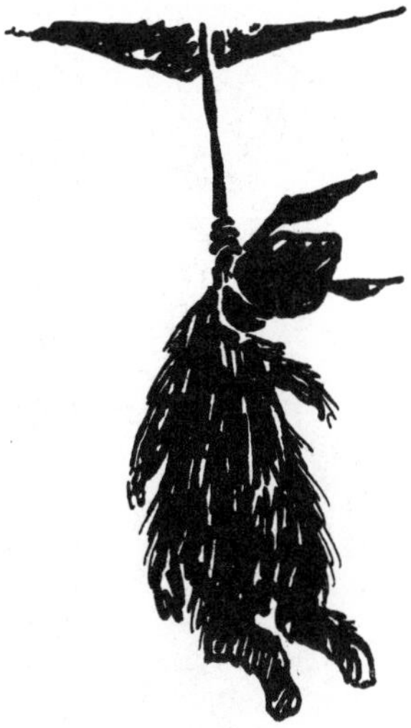

HE WAS GREASE-HUNGRY AND EAGER FOR THE FAT RABBIT HE'D SNARED THE DAY BEFORE. HOWEVER...

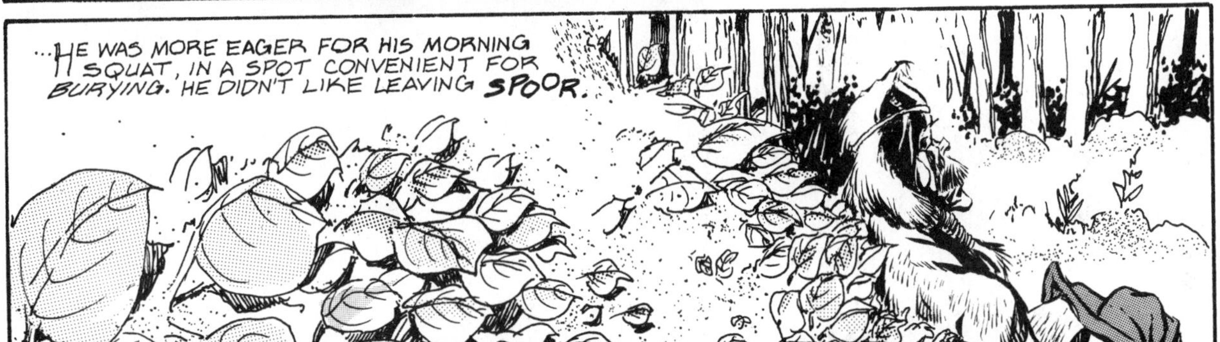
...HE WAS MORE EAGER FOR HIS MORNING SQUAT, IN A SPOT CONVENIENT FOR BURYING. HE DIDN'T LIKE LEAVING SPOOR.

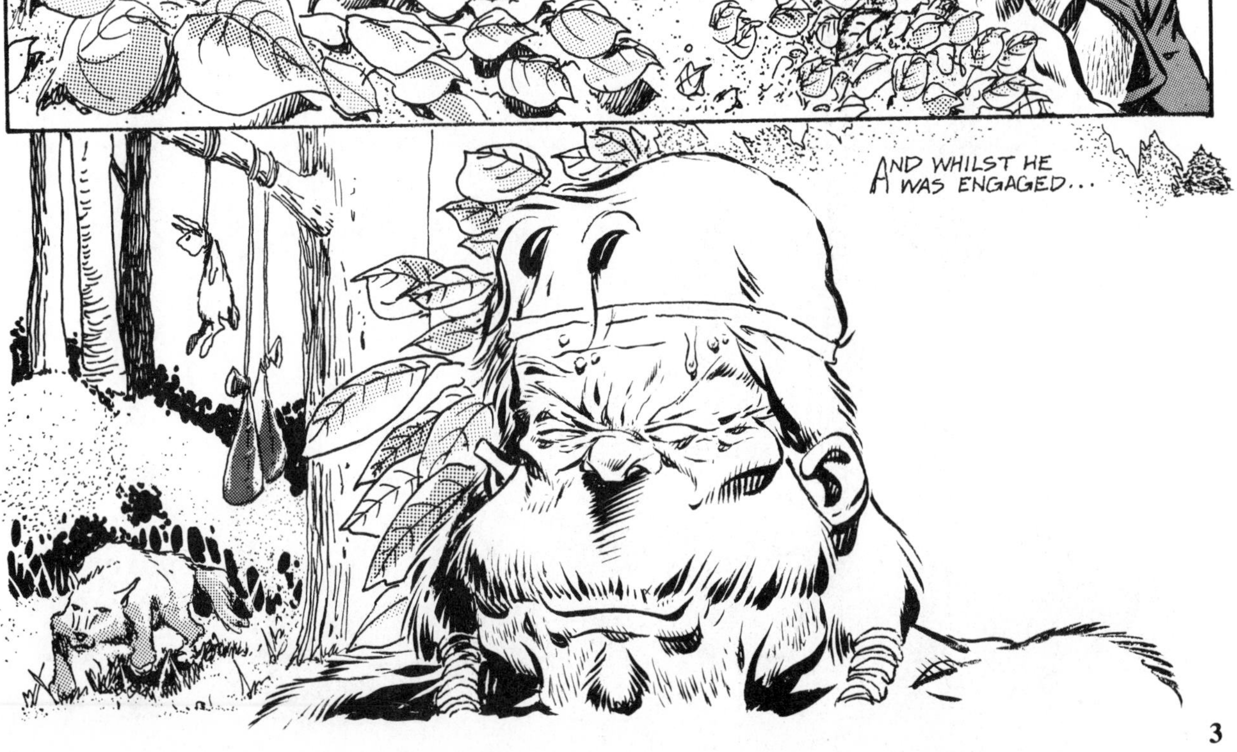
AND WHILST HE WAS ENGAGED...

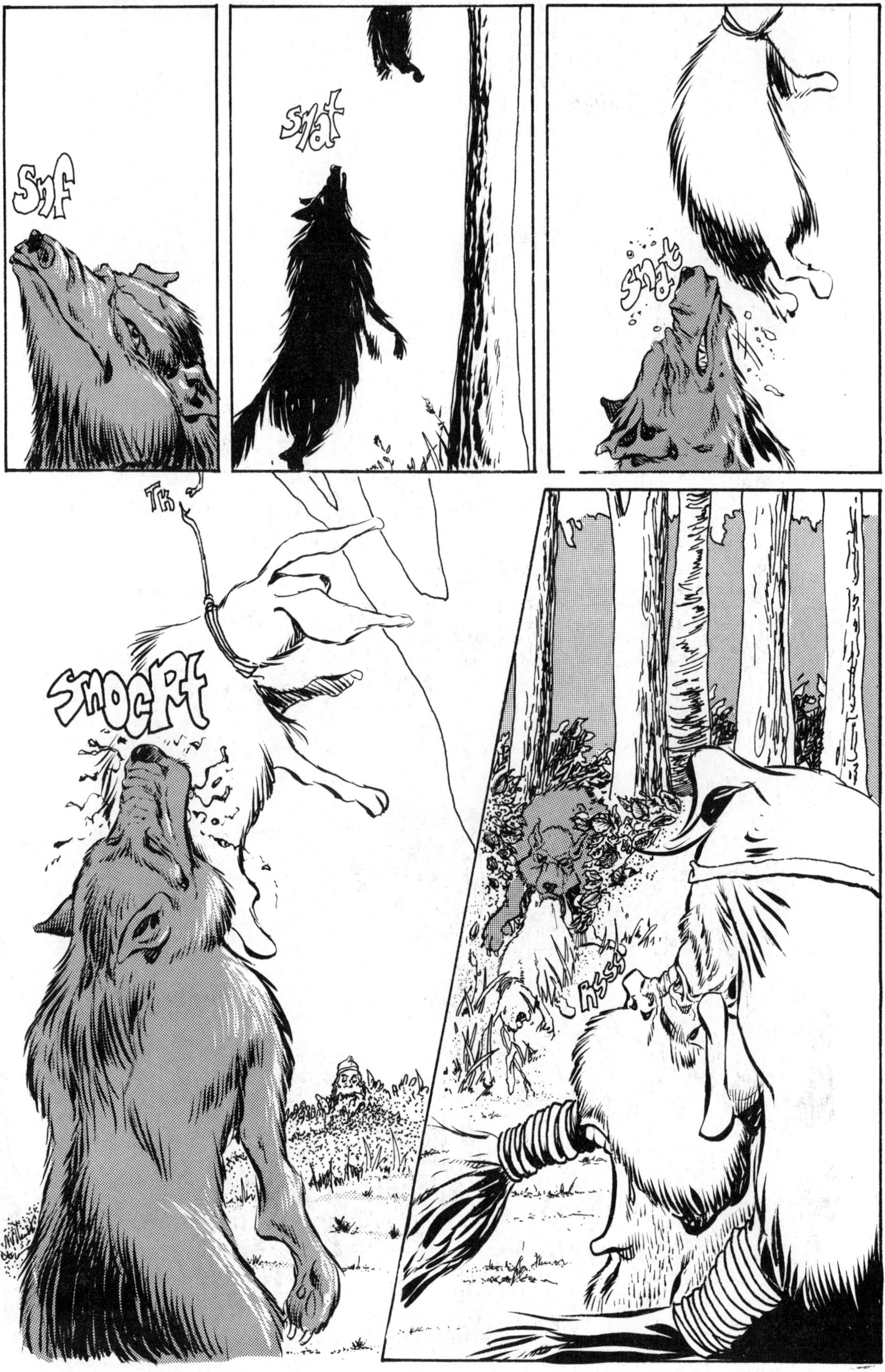
Snf
Snat
Snat
Tk
SNOCRt
Rsss

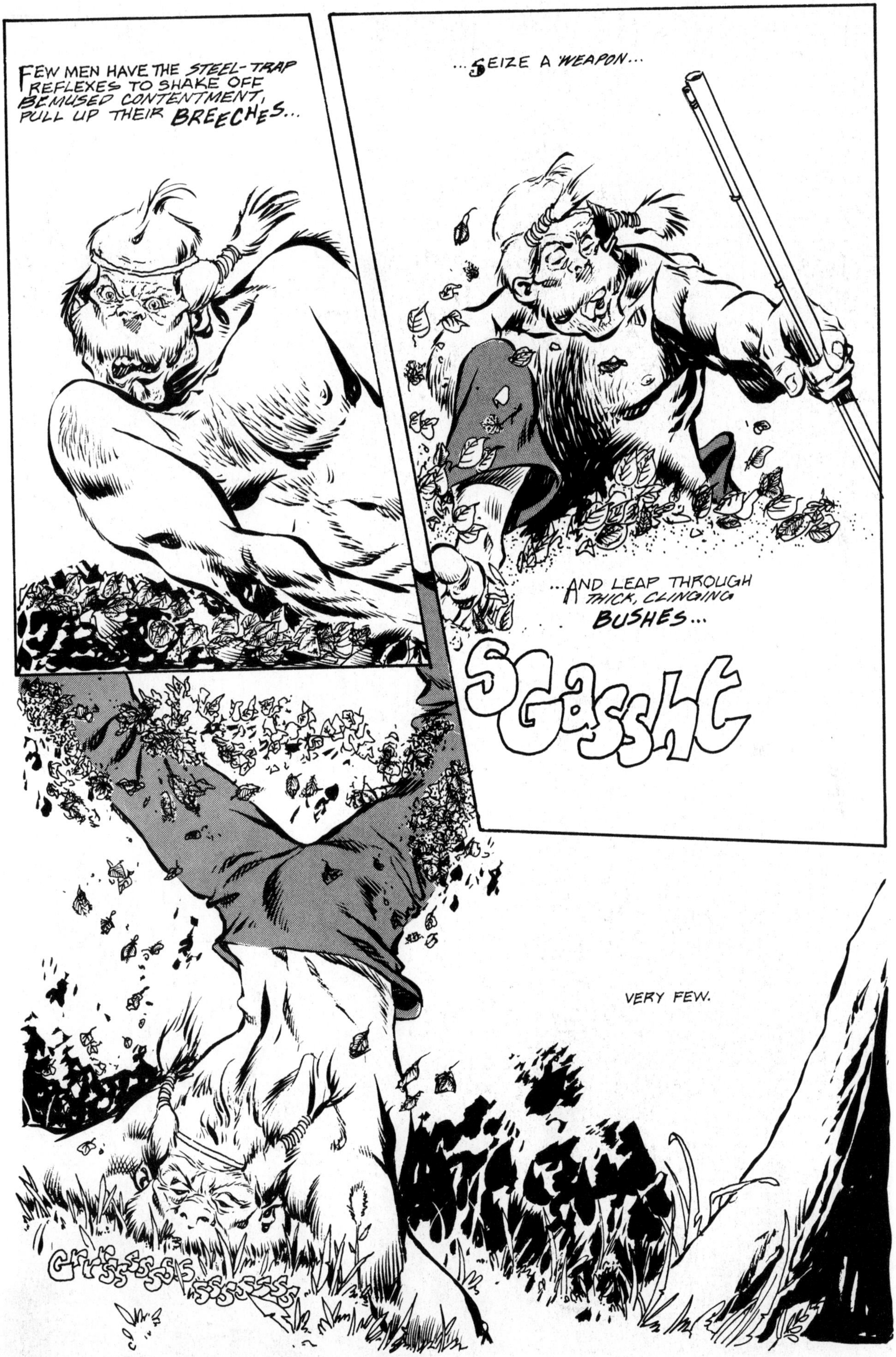

FEW MEN HAVE THE STEEL-TRAP REFLEXES TO SHAKE OFF BEMUSED CONTENTMENT, PULL UP THEIR BREECHES...
...SEIZE A WEAPON...
...AND LEAP THROUGH THICK, CLINGING BUSHES...
SGASSHT
VERY FEW.

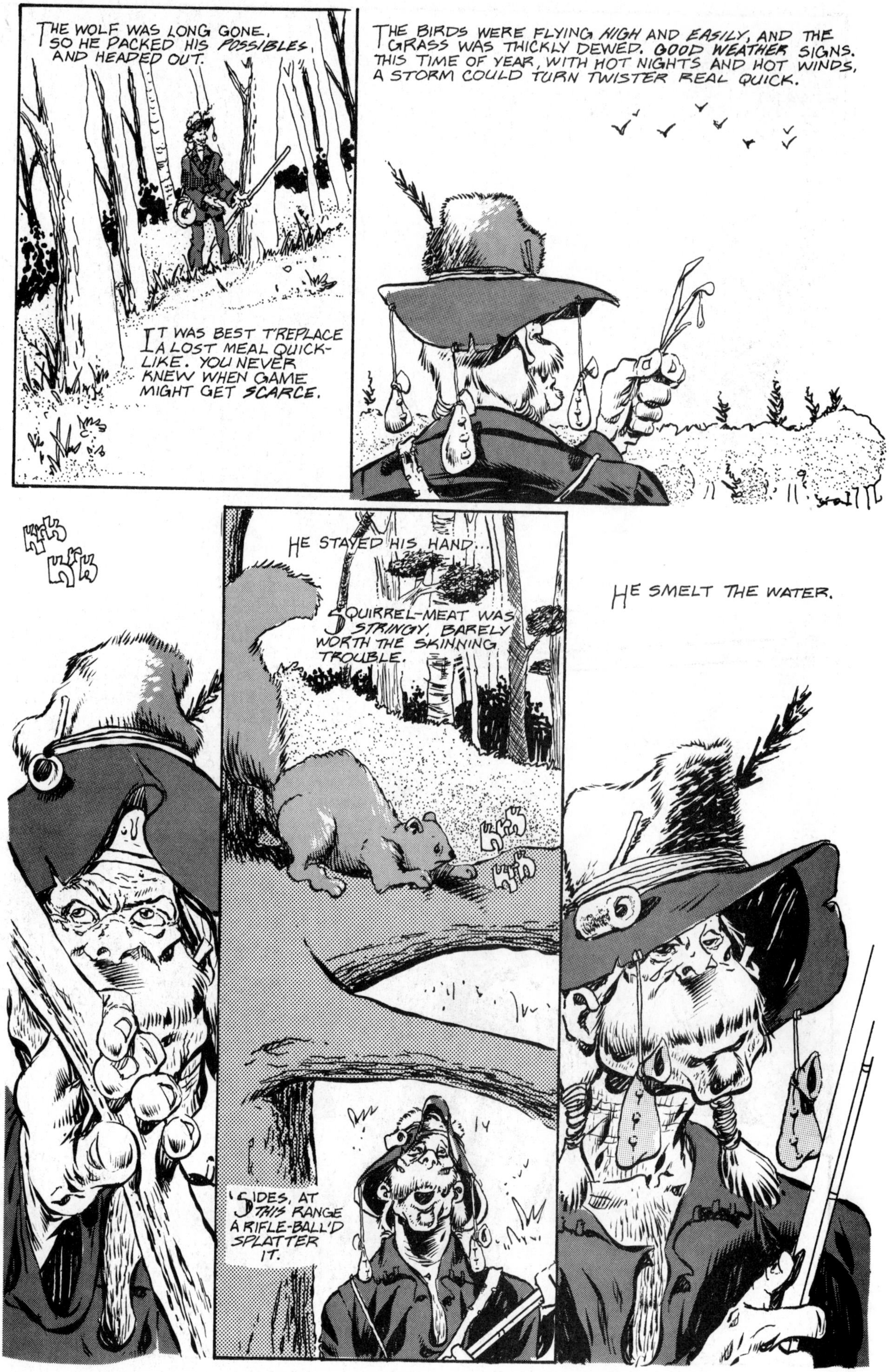
THE WOLF WAS LONG GONE, SO HE PACKED HIS POSSIBLES, AND HEADED OUT.
IT WAS BEST T'REPLACE A LOST MEAL QUICK-LIKE. YOU NEVER KNEW WHEN GAME MIGHT GET SCARCE.
THE BIRDS WERE FLYING HIGH AND EASILY, AND THE GRASS WAS THICKLY DEWED. GOOD WEATHER SIGNS. THIS TIME OF YEAR, WITH HOT NIGHTS AND HOT WINDS, A STORM COULD TURN TWISTER REAL QUICK.
HE STAYED HIS HAND...
SQUIRREL-MEAT WAS STRINGY, BARELY WORTH THE SKINNING TROUBLE.
'SIDES, AT THIS RANGE A RIFLE-BALL'D SPLATTER IT.
HE SMELT THE WATER.

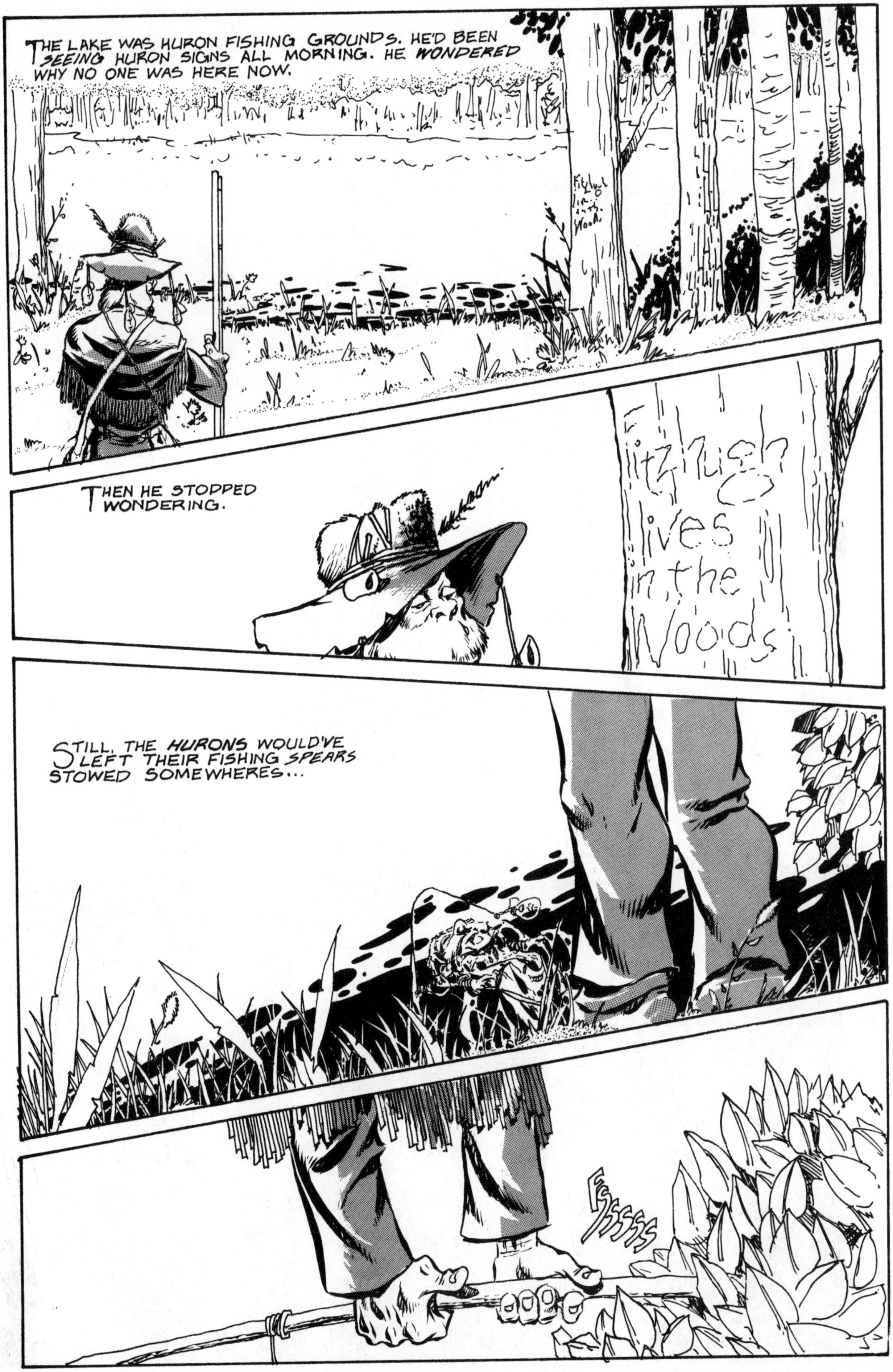
THE LAKE WAS HURON FISHING GROUNDS. HE'D BEEN SEEING HURON SIGNS ALL MORNING. HE WONDERED WHY NO ONE WAS HERE NOW.
Fitzhugh lives in the Woods
THEN HE STOPPED WONDERING.
STILL, THE HURONS WOULD'VE LEFT THEIR FISHING SPEARS STOWED SOMEWHERES...
FSSSSSS

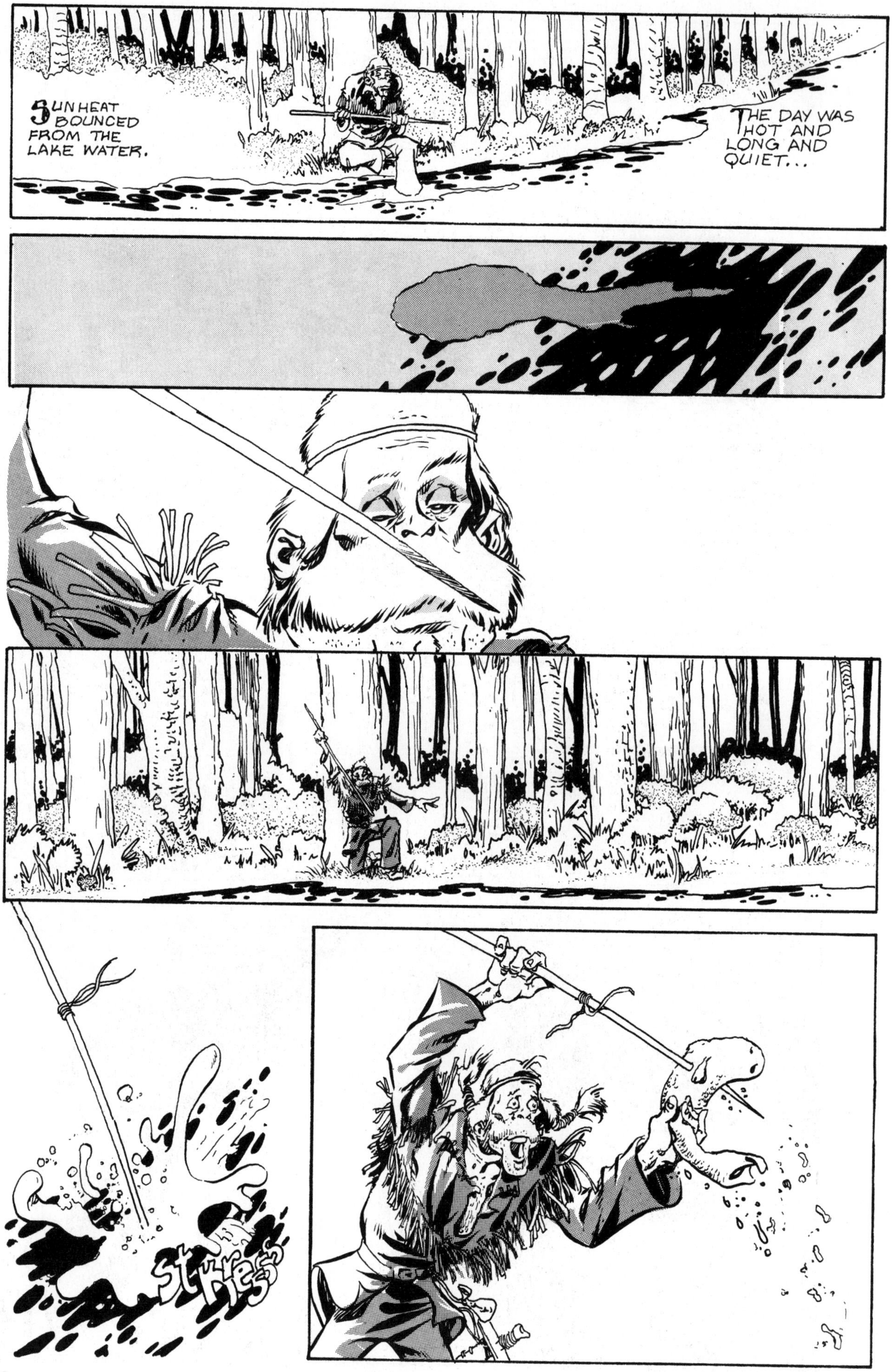
SUNHEAT BOUNCED FROM THE LAKE WATER.
THE DAY WAS HOT AND LONG AND QUIET...
STRESS

HE DRIFTED IN THE PLEASANT COOLNESS...

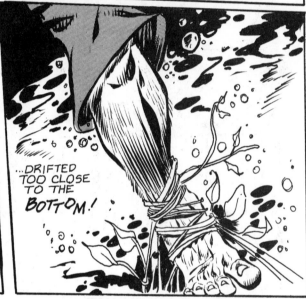

...DRIFTED TOO CLOSE TO THE BOTTOM!

HE WAS TRAPPED...

...TRAPPED UNDER THE STRAW...

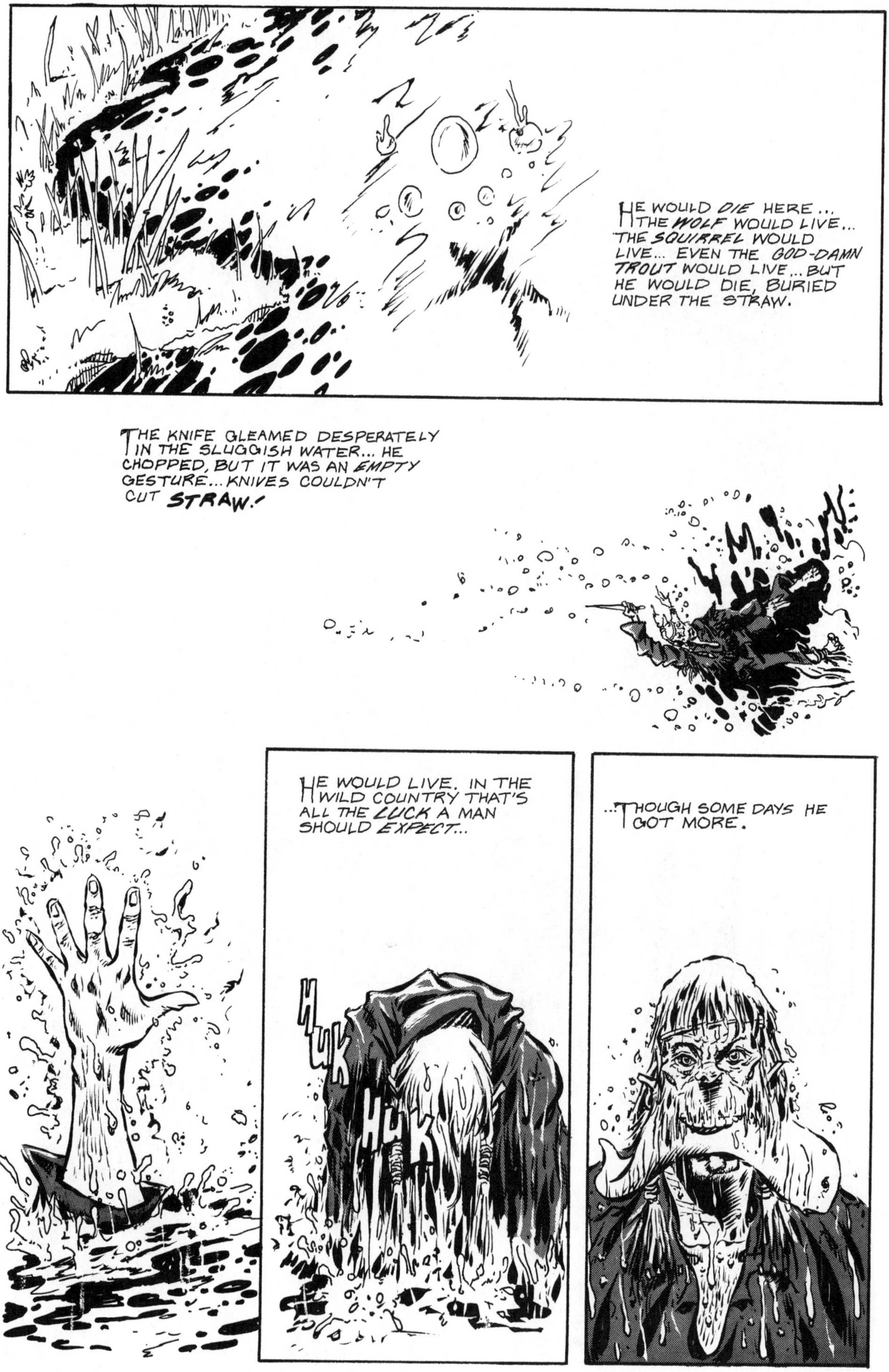
HE WOULD DIE HERE... THE WOLF WOULD LIVE... THE SQUIRREL WOULD LIVE... EVEN THE GOD-DAMN TROUT WOULD LIVE... BUT HE WOULD DIE, BURIED UNDER THE STRAW.
THE KNIFE GLEAMED DESPERATELY IN THE SLUGGISH WATER... HE CHOPPED, BUT IT WAS AN EMPTY GESTURE... KNIVES COULDN'T CUT STRAW!
HE WOULD LIVE. IN THE WILD COUNTRY THAT'S ALL THE LUCK A MAN SHOULD EXPECT...
HUK
HUK
...THOUGH SOME DAYS HE GOT MORE.

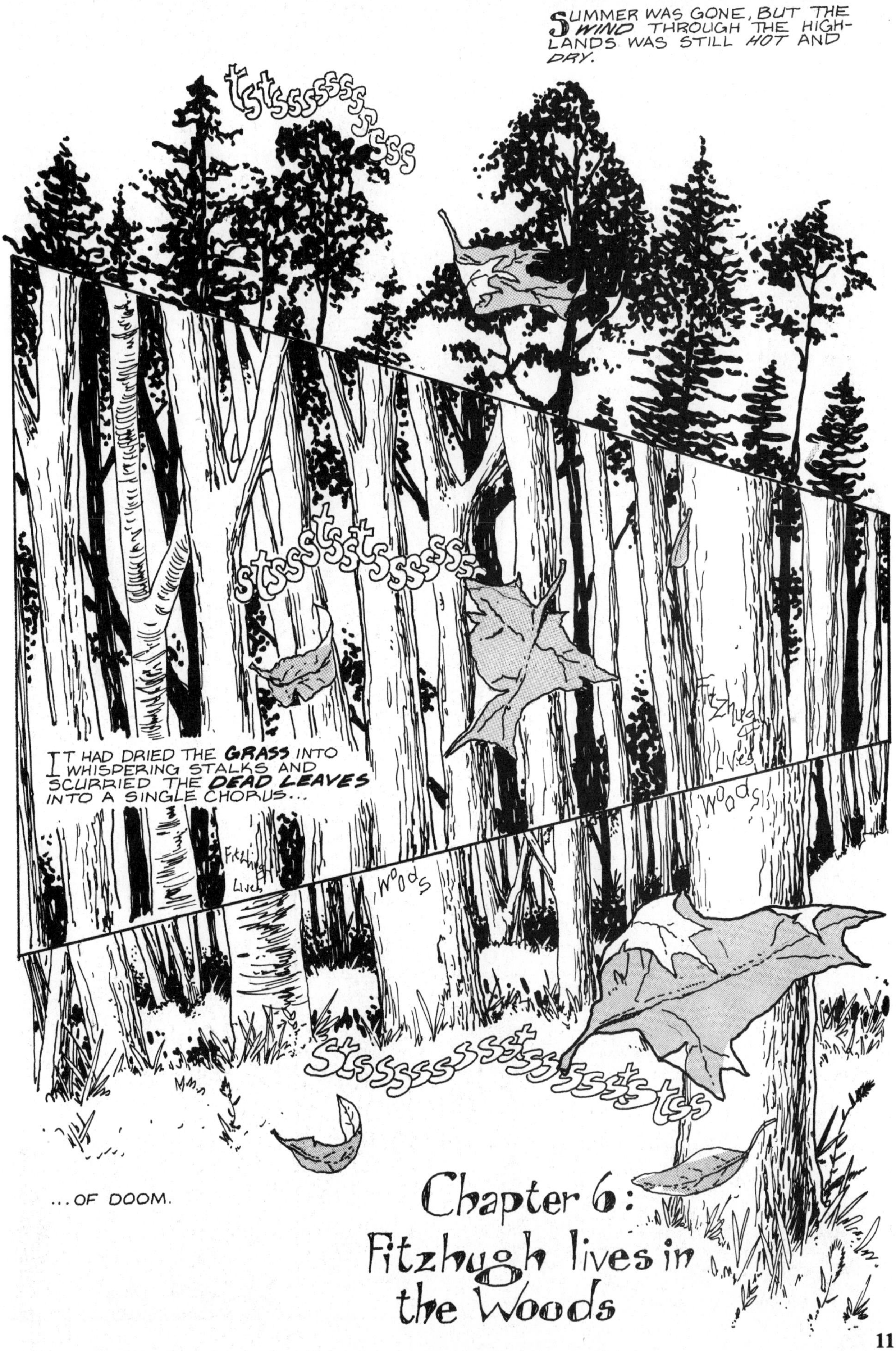
SUMMER WAS GONE, BUT THE WIND THROUGH THE HIGHLANDS WAS STILL HOT AND DRY.
tstssssssssssss
IT HAD DRIED THE GRASS INTO WHISPERING STALKS AND SCURRIED THE DEAD LEAVES INTO A SINGLE CHORUS...
stssstsstssssss
Stssssssssstsssssstss
...OF DOOM.

Chapter 6: Fitzhugh lives in the Woods

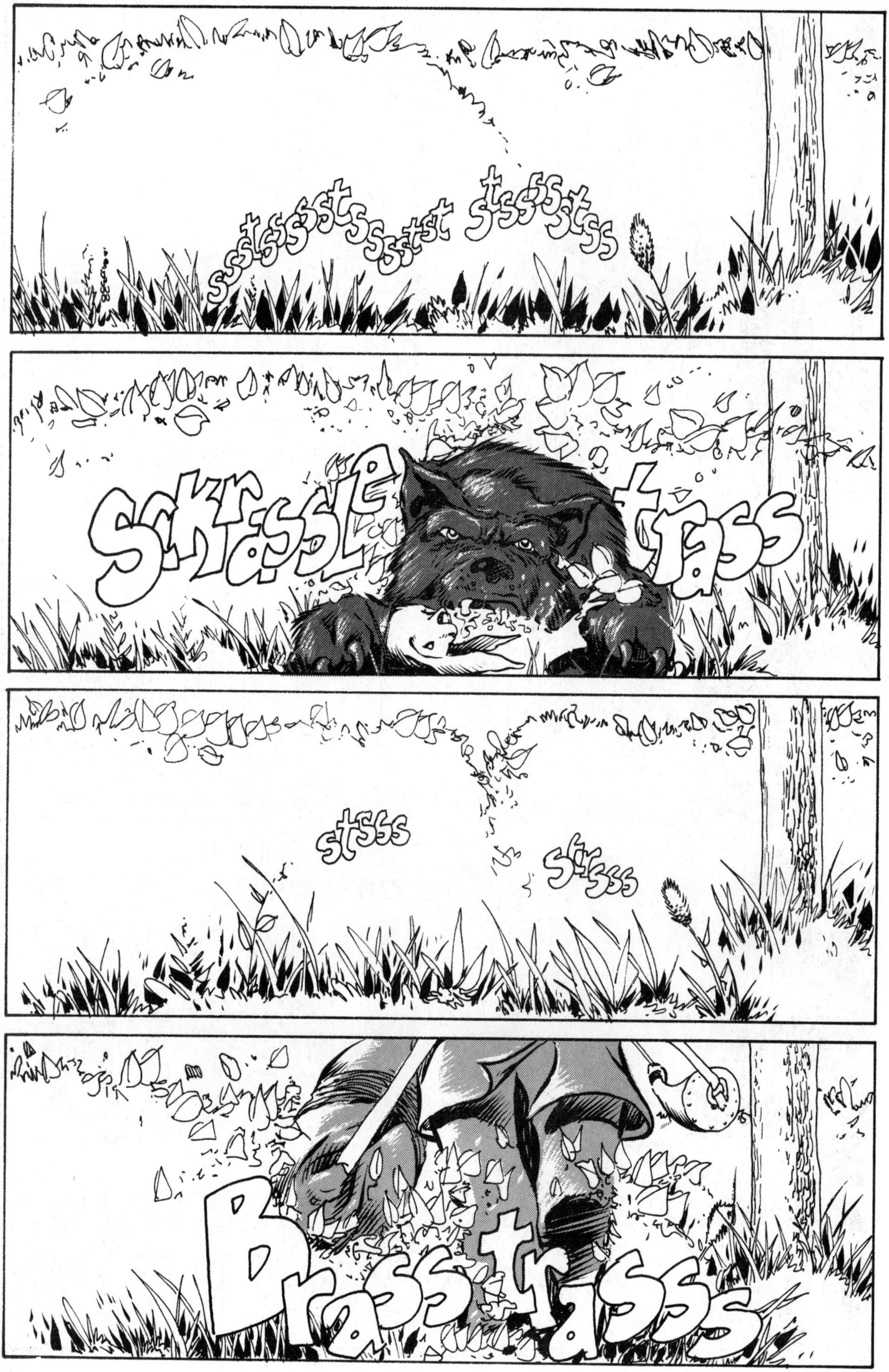
ssstsssstssssstst stsssstss
sckrassle
trass
stsss
strsss
Brasstrasss

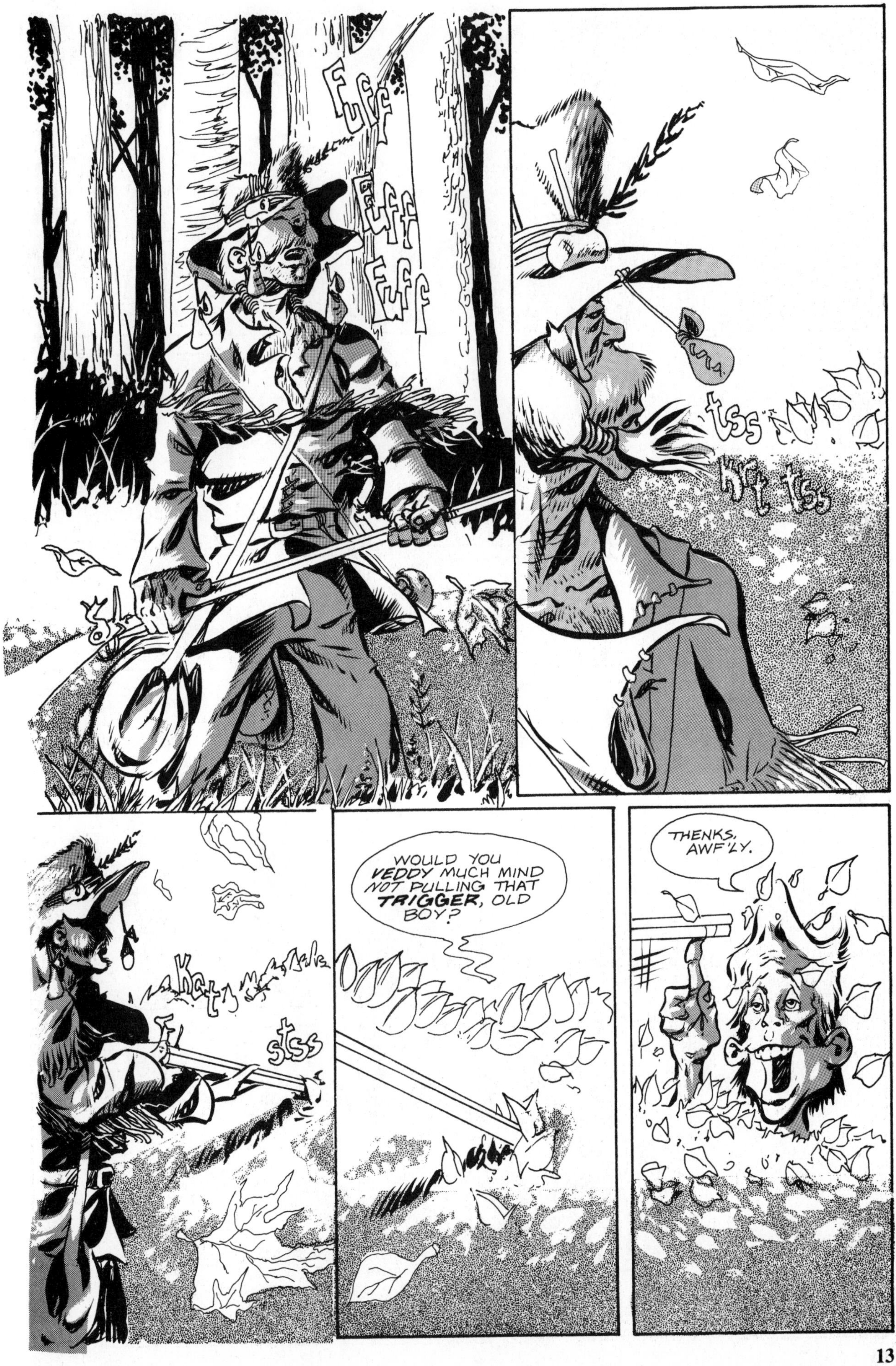
Fuff
Fuff
Fuff
tss
Kat tss
Kat
stss
WOULD YOU VEDDY MUCH MIND NOT PULLING THAT TRIGGER, OLD BOY?
THENKS, AWF'LY.

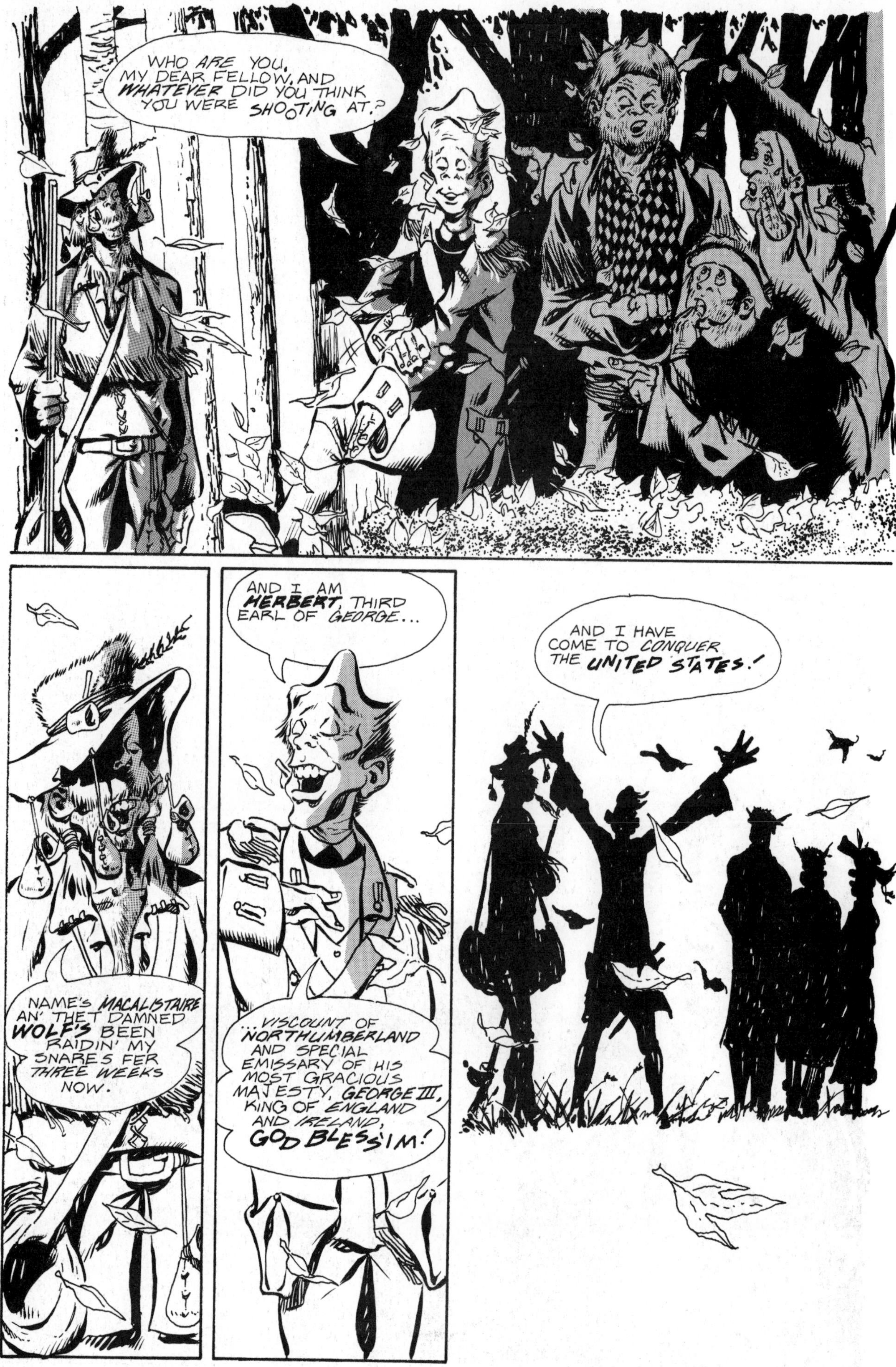
WHO ARE YOU, MY DEAR FELLOW, AND WHATEVER DID YOU THINK YOU WERE SHOOTING AT.?
NAME'S MACALISTAIRE AN' THET DAMNED WOLF'S BEEN RAIDIN' MY SNARES FER THREE WEEKS NOW.
AND I AM HERBERT, THIRD EARL OF GEORGE...
...VISCOUNT OF NORTHUMBERLAND AND SPECIAL EMISSARY OF HIS MOST GRACIOUS MAJESTY, GEORGE III, KING OF ENGLAND AND IRELAND, GOD BLESS'IM!
AND I HAVE COME TO CONQUER THE UNITED STATES.!

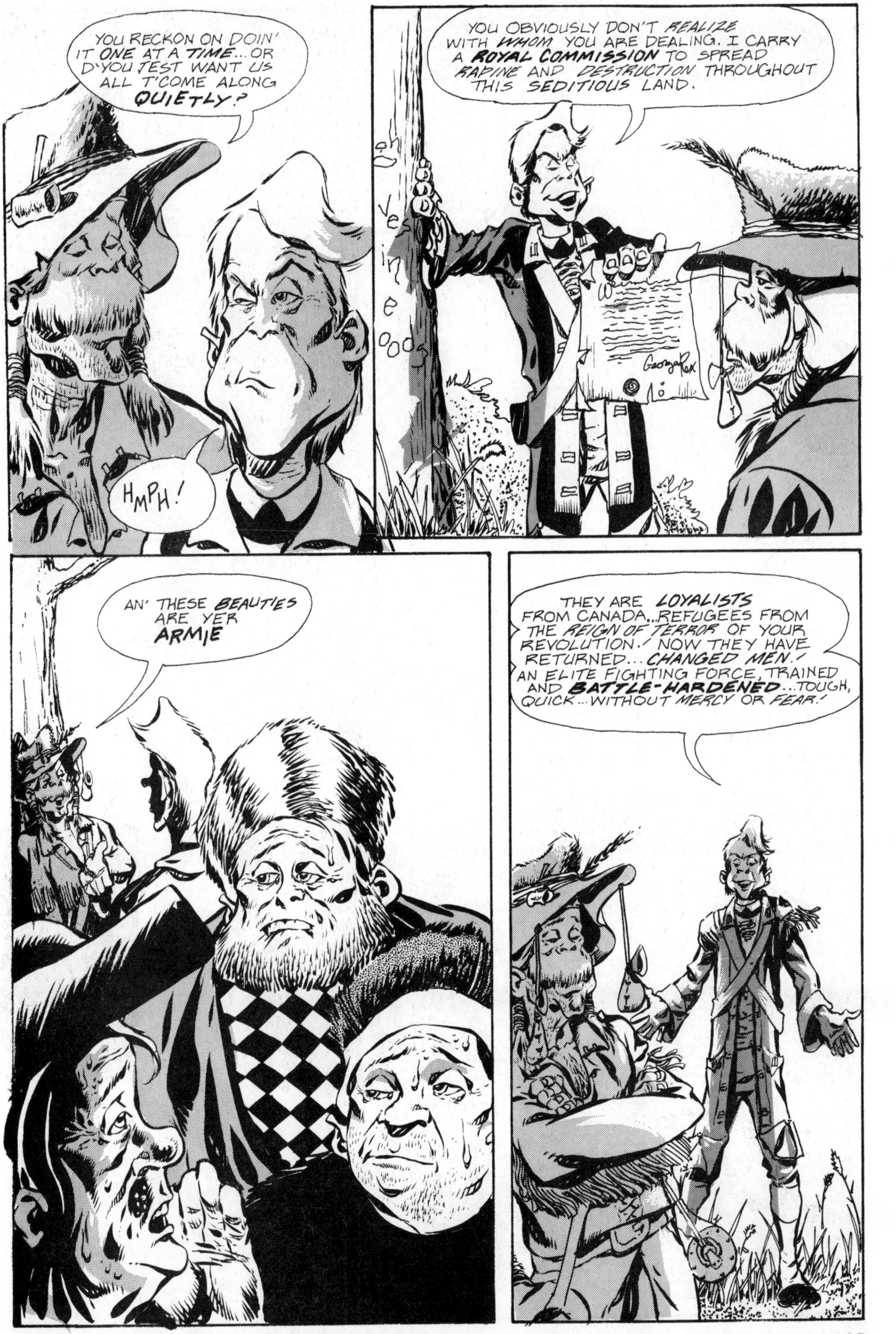
YOU RECKON ON DOIN' IT ONE AT A TIME... OR D'YOU JEST WANT US ALL T'COME ALONG QUIETLY?
HMPH!
YOU OBVIOUSLY DON'T REALIZE WITH WHOM YOU ARE DEALING. I CARRY A ROYAL COMMISSION TO SPREAD RAPINE AND DESTRUCTION THROUGHOUT THIS SEDITIOUS LAND.
AN' THESE BEAUTIES ARE YER ARMIE
THEY ARE LOYALISTS FROM CANADA... REFUGEES FROM THE REIGN OF TERROR OF YOUR REVOLUTION! NOW THEY HAVE RETURNED... CHANGED MEN! AN ELITE FIGHTING FORCE, TRAINED AND BATTLE-HARDENED... TOUGH, QUICK... WITHOUT MERCY OR FEAR!

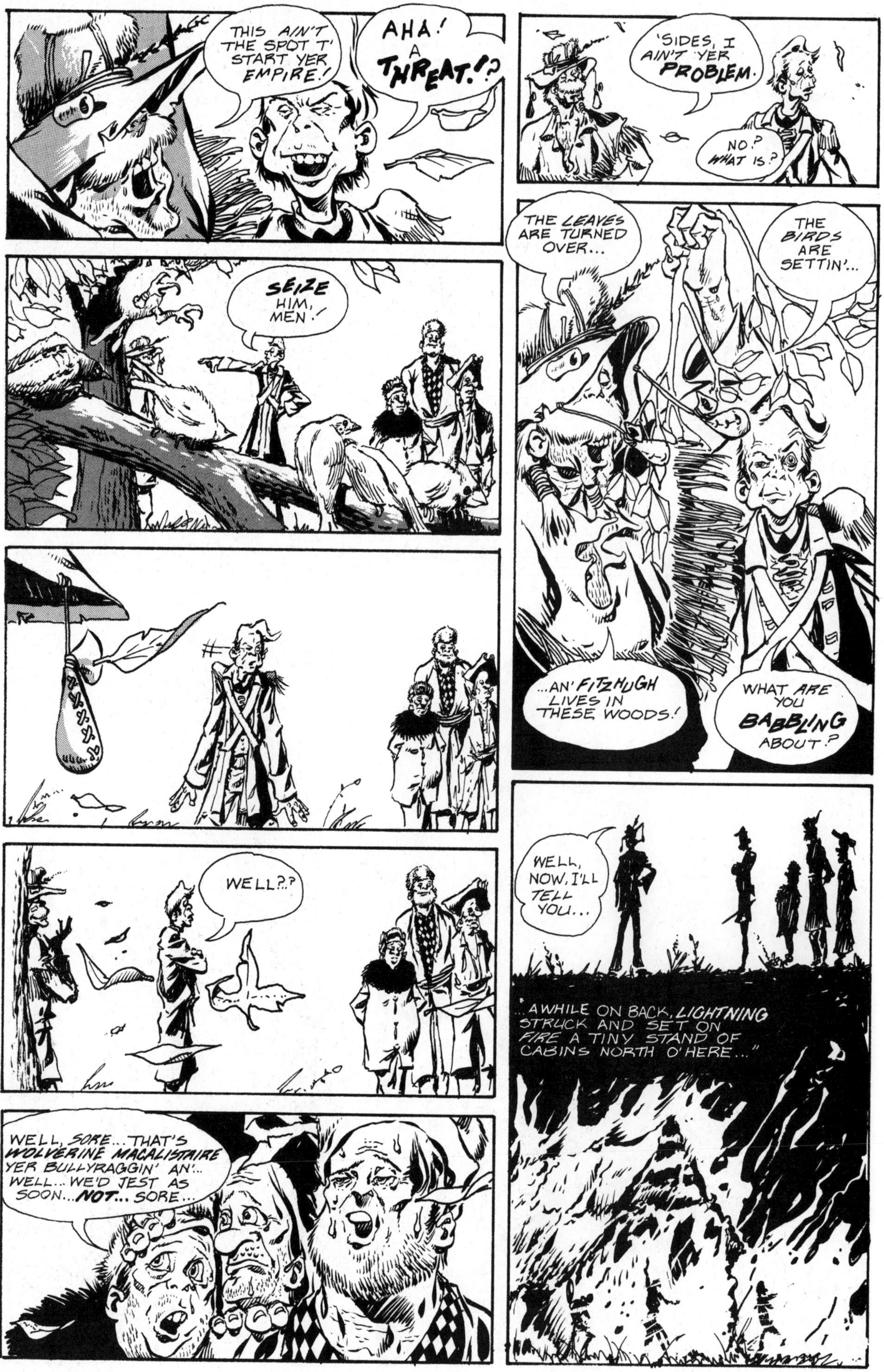
THIS AIN'T THE SPOT T' START YER EMPIRE!
AHA! A THREAT!?
'SIDES, I AIN'T YER PROBLEM.
NO? WHAT IS?
SEIZE HIM, MEN!
THE LEAVES ARE TURNED OVER...
THE BIRDS ARE SETTIN'...
...AN' FITZHUGH LIVES IN THESE WOODS!
WHAT ARE YOU BABBLING ABOUT?
WELL??
WELL, NOW, I'LL TELL YOU...
...A WHILE ON BACK, LIGHTNING STRUCK AND SET ON FIRE A TINY STAND OF CABINS NORTH O'HERE..."
WELL, SORE... THAT'S WOLVERINE MACALISTAIRE YER BULLYRAGGIN' AN'... WELL... WE'D JEST AS SOON... NOT... SORE...

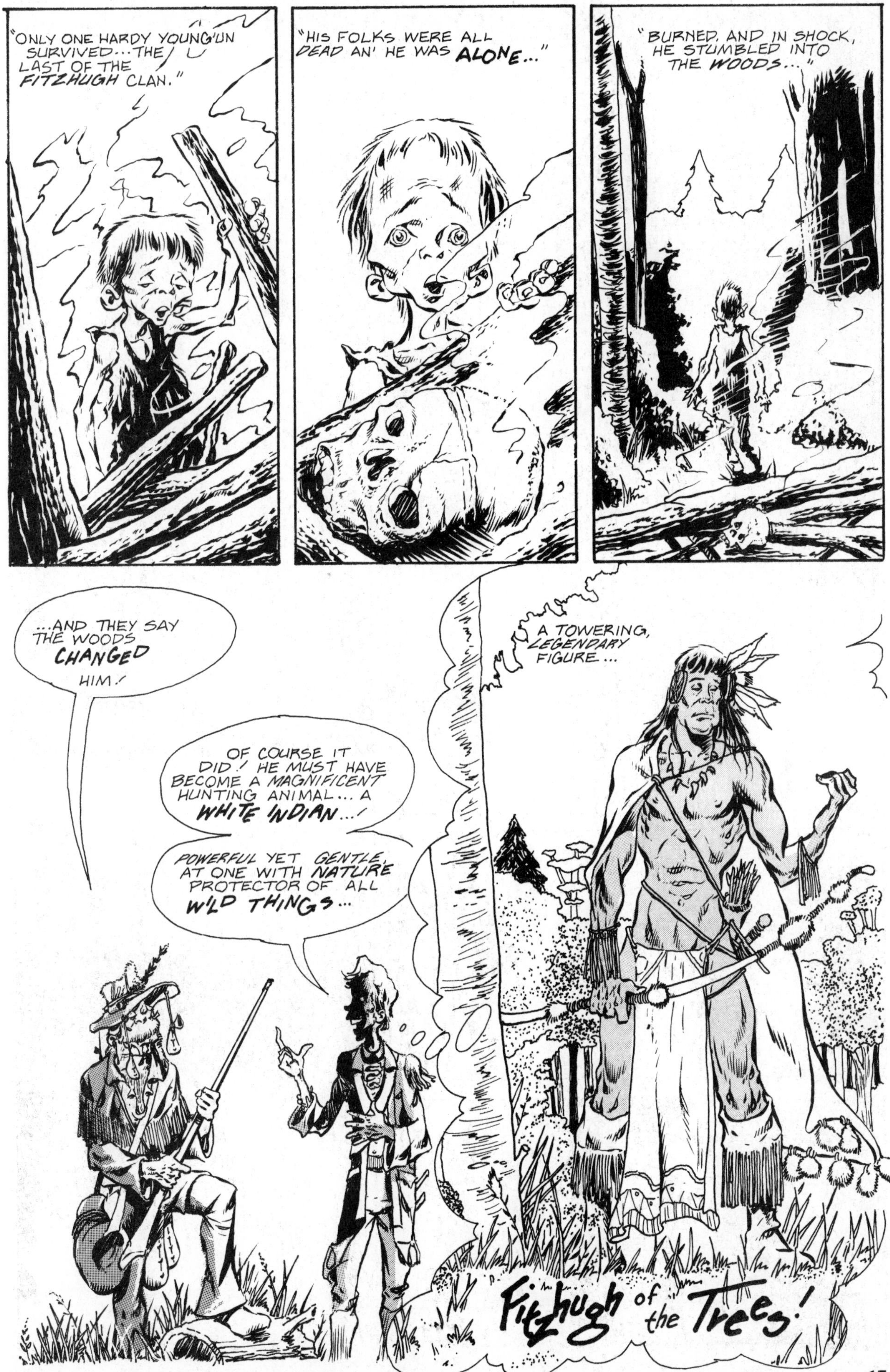
"ONLY ONE HARDY YOUNG'UN SURVIVED... THE LAST OF THE FITZHUGH CLAN."
"HIS FOLKS WERE ALL DEAD AN' HE WAS ALONE..."
"BURNED, AND IN SHOCK, HE STUMBLED INTO THE WOODS..."
...AND THEY SAY THE WOODS CHANGED HIM!
OF COURSE IT DID! HE MUST HAVE BECOME A MAGNIFICENT HUNTING ANIMAL... A WHITE INDIAN...!
POWERFUL YET GENTLE, AT ONE WITH NATURE PROTECTOR OF ALL WILD THINGS...
A TOWERING, LEGENDARY FIGURE...
Fitzhugh of the Trees!

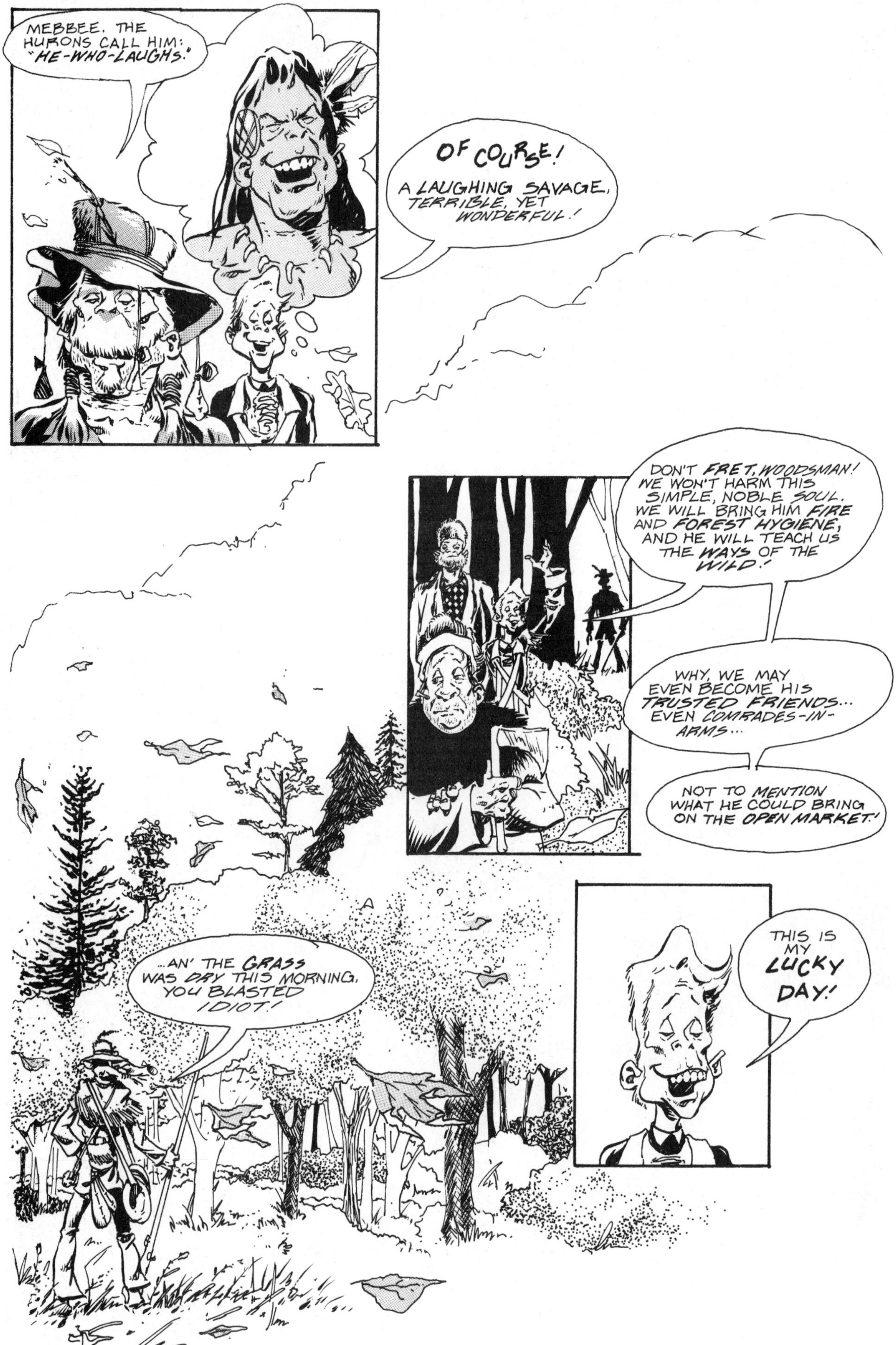
MEBBEE. THE HURONS CALL HIM: "HE-WHO-LAUGHS."
OF COURSE!
A LAUGHING SAVAGE, TERRIBLE, YET WONDERFUL!
DON'T FRET, WOODSMAN! WE WON'T HARM THIS SIMPLE, NOBLE SOUL. WE WILL BRING HIM FIRE AND FOREST HYGIENE, AND HE WILL TEACH US THE WAYS OF THE WILD!
WHY, WE MAY EVEN BECOME HIS TRUSTED FRIENDS... EVEN COMRADES-IN-ARMS...
NOT TO MENTION WHAT HE COULD BRING ON THE OPEN MARKET!
...AN' THE GRASS WAS DRY THIS MORNING, YOU BLASTED IDIOT!
THIS IS MY LUCKY DAY!

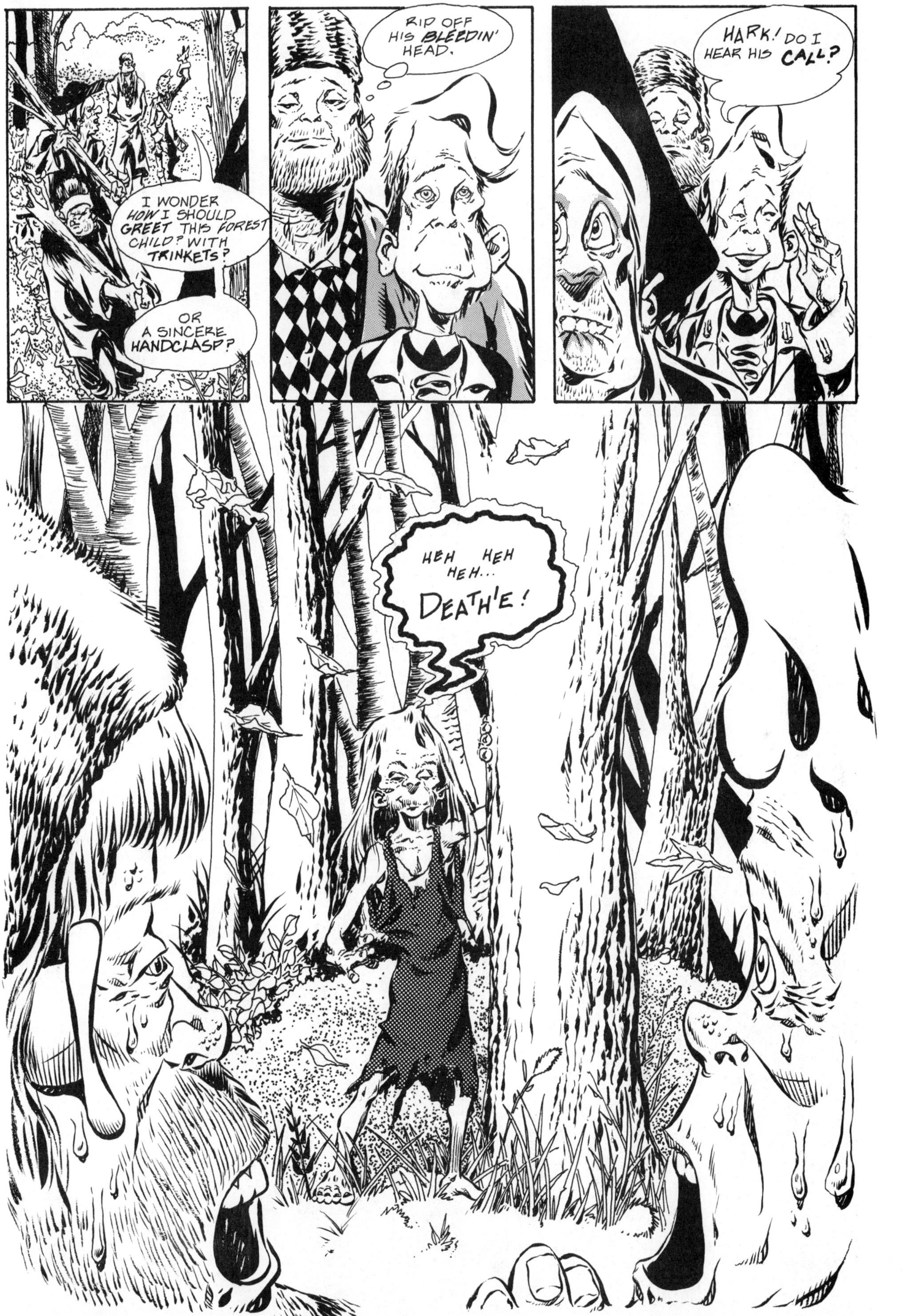
I WONDER HOW I SHOULD GREET THIS FOREST CHILD? WITH TRINKETS?
OR A SINCERE HANDCLASP?
RIP OFF HIS BLEEDIN' HEAD.
HARK! DO I HEAR HIS CALL?
HEH HEH HEH... DEATH'E!

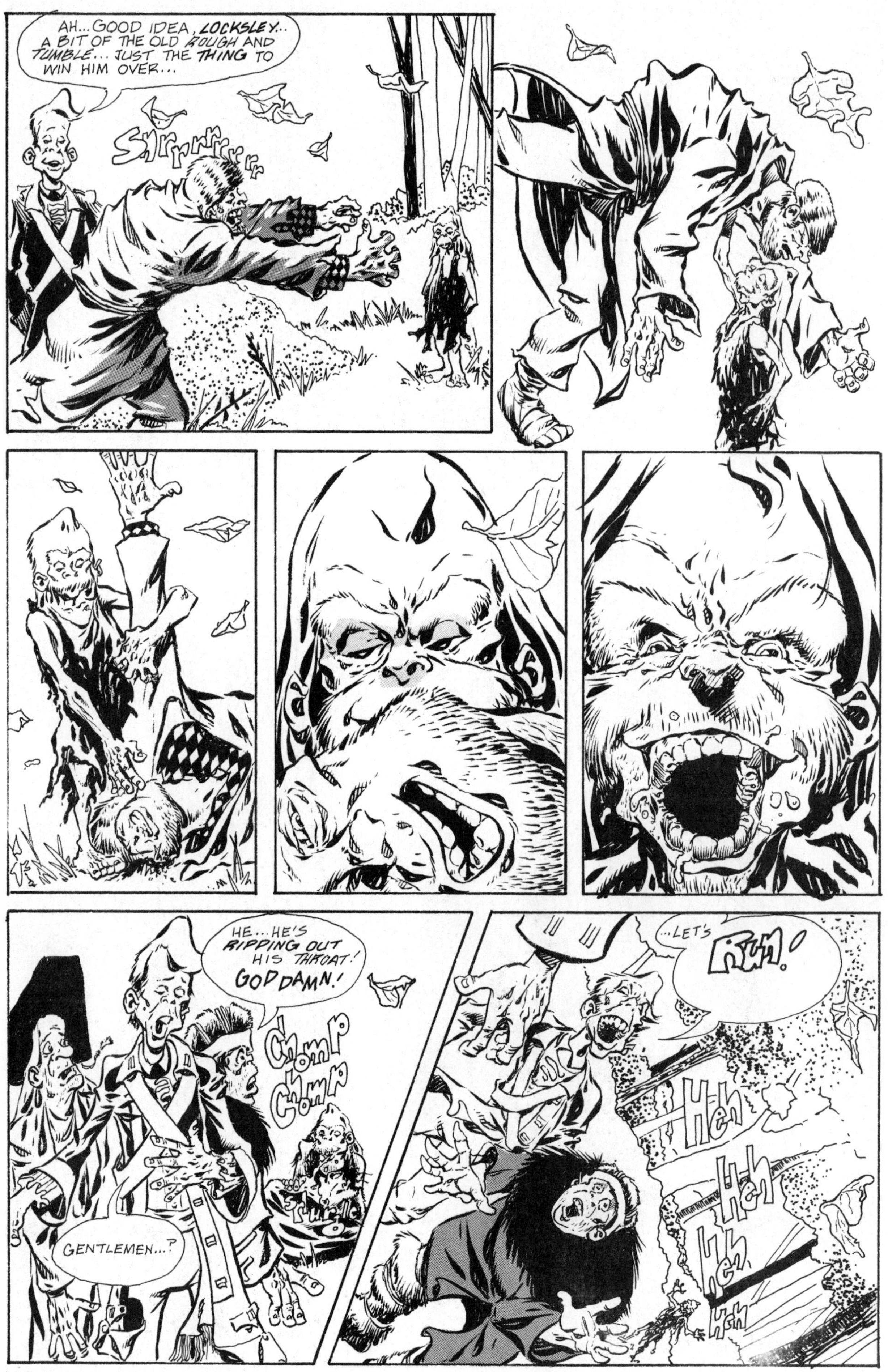
AH...GOOD IDEA, LOCKSLEY... A BIT OF THE OLD ROUGH AND TUMBLE... JUST THE THING TO WIN HIM OVER...
Syrrrrrrrr
HE...HE'S RIPPING OUT HIS THROAT! GOD DAMN!
Chomp Chomp
GENTLEMEN...?
...LET'S RUN!
Heh Heh Heh Heh

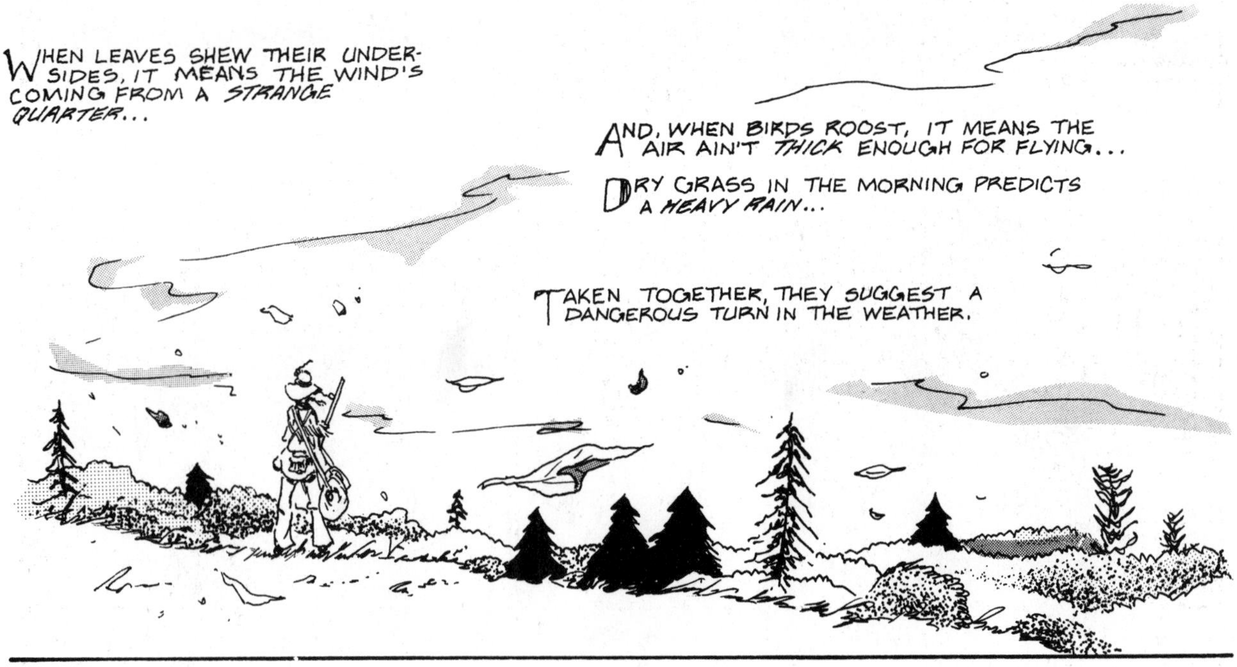
WHEN LEAVES SHEW THEIR UNDERSIDES, IT MEANS THE WIND'S COMING FROM A *STRANGE QUARTER*...
AND, WHEN BIRDS ROOST, IT MEANS THE AIR AIN'T *THICK* ENOUGH FOR FLYING...
DRY GRASS IN THE MORNING PREDICTS A *HEAVY RAIN*...
TAKEN TOGETHER, THEY SUGGEST A DANGEROUS TURN IN THE WEATHER.

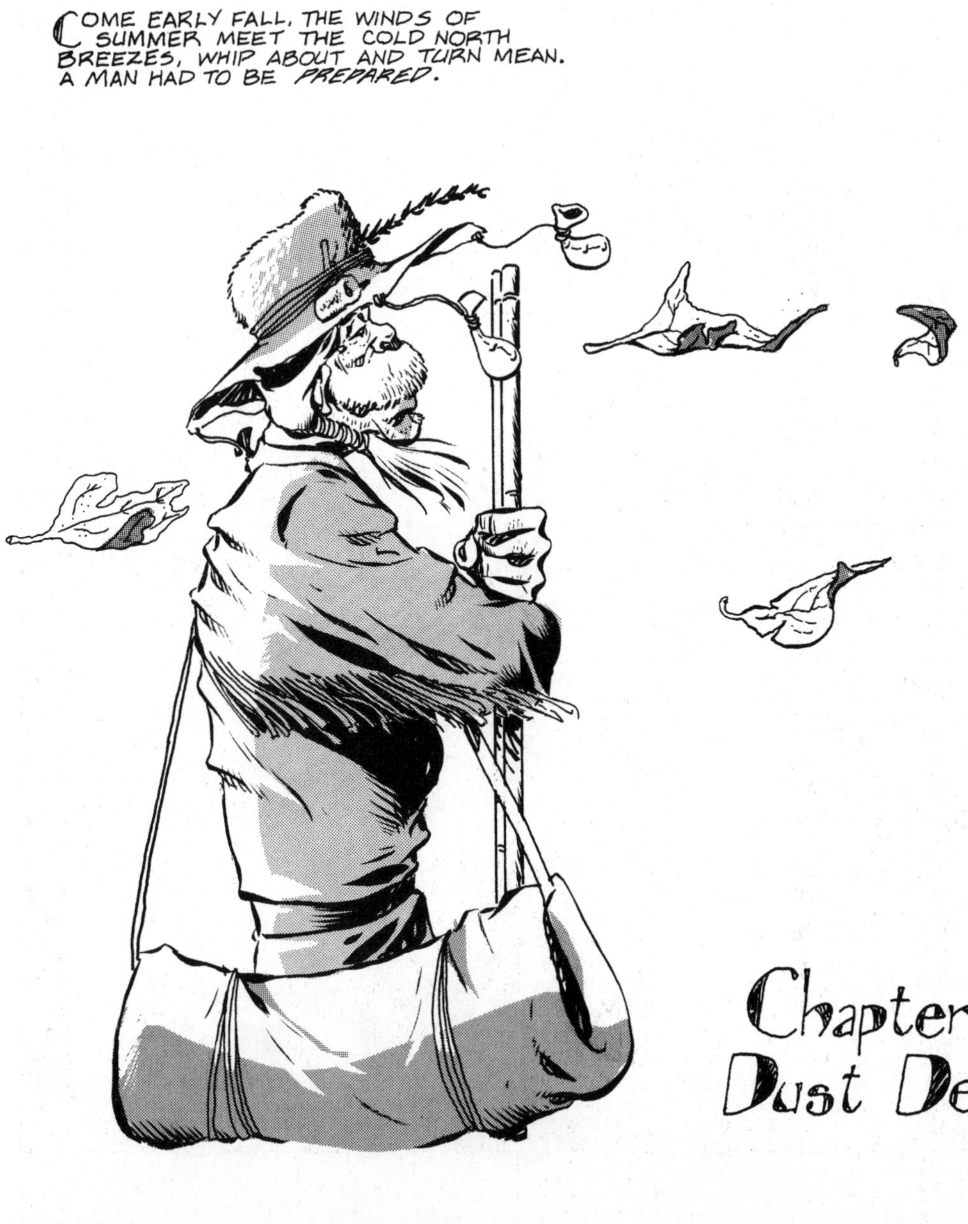
COME EARLY FALL, THE WINDS OF SUMMER MEET THE COLD NORTH BREEZES, WHIP ABOUT AND TURN MEAN. A MAN HAD TO BE *PREPARED*.

Chapter 7: Dust Devil

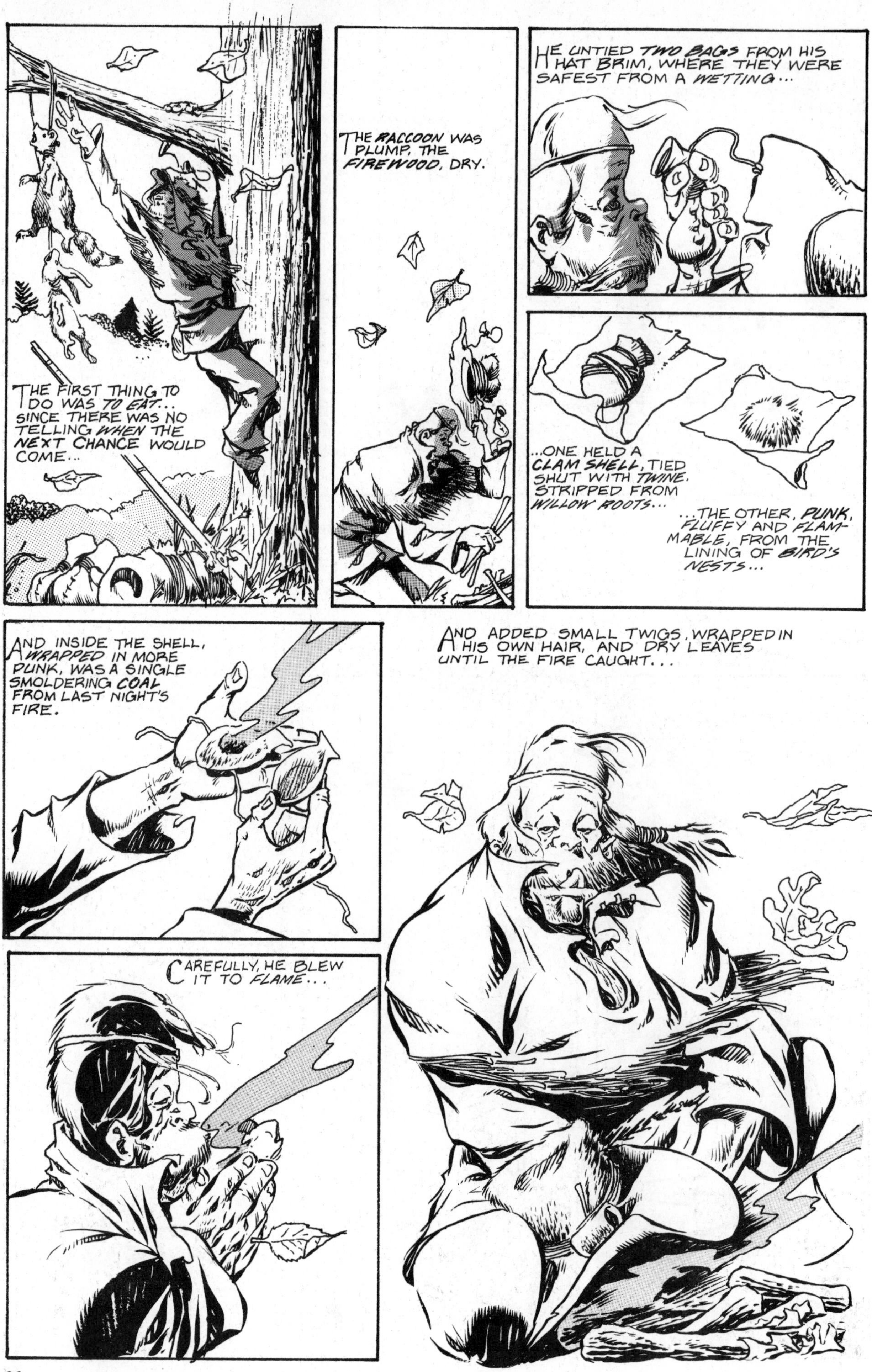
THE FIRST THING TO DO WAS TO EAT... SINCE THERE WAS NO TELLING WHEN THE NEXT CHANCE WOULD COME...
THE RACCOON WAS PLUMP, THE FIREWOOD, DRY.
HE UNTIED TWO BAGS FROM HIS HAT BRIM, WHERE THEY WERE SAFEST FROM A WETTING...
...ONE HELD A CLAM SHELL, TIED SHUT WITH TWINE, STRIPPED FROM WILLOW ROOTS...
...THE OTHER, PUNK, FLUFFY AND FLAMMABLE, FROM THE LINING OF BIRD'S NESTS...
AND INSIDE THE SHELL, WRAPPED IN MORE PUNK, WAS A SINGLE SMOLDERING COAL FROM LAST NIGHT'S FIRE.
CAREFULLY, HE BLEW IT TO FLAME...
AND ADDED SMALL TWIGS, WRAPPED IN HIS OWN HAIR, AND DRY LEAVES UNTIL THE FIRE CAUGHT...

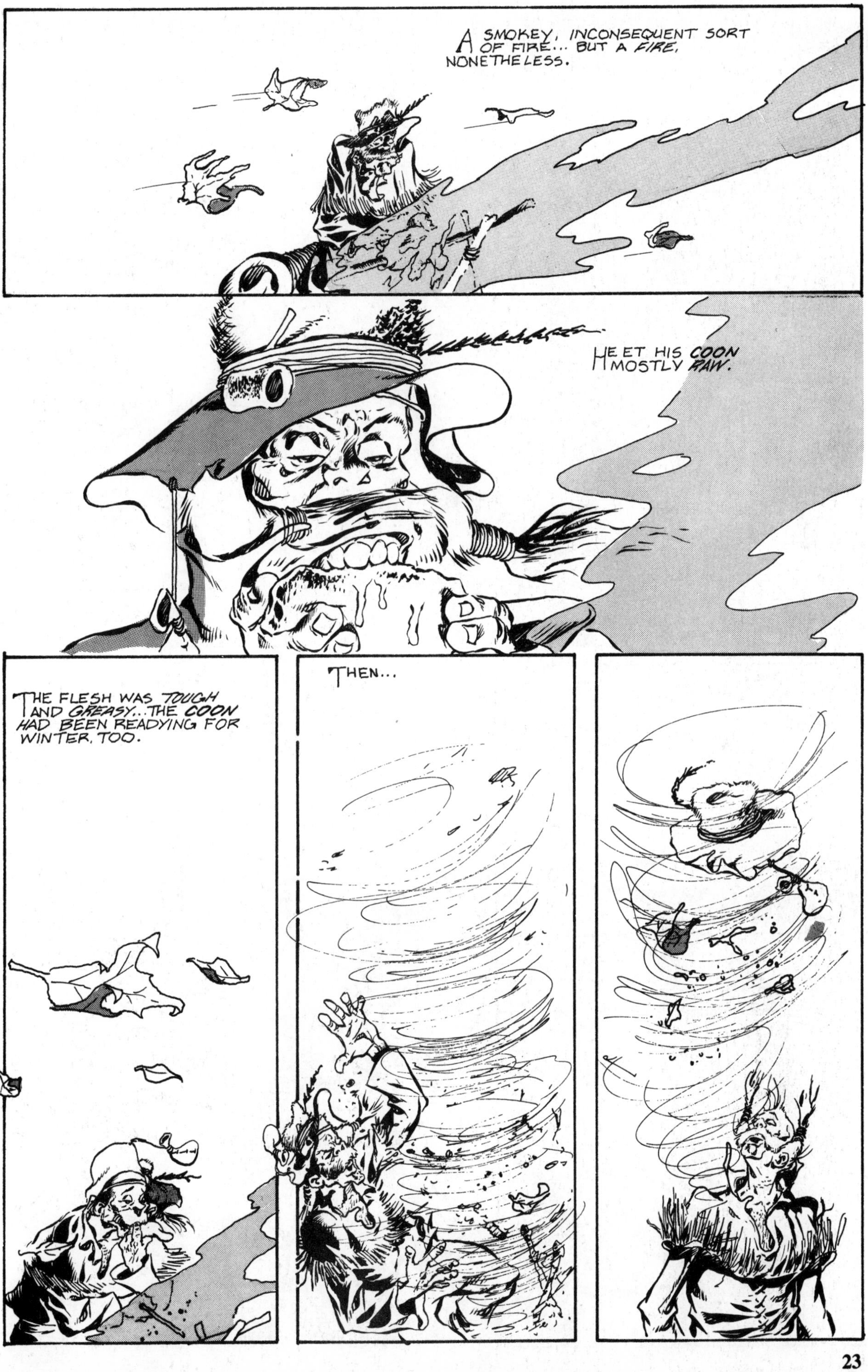
A SMOKEY, INCONSEQUENT SORT OF FIRE... BUT A FIRE, NONETHELESS.
HE ET HIS COON MOSTLY RAW.
THE FLESH WAS TOUGH AND GREASY... THE COON HAD BEEN READYING FOR WINTER, TOO.
THEN...

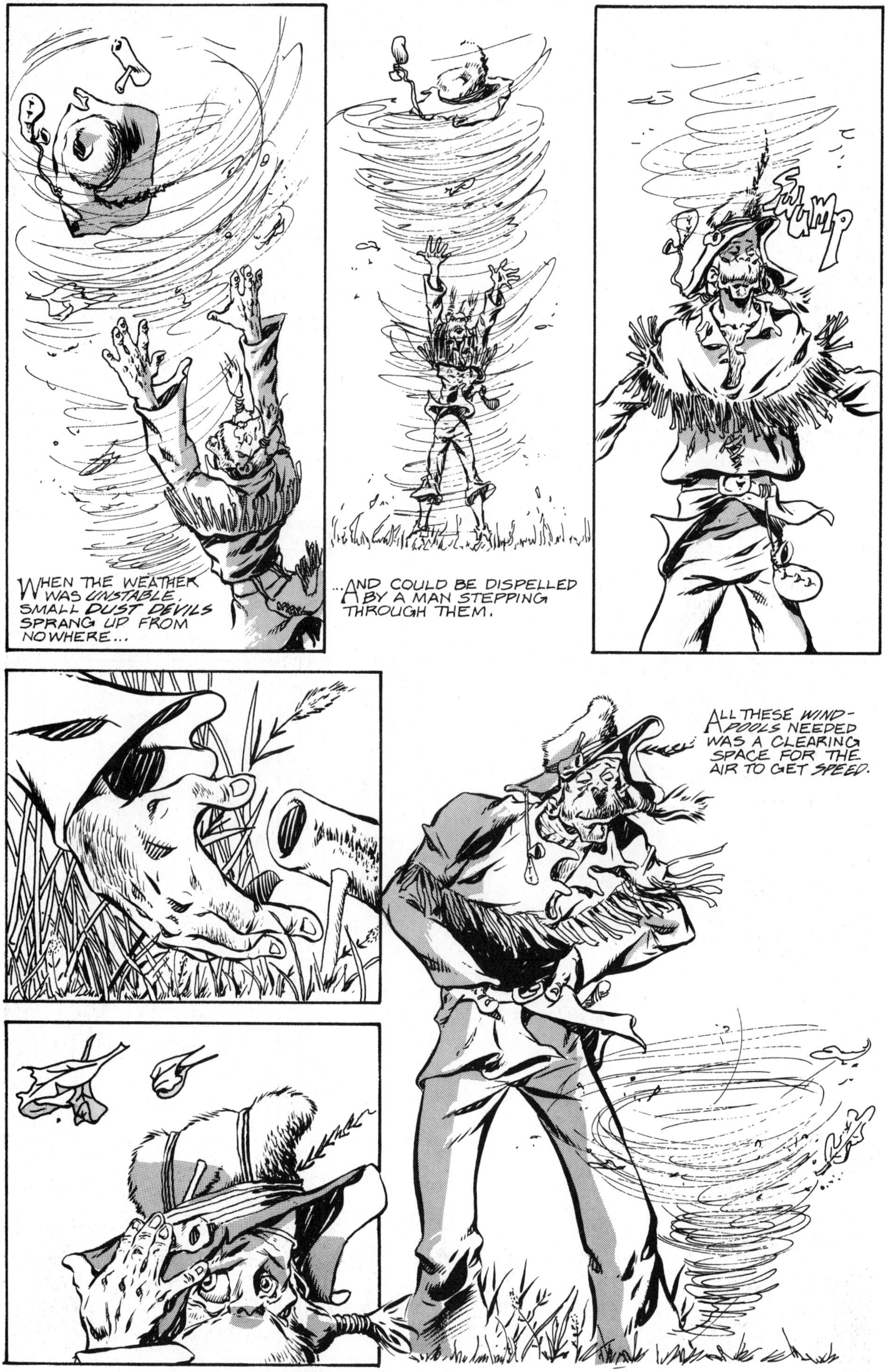
WHEN THE WEATHER WAS UNSTABLE, SMALL DUST DEVILS SPRANG UP FROM NOWHERE...
...AND COULD BE DISPELLED BY A MAN STEPPING THROUGH THEM.
SWUMP
ALL THESE WIND-POOLS NEEDED WAS A CLEARING SPACE FOR THE AIR TO GET SPEED.

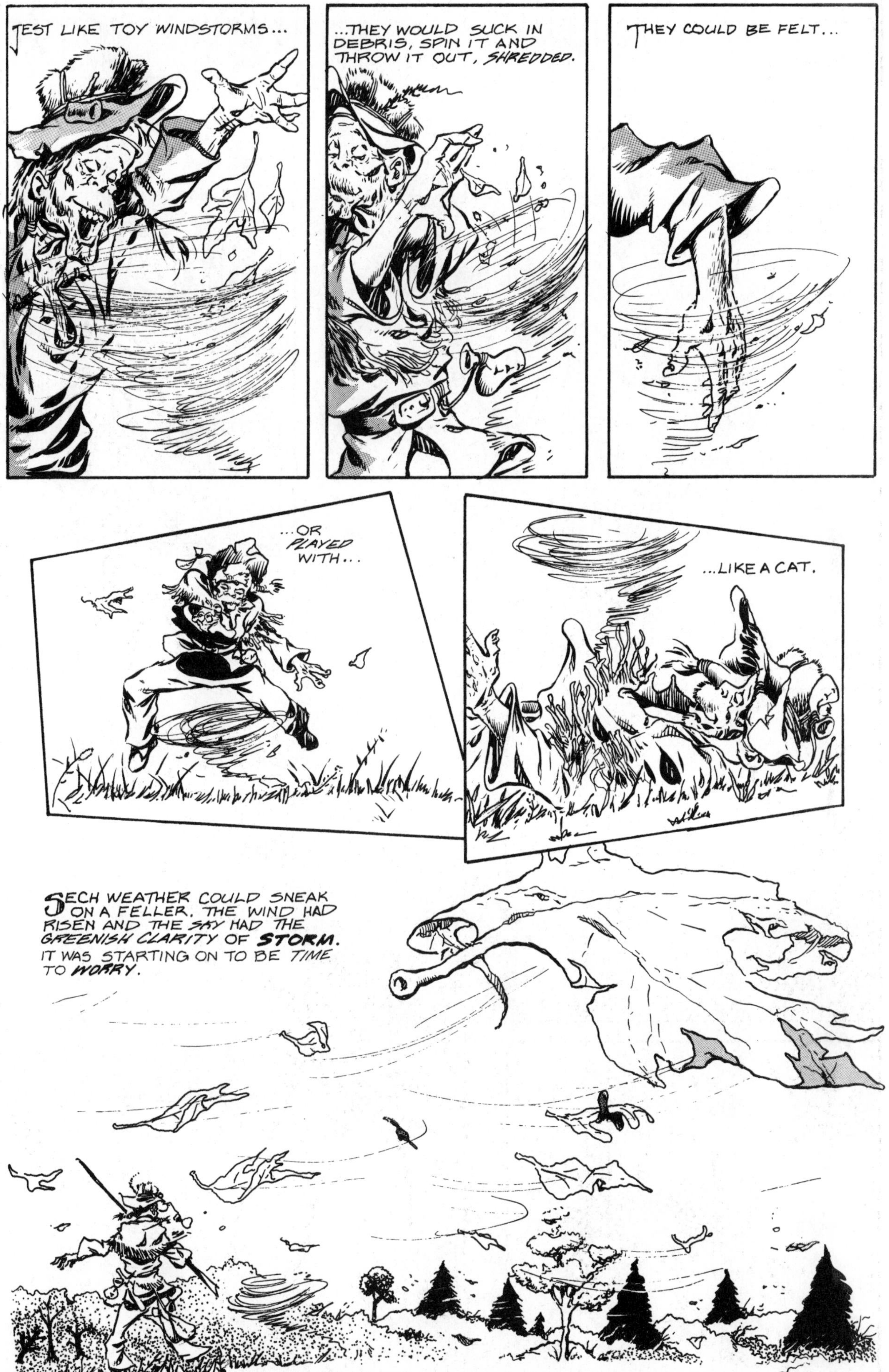
JEST LIKE TOY WINDSTORMS...
...THEY WOULD SUCK IN DEBRIS, SPIN IT AND THROW IT OUT, SHREDDED.
THEY COULD BE FELT...
...OR PLAYED WITH...
...LIKE A CAT.
SECH WEATHER COULD SNEAK ON A FELLER. THE WIND HAD RISEN AND THE SKY HAD THE GREENISH CLARITY OF STORM. IT WAS STARTING ON TO BE TIME TO WORRY.

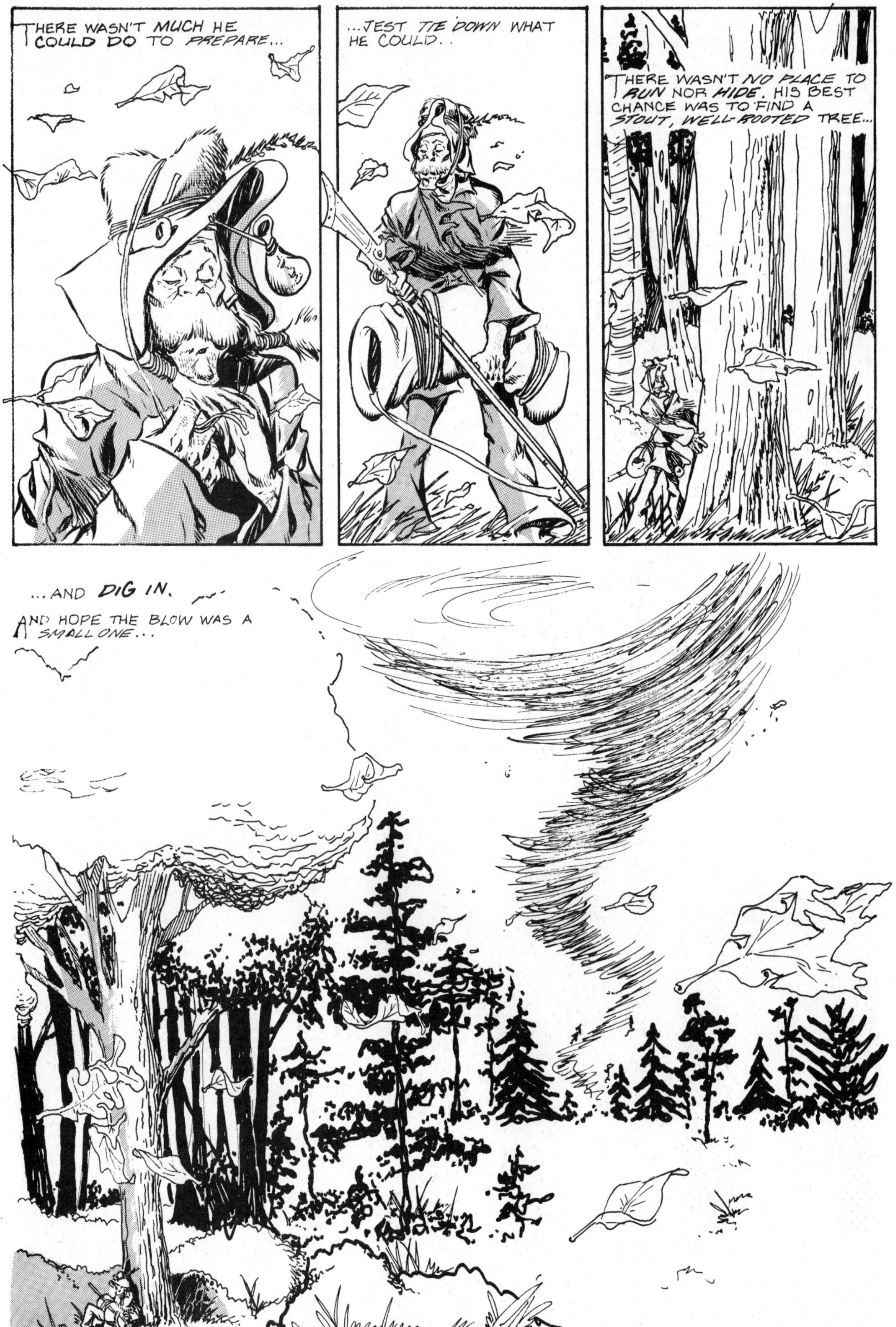
THERE WASN'T MUCH HE COULD DO TO PREPARE...
...JEST TIE DOWN WHAT HE COULD...
THERE WASN'T NO PLACE TO RUN NOR HIDE. HIS BEST CHANCE WAS TO FIND A STOUT, WELL-ROOTED TREE...
...AND DIG IN.
AND HOPE THE BLOW WAS A SMALL ONE...

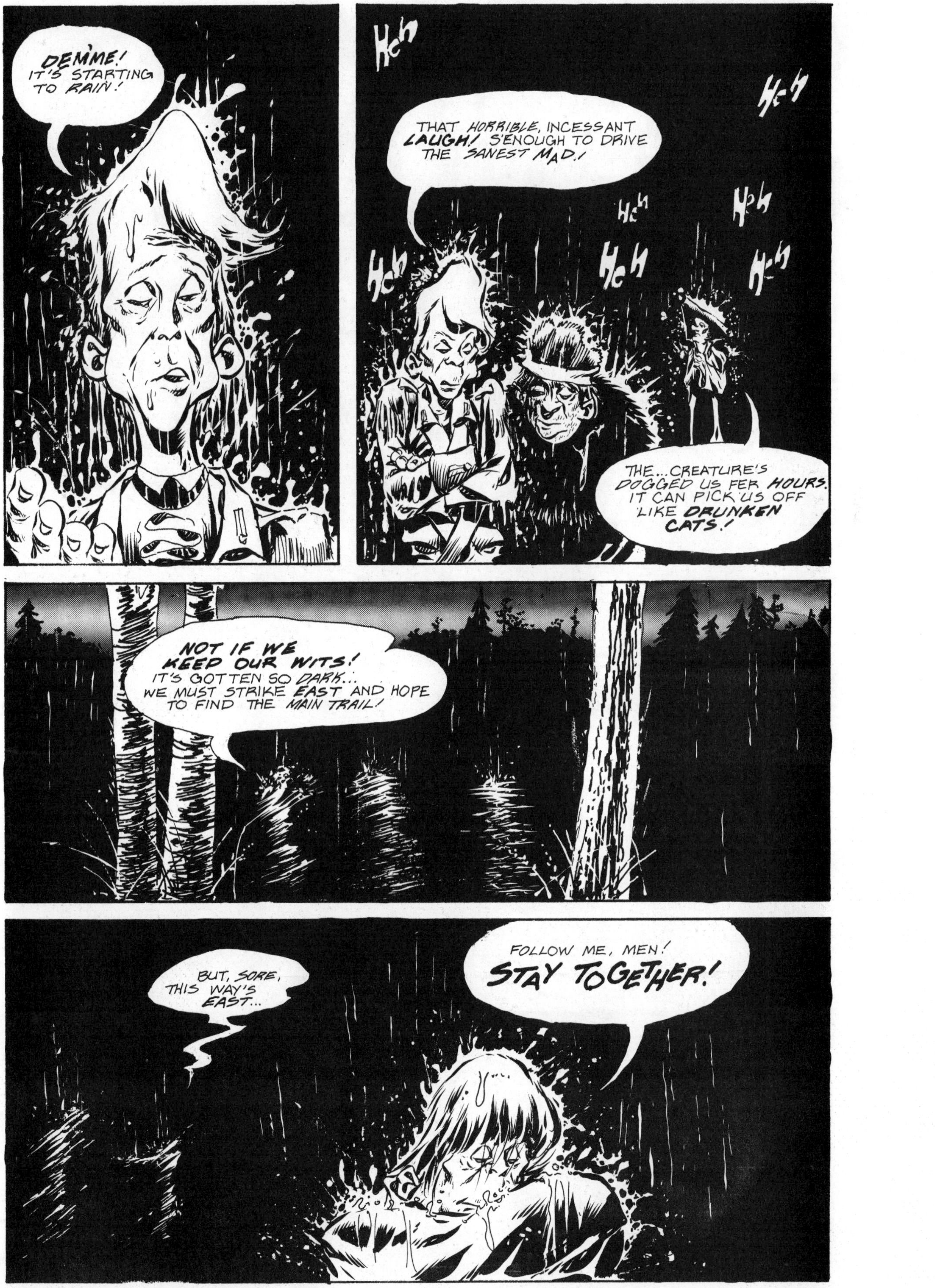
DEMME! IT'S STARTING TO RAIN!
Hch
Hch
THAT HORRIBLE, INCESSANT LAUGH! S'ENOUGH TO DRIVE THE SANEST MAD!
Hch
Hch
Hch
Hch
Hch
THE... CREATURE'S DOGGED US FER HOURS. IT CAN PICK US OFF LIKE DRUNKEN CATS!
NOT IF WE KEEP OUR WITS! IT'S GOTTEN SO DARK... WE MUST STRIKE EAST AND HOPE TO FIND THE MAIN TRAIL!
BUT, SORE, THIS WAY'S EAST...
FOLLOW ME, MEN! STAY TOGETHER!

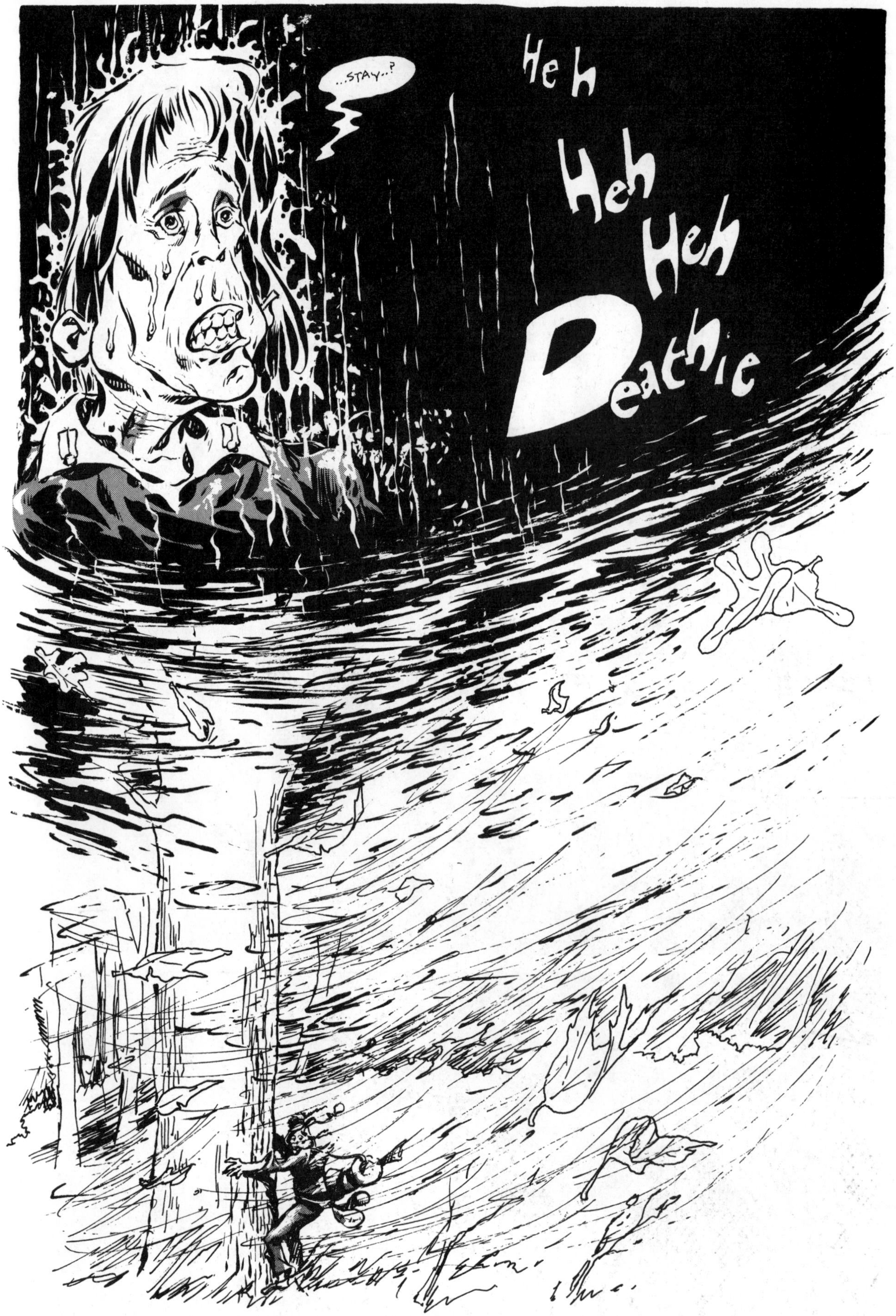
...STAY...?
Heh
Heh
Heh
Deathie

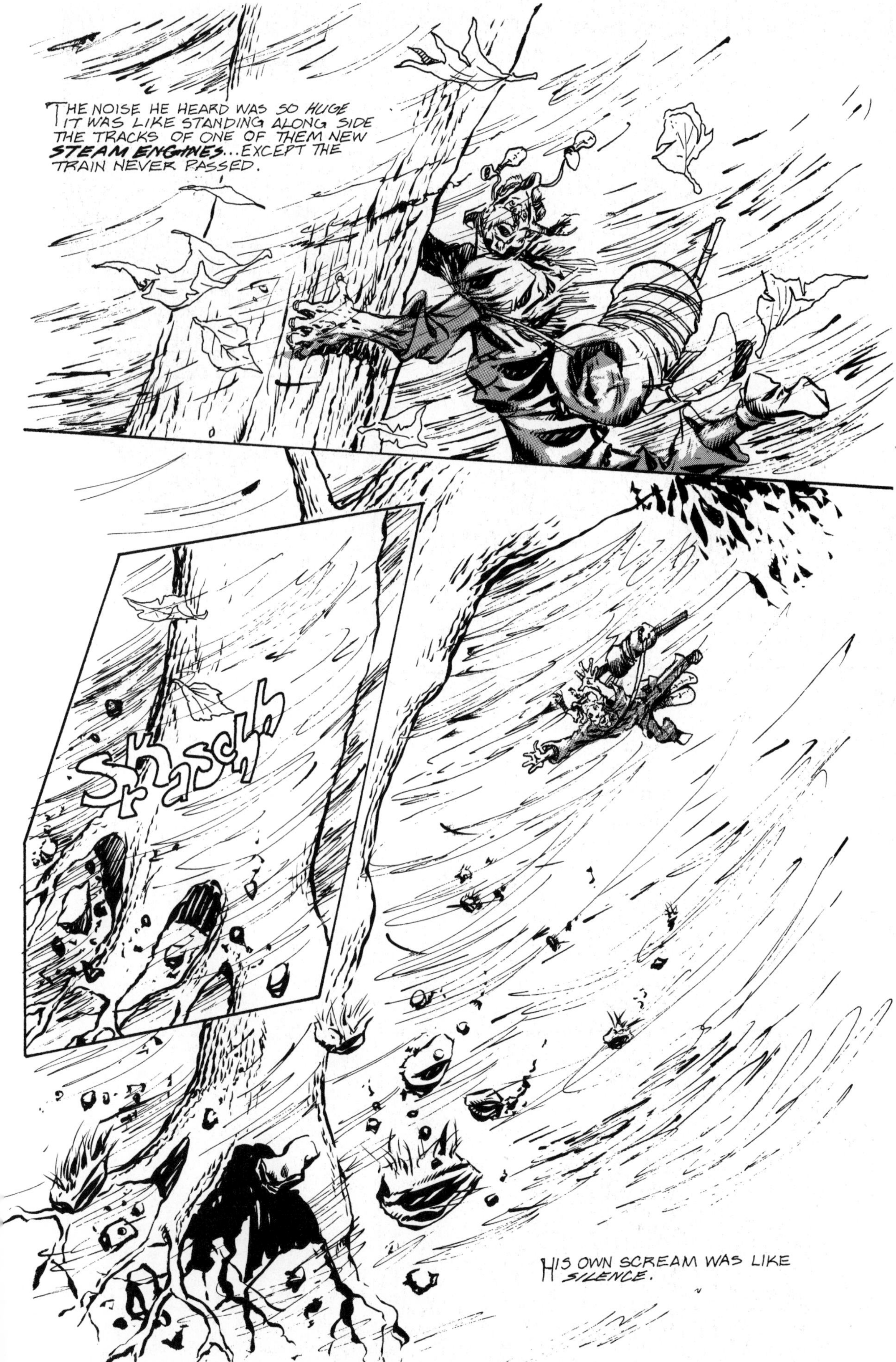
THE NOISE HE HEARD WAS SO HUGE IT WAS LIKE STANDING ALONG SIDE THE TRACKS OF ONE OF THEM NEW STEAM ENGINES... EXCEPT THE TRAIN NEVER PASSED.
Skrasch
HIS OWN SCREAM WAS LIKE SILENCE.

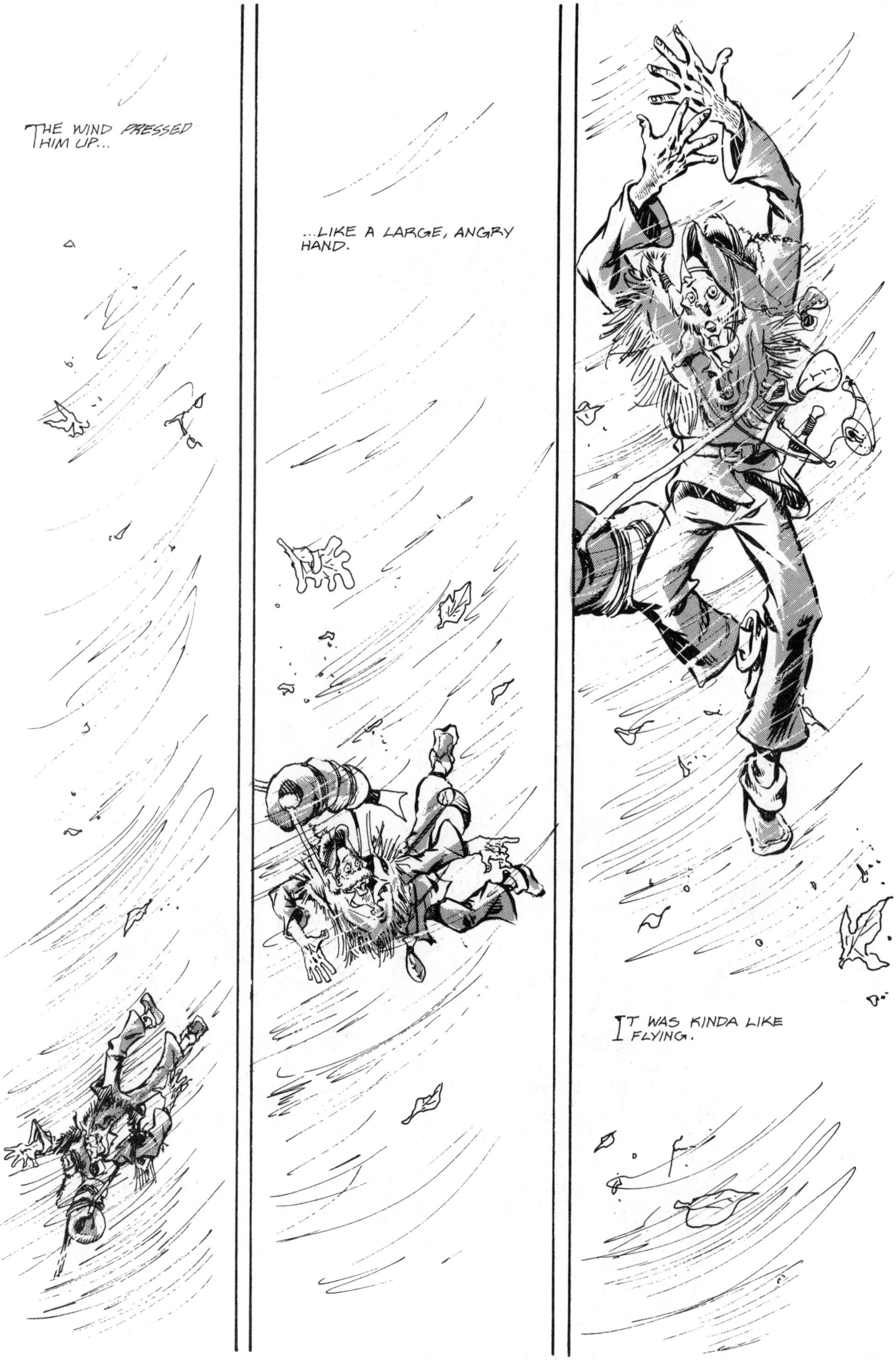
THE WIND PRESSED HIM UP...
...LIKE A LARGE, ANGRY HAND.
IT WAS KINDA LIKE FLYING.

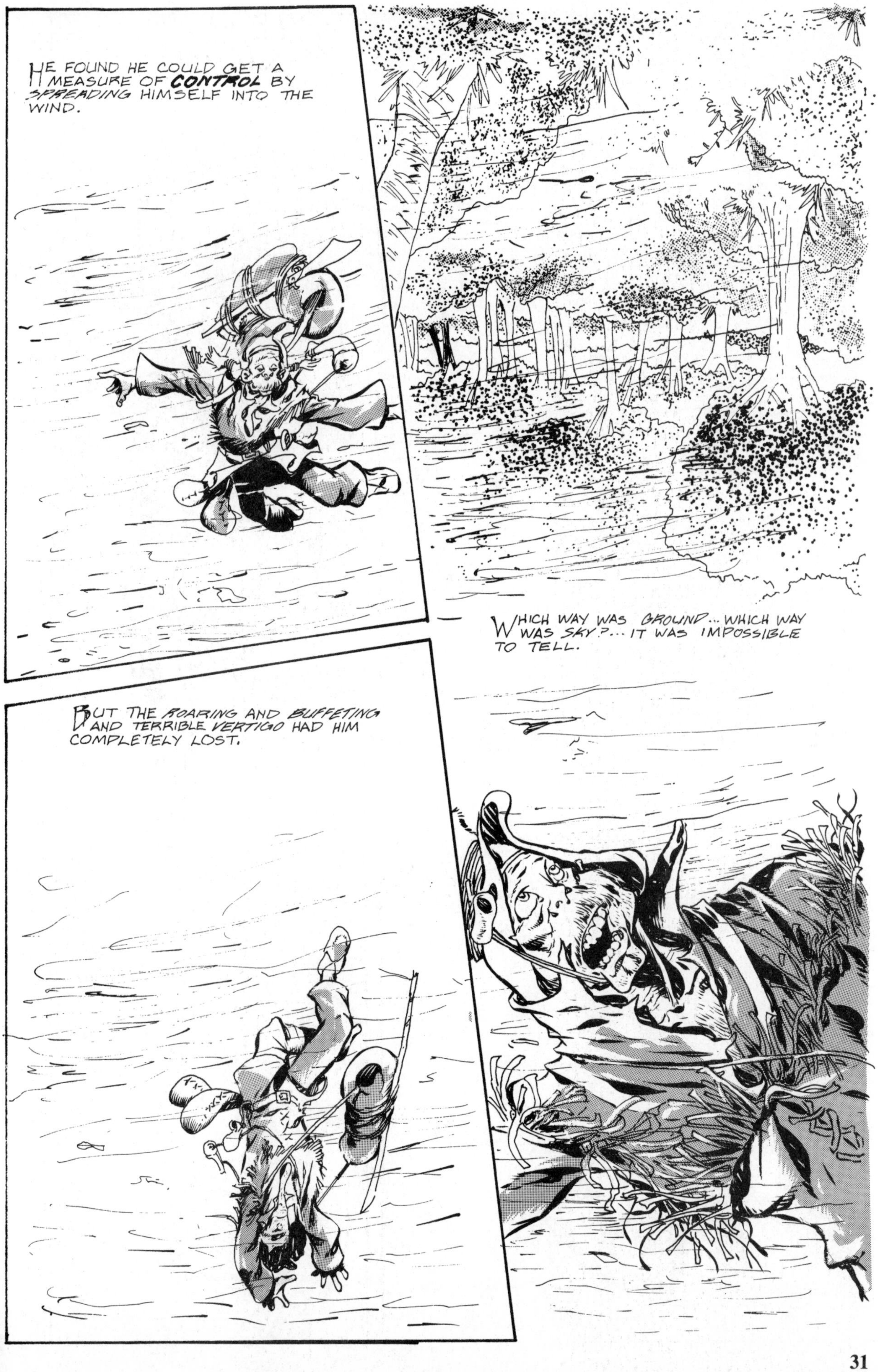
HE FOUND HE COULD GET A MEASURE OF CONTROL BY SPREADING HIMSELF INTO THE WIND.
WHICH WAY WAS GROUND... WHICH WAY WAS SKY?... IT WAS IMPOSSIBLE TO TELL.
BUT THE ROARING AND BUFFETING AND TERRIBLE VERTIGO HAD HIM COMPLETELY LOST.

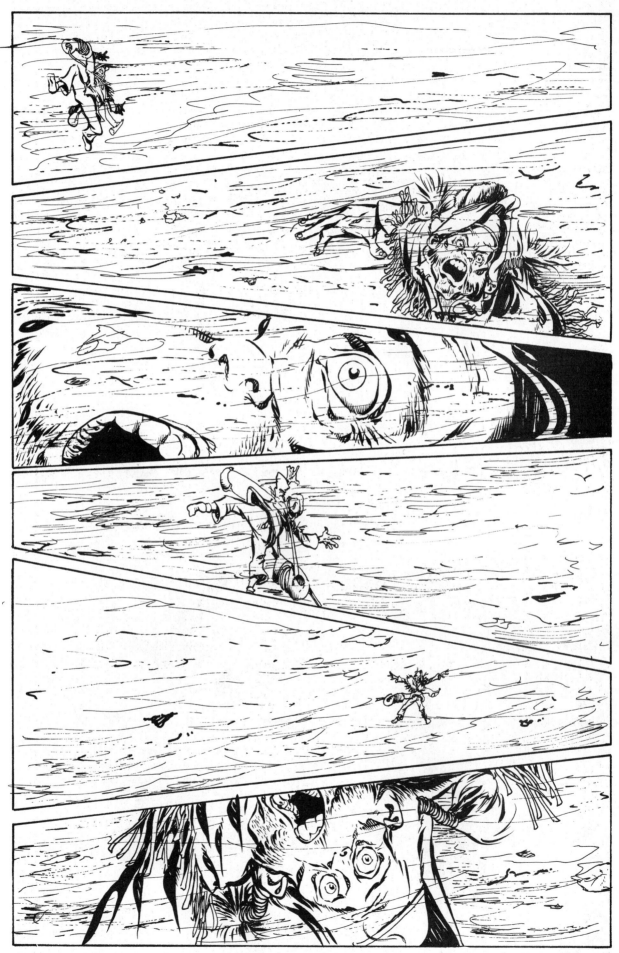

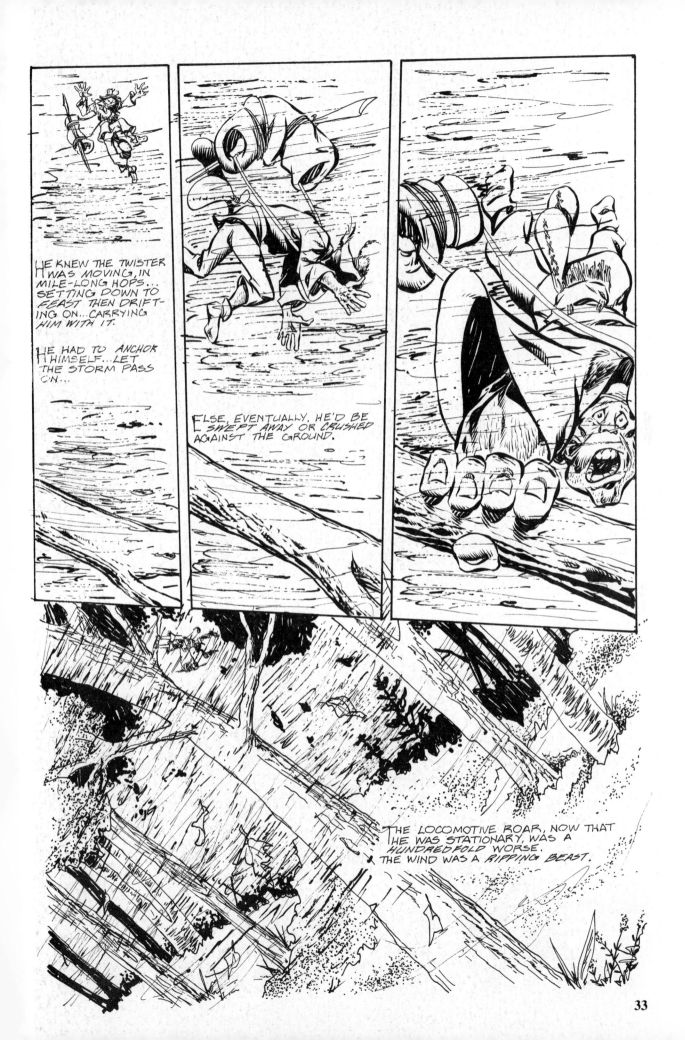

HE KNEW THE TWISTER WAS MOVING, IN MILE-LONG HOPS... SETTING DOWN TO FEAST THEN DRIFTING ON...CARRYING HIM WITH IT.

HE HAD TO ANCHOR HIMSELF...LET THE STORM PASS ON...

ELSE, EVENTUALLY, HE'D BE SWEPT AWAY OR CRUSHED AGAINST THE GROUND.

THE LOCOMOTIVE ROAR, NOW THAT HE WAS STATIONARY, WAS A HUNDREDFOLD WORSE. THE WIND WAS A RIPPING BEAST.

33

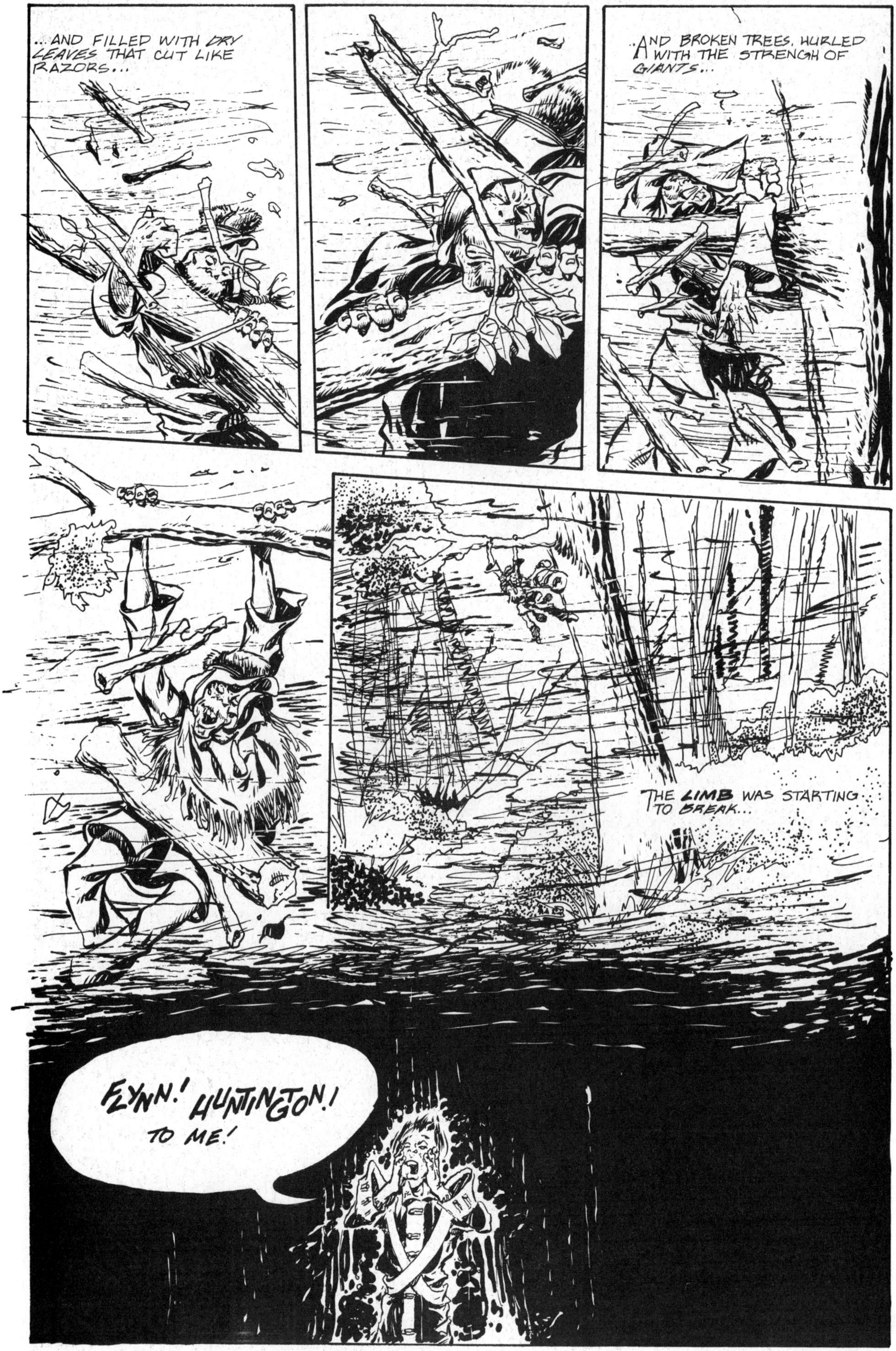
...AND FILLED WITH DRY LEAVES THAT CUT LIKE RAZORS...
...AND BROKEN TREES, HURLED WITH THE STRENGH OF GIANTS...
THE LIMB WAS STARTING TO BREAK...
FLYNN! HUNTINGTON! TO ME!

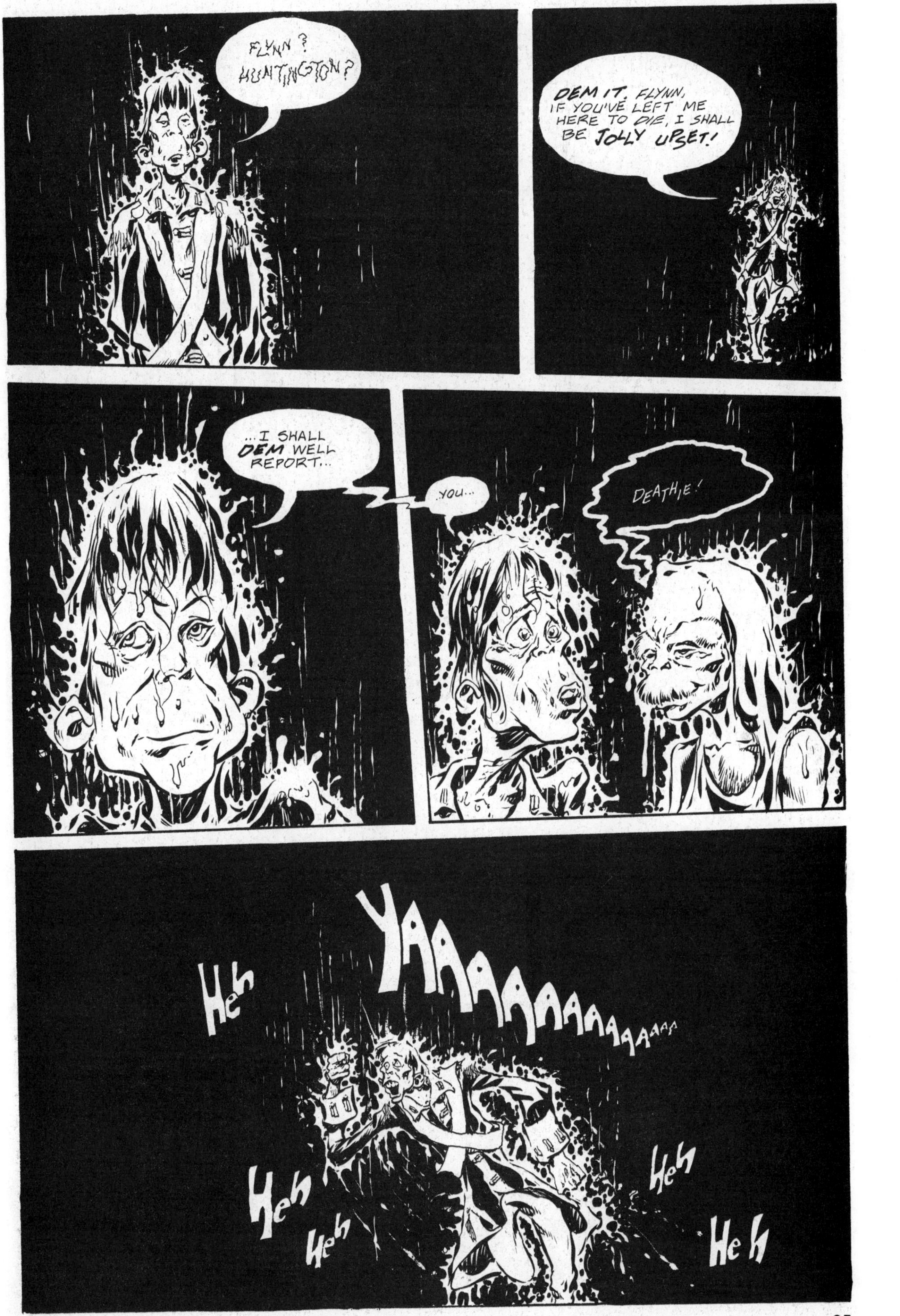
FLYNN?
HUNTINGTON?
DEM IT, FLYNN, IF YOU'VE LEFT ME HERE TO DIE, I SHALL BE JOLLY UPSET!
...I SHALL DEM WELL REPORT...
...YOU...
DEATHIE!
YAAAAAAAAAAAAA
Heh
Heh
Heh
Heh
Heh

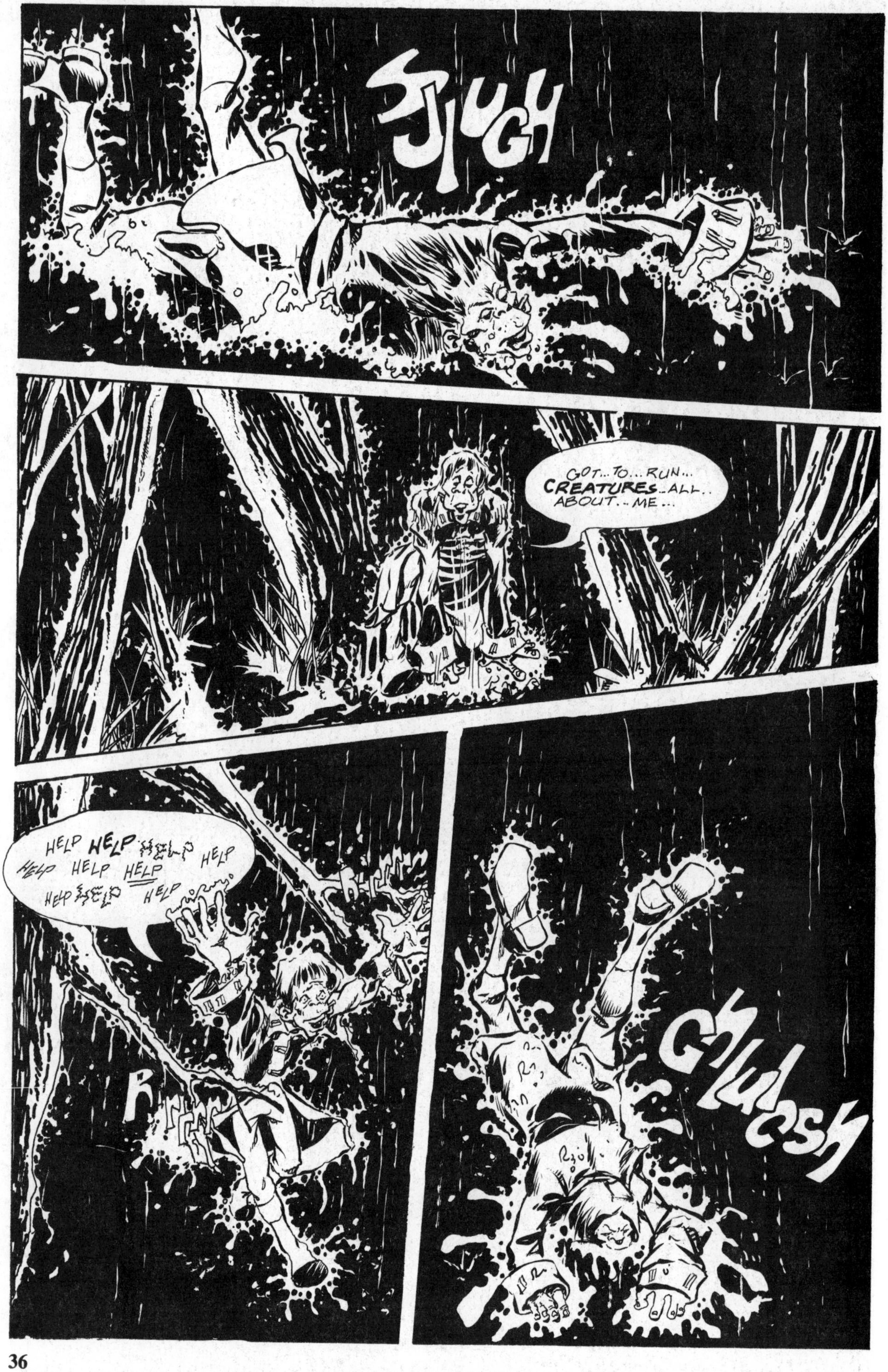
SPLUGH
GOT... TO... RUN... CREATURES... ALL... ABOUT... ME...
HELP HELP HELP HELP HELP HELP HELP HELP HELP HELP
GHLUDOSH

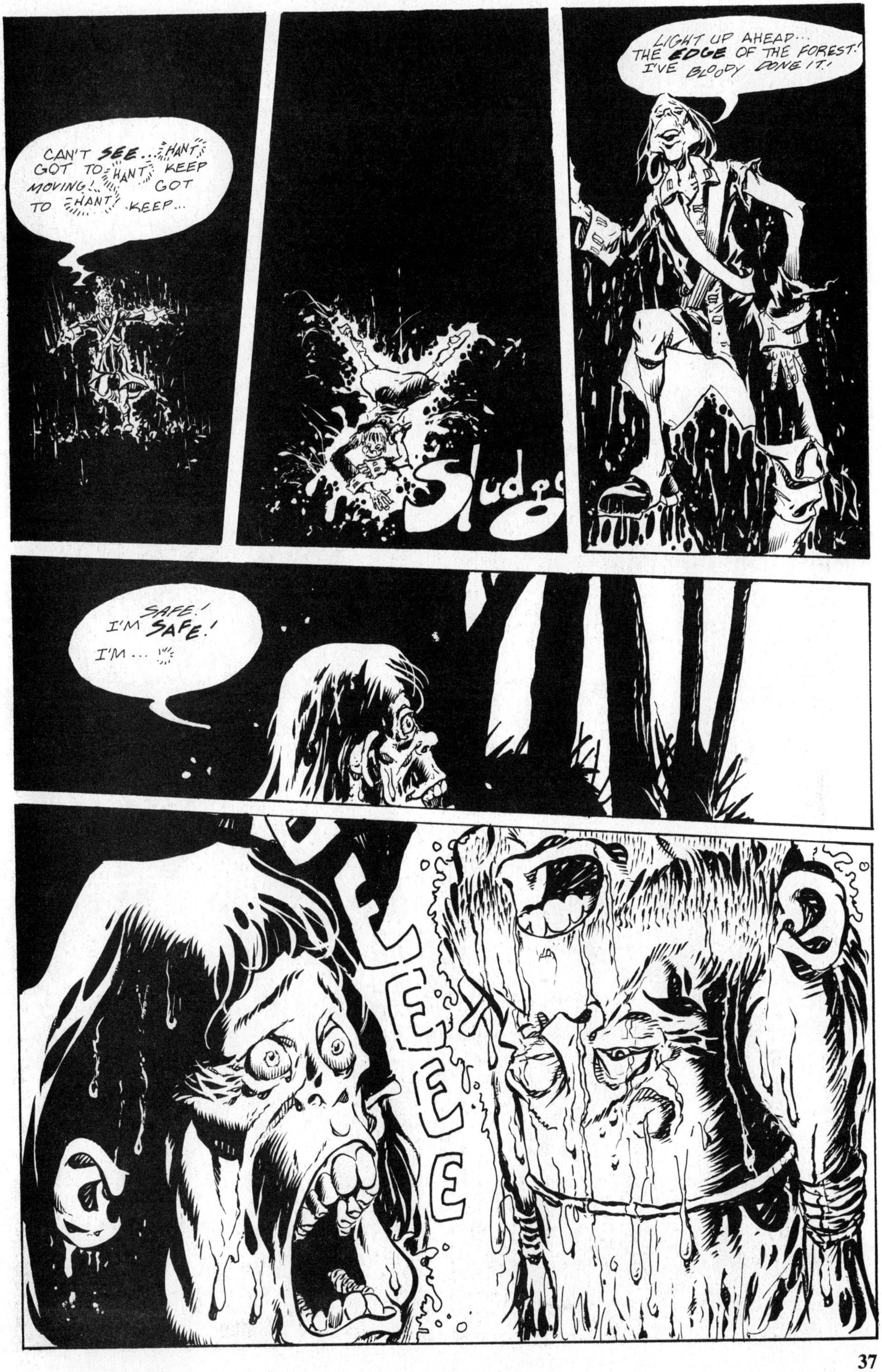
CAN'T SEE... HANT GOT TO HANT KEEP MOVING! GOT TO HANT KEEP...
Sludge
LIGHT UP AHEAD... THE EDGE OF THE FOREST! I'VE BLOODY DONE IT.
SAFE! I'M SAFE! I'M...!
EEEEEE

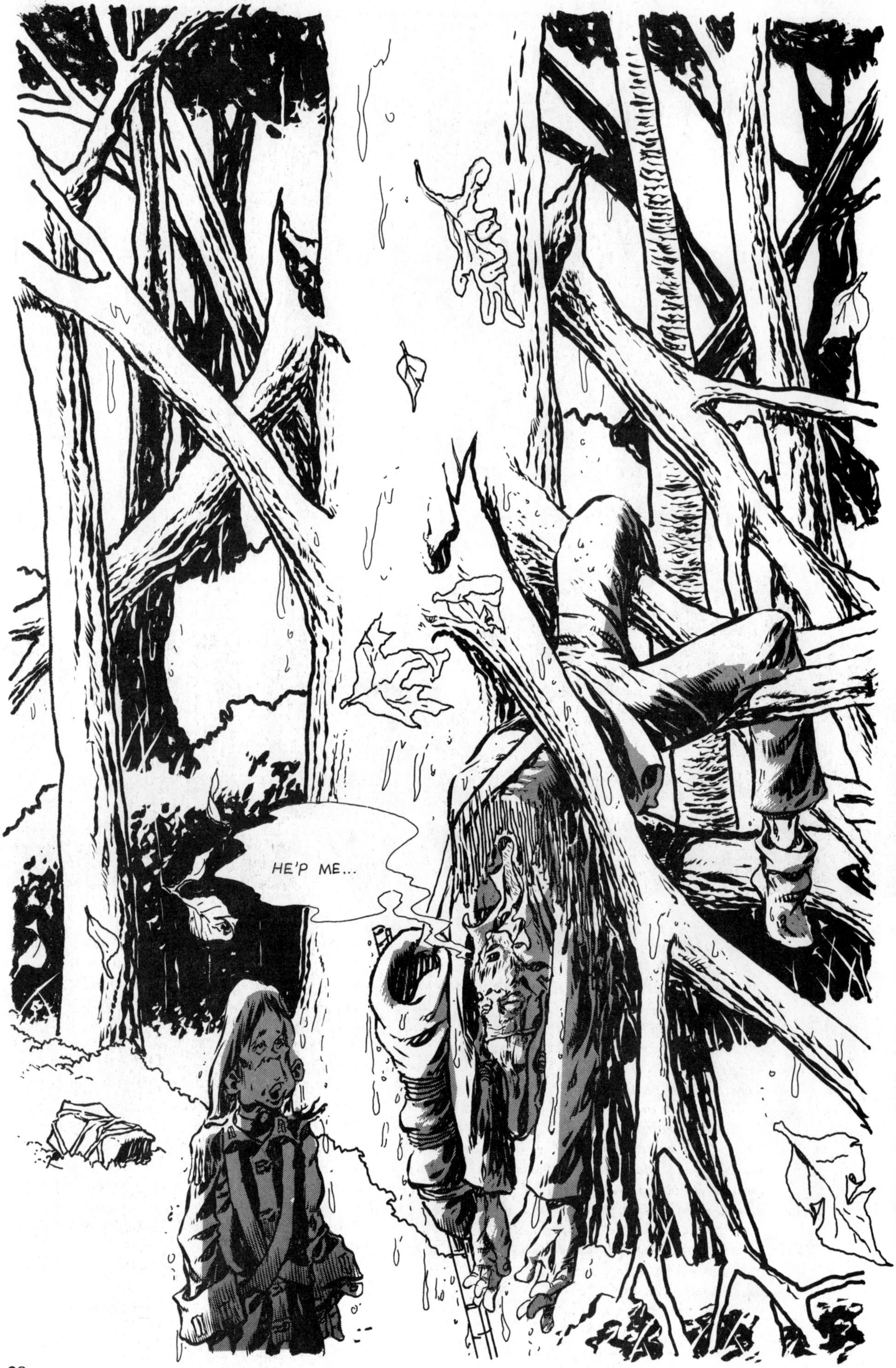
HE'P ME...

The Yarn Of The Walking Dead

"**S**lowly, squamishly, the ground beneath the pitted tombstone slowly began to move. The towering marble, shuddering like some tortured hemibeast, slowly toppled onto the squamish loam, and where it had lately been, a single hand, blackened by decay, save where the bone shewn through, wiggled serpent-like into the fetid air, waving like some tattered pennant of daemonic despair.

"*Then from that decayed loam, from dank unwholesome realms of the dead, arose Marcus DeQuincy, his white, bewormed flesh still bejeweled with the pulpy shards of the coffin he had so lately quitted. It had taken him all of the five years since he had been buried to burst free of the suffocating coffin and claw his way upward, through the stinking muck, to stand as he did now, under the gibbenous moon. Swaying, his desiccated muscles barely able to hold him upright, his face, noseless, with eyes like wet black marbles, half covered with*

clotted earth, he took one step, then another, his feet making squamish dents in the soil..."

"Dat's de third time you use dat 'squamish' fella in dis story," offered the Indian boy. "Dere was de ground an' de loam an' now..."

"I see your point," said the Poet. "There's no need to count." He stared briefly at the dying fire before which he was crouched, then began reading again from the tattered foolscap.

"*Sluggishly, he began to move across the fields to the town, a vile puppet with strings pulled by a Mad God from Hell. Behind him he left an unmentionable slime upon the furrowed ground, whose dead...*"

"An' you use 'slime' a buncha times, too," said the Indian boy.

"Ya," said the Hessian. "Undt 'tattered.' You said 'tattered' a goodt lot."

"Et pourquoi ees thees 'slime' unmentionable if

you 'ave joos *mention* him?" asked Three Finger Pierre. The Poet sighed.

"Could we try to keep this to *constructive* criticism? I'd like to hear what you really think of the story thus far. What you *enjoyed* about it." There was a pause. The various members shuffled about the fire or hunched a bit against the cool night air. Finally, the Indian boy said:

"Well, I sure like dat 'vile puppet' part. Dat was swell, you bet. An' I like de part where 'is wife feed him poison chard, so he died. Dat was plenty exciting."

"Thank you."

"Only. . ."

"What now?"

"What's dis 'chard' t'ing? I never hear of him."

"It's like lettuce, only it tastes like weak cabbage," said Wolverine MacAlistaire from his spot by the fire. "An' it's stalked, like celery."

"Oh. I t'ink it was a melon 'cause it had de poison."

"Nope. It's lettuce."

"Can we return to the *point*?" asked the Poet. He looked with some pain at the shadowed pine trees that loomed over and protected the little group of travelers, as though to ask for strength. "What I was *hoping* for was intelligent criticism of my basic *theme*, my *character development* and *technique*. Now please pay attention and I'll ask again when I'm done." Everyone shifted helpfully, striving to look attentive.

"At last he reached the house, and looking within, saw his doll-like, feral wife, Esmeraltine, locked in a disloyal carnality with his best friend, the slyly handsome Vernon Pelesque. . ."

"What's 'carnality'?" asked the Indian.

"It's a flower," opined the Woodsman. "Red."

"Dey were locked in a red flower?"

"*Kissing*. They were *kissing*," said the Poet, with a venomous look. "May I *please* finish this?" He took a deep breath. *"Suddenly, the window casement burst open and there before them was the crumbling, vengeance-animated husk of he whom they had hoped to dispose of, so as to clear the way for their own lusts and profits. Dismay and fear warred equally for dominance upon each candle-illumined countenance.*

"'Marcus!' cried Esmeraltine, the scream torn unwillingly from her alabaster throat. Vernon reached for the gleaming fireplace poker, but the dead man was quicker, leaping on him like a cat. There was a single desperate wrench, a muffled gurgle, and then a liquefied, triumphant chuckle. DeQuincy stood before his wife, whose pale limbs trembled like fauns in a winter breeze.

"'Marcus,' sobbed the disloyal beauty. 'With what intent have you broken the laws of God and Man, and snapped thus the indisoluable chains of Death itself? Why have you come?' The hideous grinning features gazed down at her, with scant sympathy.

"'Only for THIS, my dear,' hissed the oily corpse, and he plunged his mouth down upon hers in a desanctified kiss of unholy passion." The Poet

lowered his manuscript. *"The next day, the neighbors discovered a horrid tableau. To wit: One body, its neck snapped like a twig; the second, the beautiful Esmeraltine, her mind gone, laughing without cease; and the third, a single mound of jellied waste, which the summoned physicians agreed ONCE had been HUMAN!"*

The little group of travelers was still. Then, the Indian boy said, "I like de part of about dat twig snapping t'ing. I like dat plenty." The German trader shook his head. "Vhat iss zer idea of zo much rot undt stink. It makes me queasy."

"Oh, I put that in there for the *realism*," remarked the Poet, a bit smugly.

"Funny thing about thet." The big woodsman stretched and hitched himself into a position where he could see the smaller man more easily. "I never seed an actual case where a man was kilt by his wife. Oh, I heerd yarns about sech an' songs an' broadsides a'plenty. But I never actually knowd of a *real* happening. Whilst I do know of my own reason about men what have put their wives under. Two, in fact. If we're talkin' *real*." He was regarding the poet with a mild gaze that the other man found infuriating. He could never tell when the man was joking. For example, he was reasonably sure that the woodsman knew what *carnality* meant.

"I suppose *you* could tell a *real* story about a walking corpse?" snapped the Poet, nettled. The Woodsman lit his pipe on a cinder.

"Reckon I could try," he said. And began.

"**T**hey *was a man named Hugh Glass, who I knew t'look at. He was an adopted son of th' Pawnee. An' several year ago he was on a expedition t' punish th' Rees. A company o' trappers had planned t' punish th' Rees sore an' rid 'em o' their man-killin' ways. The only fault in thet plan lay in th' Rees, who figgered out their plan an' was waitin' f'r 'em. So they was soon on th' prod, with th' Rees aroused an' in pursuit. A few days later, Glass went out by hisself fer huntin' an' blundered upon a mother Ephraim an' her cubs. He knowd she'd. . ."*

"Mother Ephraim?" inquired the Poet.

"B'ar," said the Woodsman. "Grizz. Stood 10 foot

high, weighed close on two ton. I've seen 'em break a..."

"No need to elucidate. Sweet frontier jargon. Pray proceed."

"He knowd she'd stand 'fore strikin' him. So stood an' potted her through th' core. Should've kilt her, but didn't. He run. She caught 'im. Swatted him several. Crushed his chest bones. Slashed at him like a slit pig an' tore a chunk outer his back t' feed her young.

"When th' rest come runnin' at his screams, they found th' b'ar worryin' him like a rat an' him hollerin' an' slashin' with his Johnson..."

"Johnson?"

"Knife. They's this company back east..."

"Forget I asked."

"Ennyhow, they shot into her, until at last she keeled over from Hugh's ball in her. But Hugh Glass was in shreds, had lost most o' his blood, an' yet was still livin'.

"The crew hunkered down on thet spot, a-waitin' on him t' kick. They waited all night an' on to th' next day. By thet time they was near t'panic. They knowd th' Rees was about some'eres an' powerful eager t' find 'em. It didn't reason t' use up seven lives t' bury a feller what was spent.

"So they asked f'r volunteers; two men who would wait with Hugh till his husk was empty an' then plant him. For thet they get forty dollar each. That was as much as a trapper could make in a half season. As it passed, th' two who stepped forward was a old feller name Fergusen an' a green kid name Jim Bridger.

"Them two settled down t' wait with th' best intentions. Hugh seemed t' have ev'ry best reason t' die an' none t' live. He was still bleedin', big chunks o' him was gone, an' his breathin' was a death rattle. But he still hadn't kicked. Th' men was startin' t' sweat. Ev'ry shadow, ev'ry grass rustle or bird call might be th' Rees returnin'. An' th' Rees might play with a man f'r a week 'fore they'd let him die.

"On th' mornin' of th' fifth day, Fergusen put his ear t' Hugh's chest. 'Seems like he's dead finally. Time t' go.' Th' kid looked relieved.

"'Thet's fine. We kin bury him an' get th' blazes gone from 'ere.' Th' older man looked sidewise, stabbin' at th' berry bush with his deer-shod foot.

"'Don't think buryin's called f'r. He ain't th' kinda dead I'd be comfortable buryin'.' Th' kid looked suspicious.

"'What kinda dead is he?'

"'Near enough dead, not t' worry on. He ain't breathin' thet I kin hear, but he's still warm. Th' life in him ain't enough t' fill a cricket, an' I won't die f'r a cricket!' The boy argued some, but give in at last. Fergusen stripped off Hugh Glass's clothes an' took his weapons an' possibles. 'No p'int leavin' 'em f'r th' Rees,' he informed th' boy. They left Hugh Glass stripped naked an' bled dry under thet berry bush. F'r all intents, he was dead. Later on thet same day, Hugh Glass woke up.

"'Sonuvabitch,' Hugh Glass remarked. 'Th' bastids left me.'

*"**H**ugh Glass commenced to crawl. He had first pulped an' chawed all th' berries on th' little tree. Thet cost him considerable pain an' he blacked out once jest raisin' his arm. But he was powerful thirsty an' he knowd he'd never live without water. So he rolled hisself down the four feet to th' little stream thet fed this clearin'. He black out again an' started all his wounds a-bleedin'. When he roused f'r th' second time, he reasoned he'd have t' start out to-day. The nearest fort was to th' west an' he could follow the stream bed awhile an' eat th' small plants an' grubs an' sech along it. He had a strong desire t' meet up with Fergusen an' Bridger again an' rip out their eyes with his thumbs an' shatter their skulls against a rock. They had left him without gun or knife, flint or steel. A man who was fit could make th' walk t' th' fort in about a month. It was only 300 miles. He figgered in his present state it would take him longer. Th' first day he covered seventeen feet.*

"He crawled, mostly, f'r th' first two weeks. Once he stood up an' waved his arms t'scare off some wolves from their kill. Thet got him some fresh, raw meat an' he was able t'drink back a deal o' th' blood he'd lost from his wounds tearin' open. He stayed with the meat another week, till th' smell drove him off. He was crawlin' three mile a day, by thet time.

"Finally, he was able t'stand, an' walk for'ard like a man. An' with each step, he thought up more an' uglier things t' do to th' men what had kilt him. Finally, th' gatesman at th' fort sighted him, an'..."

"An' he was dis powerful mass o' gristle an' muscle, harden' by de wilderness into lean, yet massive, near-savage beauty, with de nobility of sufferin' deep in 'is clear eyes," guessed the Indian boy.

"Wall, not quite. *"He was a wisp o' a skeleton, th' human grease an' dust burnt black t' him, hairy an' near mad. His body was criss-crossed with scars an' he had near forgot how t' talk, he'd been alone so long.*

"He rested a week or so, but when a expedition was fitted up t' head to th' next nearest fort, he borrowed a gun an' kit against his company's credit an' j'ined 'em. F'r there was where he reckoned t' find th' crew what had left him.

"They was a number o' other adventures, including another run-in with th' Rees, an' he lost th' rest o' his new party. But finally he stood covered with crusted snow outside th' fort. He was let in an' he went at once t' th' tavern where Jim Bridger sulked over an ale an' thought about th' man he'd left t' die so many months before. It was a subject he thought on often, but today was different. He was interrupted by a terrible bellow an' looked up t' see Hugh Glass, covered with ice, p'intin' at him like th' crack o' doom.

"'You dastard mulefoot!' hollered Glass. 'Why'd you leave me t' DIE?' An' young Bridger had hisself a accident.

"Once he had got it straight thet th' man before him was livin', Bridger commenced to explain his actions, not puttin' all the blame on Fergusen, but not lettin' him clear too much neither. He was prepared t' die, f'r he had seen a terrible vengeance glintin' in th' old man's eye. F'r his part, the almost year he had been at trackin' Bridger had cooled Hugh Glass some. Seein' th' young, sweatin' boy right before him, it became harder an' harder t' picture killin' him in cold blood. So thet when th' boy had done, Glass shrugged an' had him tell where Fergusen had been headed. Then he turned his back an' went f'r th' door. 'But...but...wait,' gasped th' boy. 'Is thet all you want from me?' Glass sized him up with an angry eye.

"'You kin gimme thet raw-hide shirt, if it fits. Boots, too.' Bridger took thet deal like th' best trade he'd made in his life. Was, too.

"Turned out Fergusen was now a official scout at a army post in country even more blank an' mis'rable than th' first. But, even though they were in a spot so blasted thet civilization was a dim memory (or mebbe BECAUSE o' thet), th' commandant o' th' fort didn't feel he could allow his chief scout t' be stomped t' death. Bad f'r morale. An' Hugh Glass could see th' wisdom in thet.

"So they struck a compromise. It had taken till summer f'r Glass t' reach th' fort, so's there was a deal o' humanity, trappers, injuns an' soldiers, traders, farmers an' sech like, crammin' the fort. All o' them was assembled an' then Fergusen was made t' stand before 'em whilst Glass told all o' his story about Bridger an' Fergusen's cowardly desertion an' theft o' Glass's possibles.

"After which the commandant supplied him with a new kit an' he was encouraged t' leave as soon as possible, lest his temper get th' better o' him in sech close proximity t' him what had wronged him.

"Truth t' tell, Glass was glad hisself t' be goin'. His anger was most burnt out, even at Fergusen, an' he was as pleased with th' man's humiliation as he would've been with his blood. He did some more trappin', then retired some year ago t' farm."

"**E**el's feet!" said the Indian boy. "Did all dat stuff really 'appen to him?"

"Close as I kin recall," said the big man carefully. "Ev'rybody tells it varied."

"Of course it's true!" said the Poet. "It's *much* too boring for *fiction*! Was there a *point* to all that?" MacAlistaire considered.

"Only thet each man finds his own revenge f'r his own wrongs. An' even a man what's come back from th' grave don't always crave revenge th' way he'd thought he would."

"Revenge," said the Poet, settling down in his blanket, "is the noblest motif in fiction. Everyone uses it. Your story would be much improved if he hunted them down and slew them in ironic ways, perhaps then dying himself."

"Even if it weren't true?"

"*Especially* if it's not true. People only accept the truth of nonfiction if it corresponds to the truth they have been trained to accept in fiction. Even if that truth is false."

Then he fell asleep. One after the other, they all dozed around the coals of the dying fire. MacAlistaire thought about the Poet's last words, and for a long time he lay awake and grinned to himself in the darkness until he, too, fell asleep.

The author would like to recommend *Give Your Heart to the Hawks* to anyone interested in wilderness tales, or mountain men in particular. I have cribbed from it shamelessly for this story about Hugh Glass and have found it unparalleled in covering the entire period of the Mountain Men with authority and wit. And if my dog hadn't carried it away the night before deadline I'd be able to tell you *who wrote it*, too. Oh, well. No one's perfect.

My publisher informs me that a just-released movie, *Grim Prairie Tales*, features a city slicker and a grizzled bounty hunter trading horror stories in a Western setting. I can assure suspicious readers that I had not seen the movie when I wrote this story—haven't in fact, as of this writing—and submit this as further proof that since all writers tap the same river, they will upon occasion wind up with a near identical bucketful.

THE WEATHER HAD TURNED...

...THERE WAS RIME ON THE GROUND IN THE MORNINGS...

K^at_hh

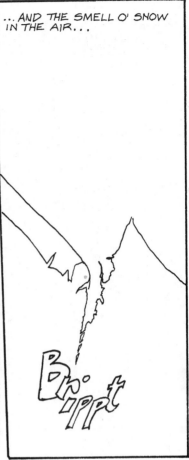

...AND THE SMELL O' SNOW IN THE AIR...

B_rn_i^p_pt

T_sr_rt_th

MACALISTAIRE HAD ONCE HEARD A FELLER SAY THET THIS TIME O' YEAR... 'TWEEN *FALL* AN' *WINTER* WHEN THE GRASS WAS *GREEN* AND THE AIR WAS *DANGEROUS WITH COLD*... WAS A *WITCHY TIME*, FULL OF MAGICKS AND SURPRISE...

AAAAARRRG!

43

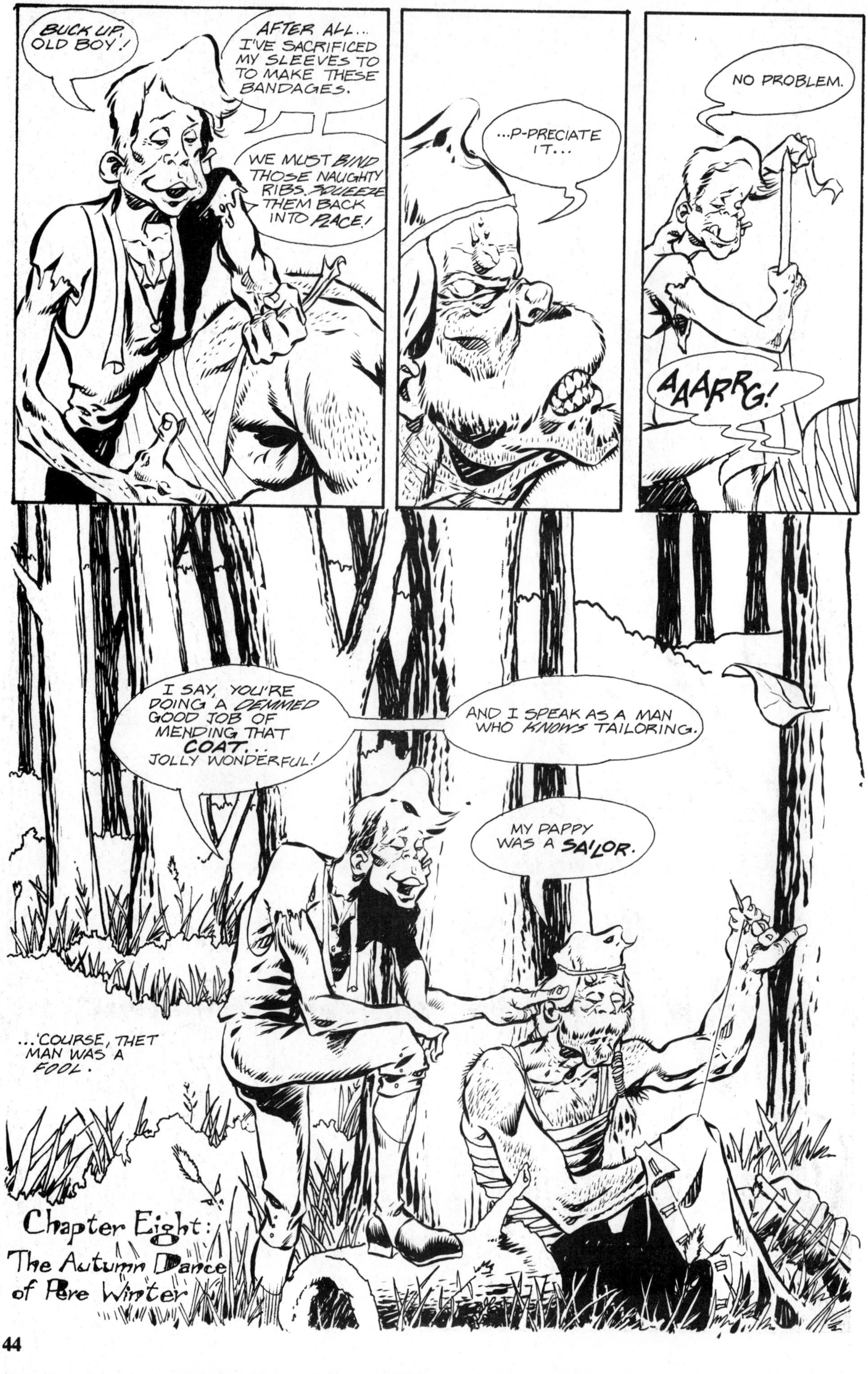
BUCK UP, OLD BOY!
AFTER ALL... I'VE SACRIFICED MY SLEEVES TO TO MAKE THESE BANDAGES.
WE MUST BIND THOSE NAUGHTY RIBS. SQUEEZE THEM BACK INTO PLACE!
...P-PRECIATE IT...
NO PROBLEM.
AAARRG!
I SAY, YOU'RE DOING A DEMMED GOOD JOB OF MENDING THAT COAT... JOLLY WONDERFUL!
AND I SPEAK AS A MAN WHO KNOWS TAILORING.
MY PAPPY WAS A SAILOR.
...'COURSE, THET MAN WAS A FOOL.
Chapter Eight:
The Autumn Dance of Pere Winter

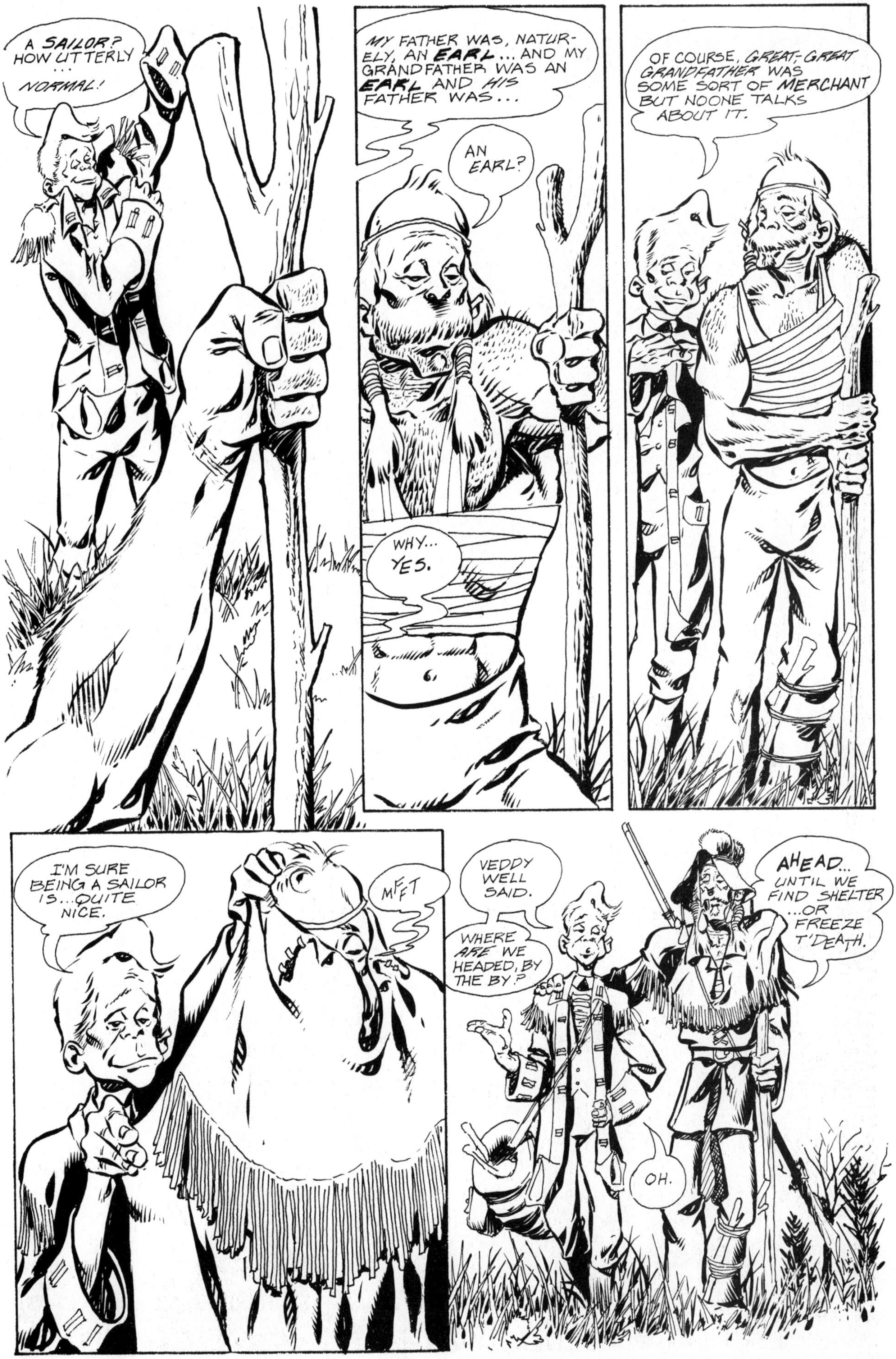
A SAILOR? HOW UTTERLY ... NORMAL!
MY FATHER WAS, NATUR-ELY, AN EARL... AND MY GRANDFATHER WAS AN EARL AND HIS FATHER WAS...
AN EARL?
WHY... YES.
OF COURSE, GREAT-GREAT GRANDFATHER WAS SOME SORT OF MERCHANT BUT NOONE TALKS ABOUT IT.
I'M SURE BEING A SAILOR IS... QUITE NICE.
MFFT
VEDDY WELL SAID.
WHERE ARE WE HEADED, BY THE BY?
AHEAD... UNTIL WE FIND SHELTER ...OR FREEZE T'DEATH.
OH.

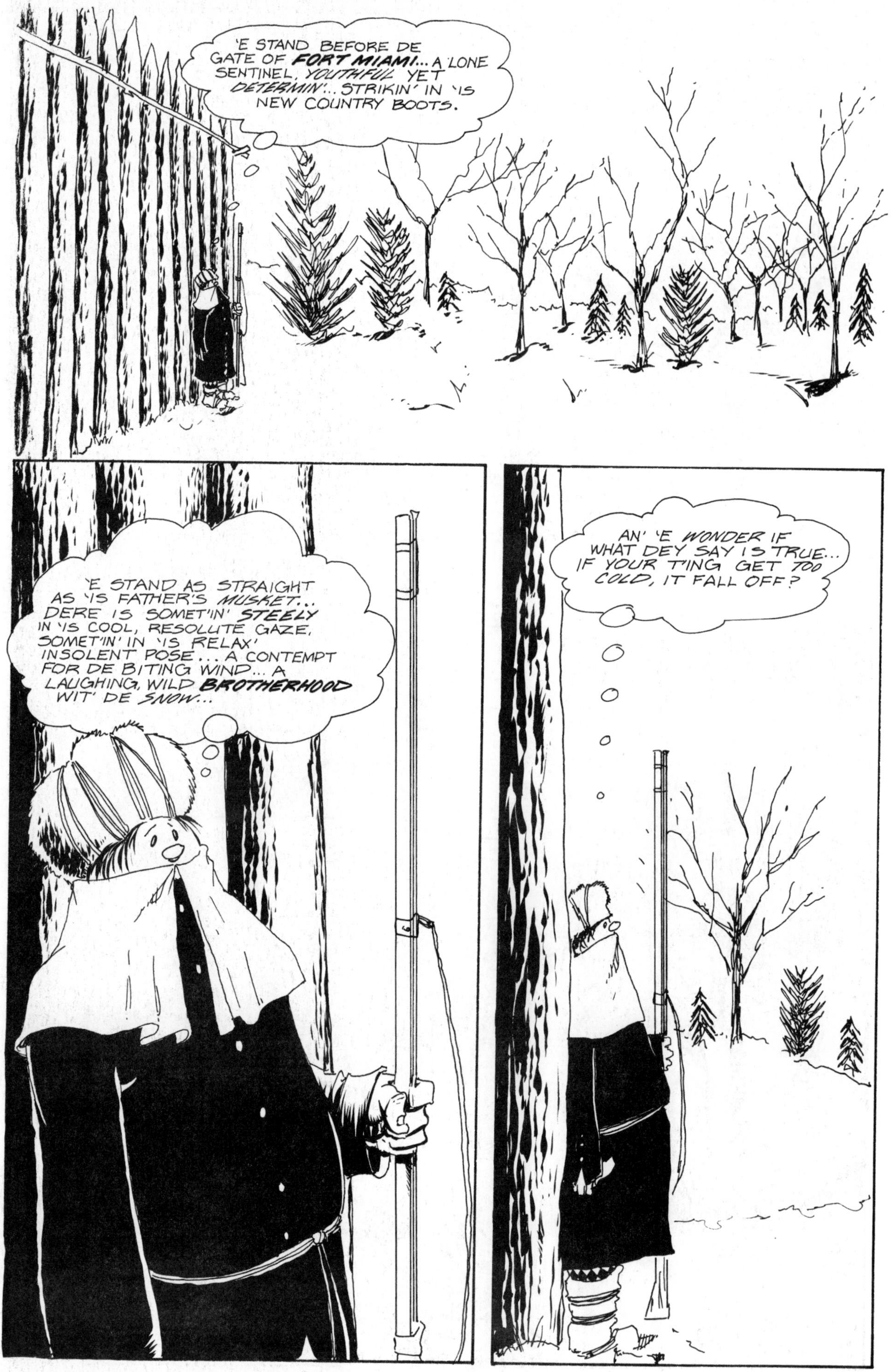
'E STAND BEFORE DE GATE OF FORT MIAMI... A LONE SENTINEL, YOUTHFUL YET DETERMIN'... STRIKIN' IN 'IS NEW COUNTRY BOOTS.
'E STAND AS STRAIGHT AS 'IS FATHER'S MUSKET... DERE IS SOMET'IN' STEELY IN 'IS COOL, RESOLUTE GAZE, SOMET'IN' IN 'IS RELAX' INSOLENT POSE... A CONTEMPT FOR DE BITING WIND... A LAUGHING, WILD BROTHERHOOD WIT' DE SNOW...
AN' 'E WONDER IF WHAT DEY SAY IS TRUE... IF YOUR T'ING GET TOO COLD, IT FALL OFF?

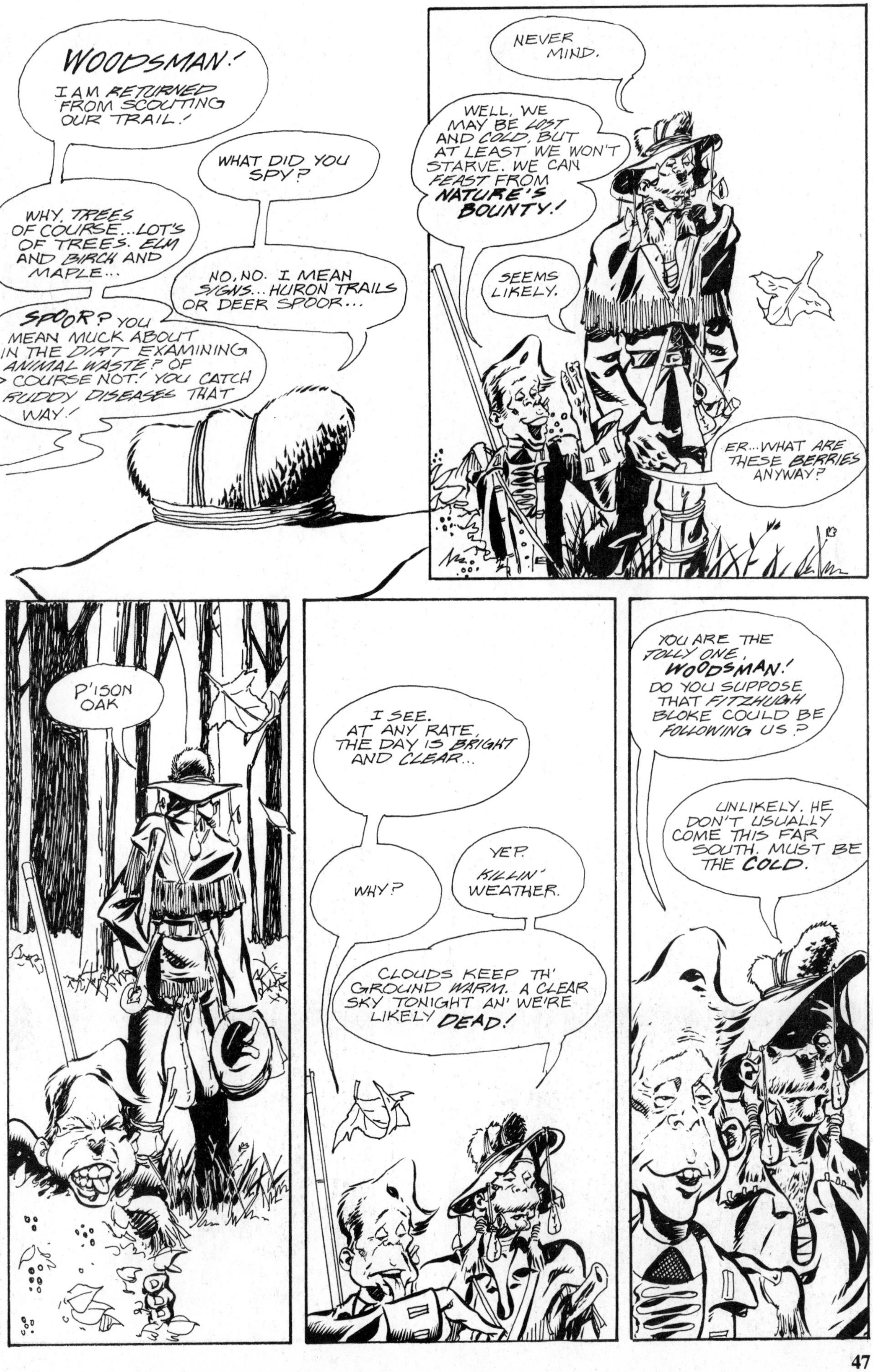

WOODSMAN! I AM RETURNED FROM SCOUTING OUR TRAIL!
WHAT DID YOU SPY?
WHY, TREES OF COURSE... LOT'S OF TREES. ELM AND BIRCH AND MAPLE...
NO, NO. I MEAN SIGNS... HURON TRAILS OR DEER SPOOR...
SPOOR? YOU MEAN MUCK ABOUT IN THE DIRT EXAMINING ANIMAL WASTE? OF COURSE NOT! YOU CATCH RUDDY DISEASES THAT WAY!
NEVER MIND.
WELL, WE MAY BE LOST AND COLD, BUT AT LEAST WE WON'T STARVE. WE CAN FEAST FROM NATURE'S BOUNTY!
SEEMS LIKELY.
ER... WHAT ARE THESE BERRIES ANYWAY?
P'ISON OAK
I SEE. AT ANY RATE, THE DAY IS BRIGHT AND CLEAR...
WHY?
YEP. KILLIN' WEATHER.
CLOUDS KEEP TH' GROUND WARM. A CLEAR SKY TONIGHT AN' WE'RE LIKELY DEAD!
YOU ARE THE JOLLY ONE, WOODSMAN! DO YOU SUPPOSE THAT FITZHUGH BLOKE COULD BE FOLLOWING US?
UNLIKELY. HE DON'T USUALLY COME THIS FAR SOUTH. MUST BE THE COLD.

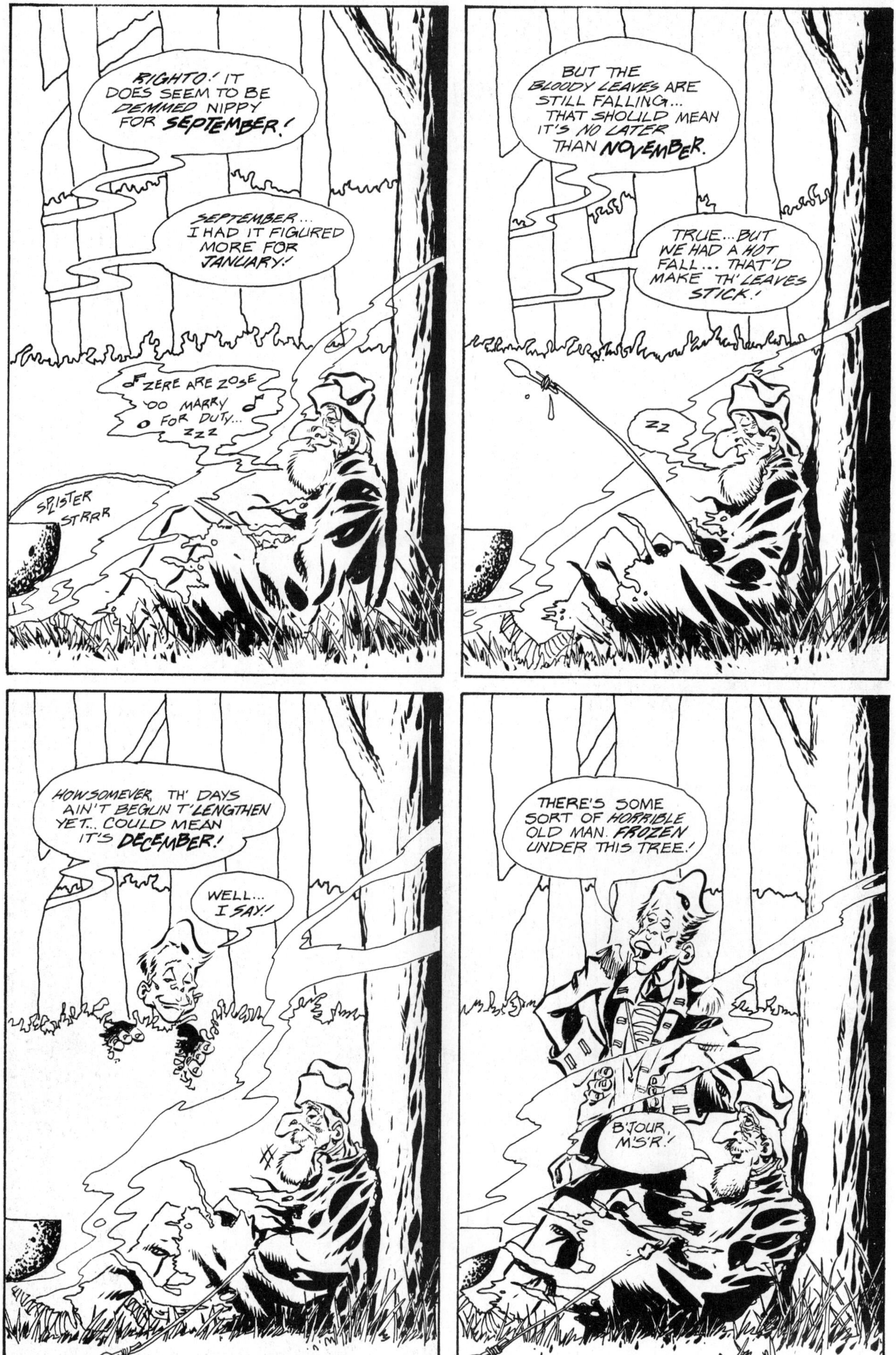
RIGHTO! IT DOES SEEM TO BE DEMMED NIPPY FOR SEPTEMBER!
SEPTEMBER... I HAD IT FIGURED MORE FOR JANUARY!
ZERE ARE ZOSE 'OO MARRY FOR DUTY... ZZZ
SPISTER STRRR
BUT THE BLOODY LEAVES ARE STILL FALLING... THAT SHOULD MEAN IT'S NO LATER THAN NOVEMBER.
TRUE... BUT WE HAD A HOT FALL... THAT'D MAKE TH' LEAVES STICK!
ZZ
HOWSOMEVER, TH' DAYS AIN'T BEGUN T'LENGTHEN YET... COULD MEAN IT'S DECEMBER!
WELL... I SAY!
THERE'S SOME SORT OF HORRIBLE OLD MAN, FROZEN UNDER THIS TREE!
B'JOUR, M'S'R!

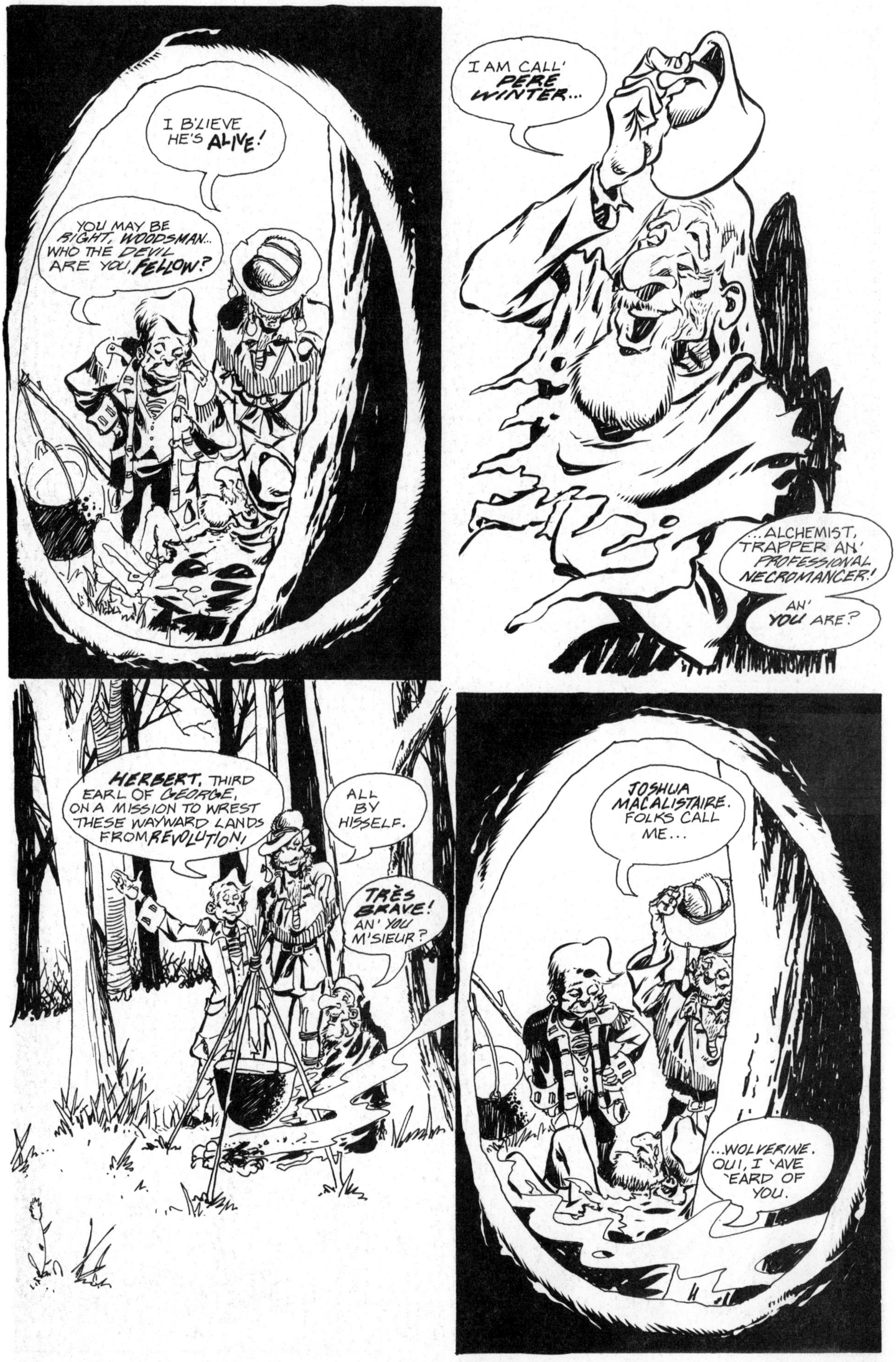
I B'LIEVE HE'S ALIVE!
YOU MAY BE RIGHT, WOODSMAN... WHO THE DEVIL ARE YOU, FELLOW?
I AM CALL' PERE WINTER...
...ALCHEMIST, TRAPPER AN' PROFESSIONAL NECROMANCER!
AN' YOU ARE?
HERBERT, THIRD EARL OF GEORGE, ON A MISSION TO WREST THESE WAYWARD LANDS FROM REVOLUTION,
ALL BY HISSELF.
TRÈS BRAVE! AN' YOU M'SIEUR?
JOSHUA MACALISTAIRE. FOLKS CALL ME...
...WOLVERINE. OUI, I 'AVE 'EARD OF YOU.

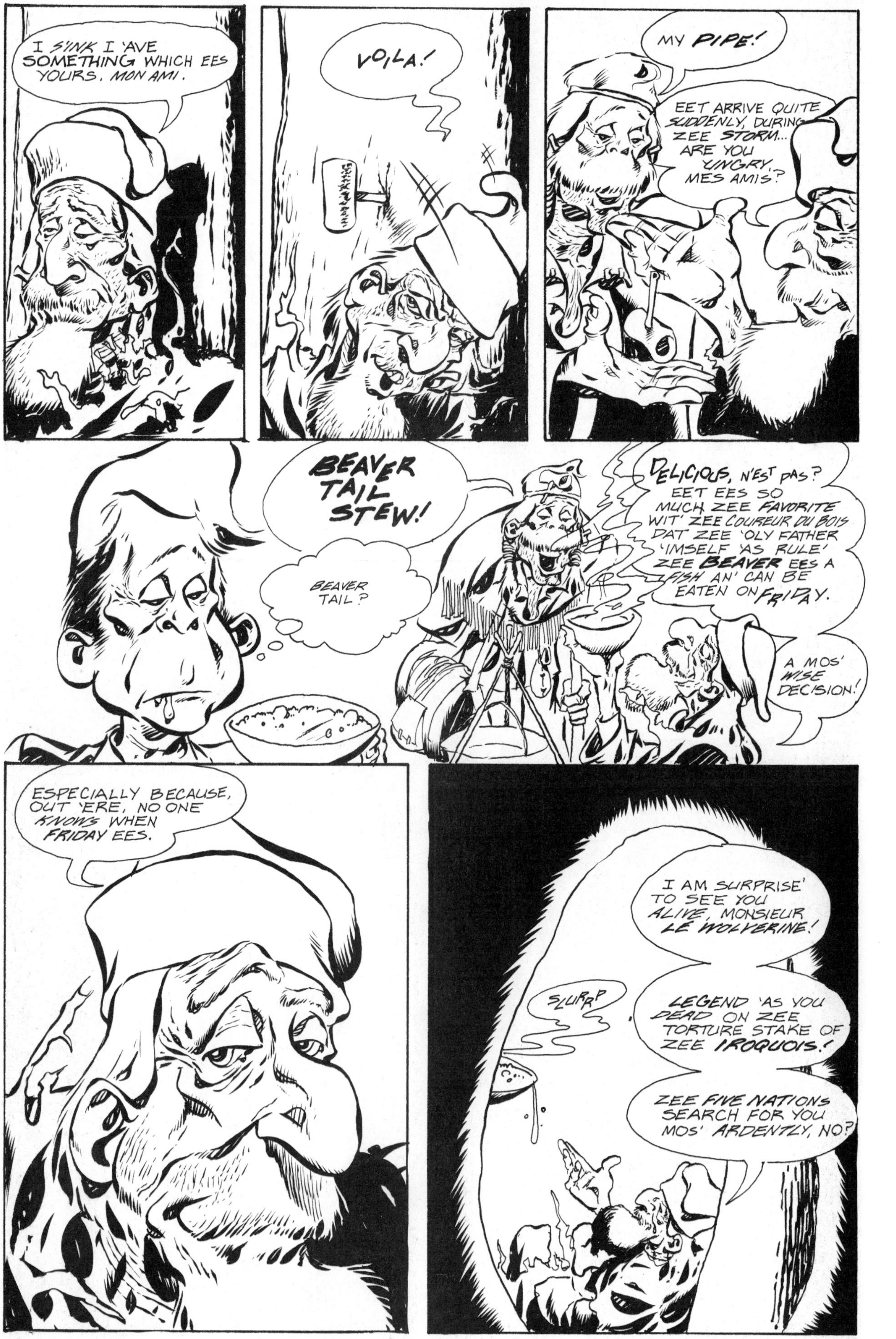
I SINK I 'AVE SOMETHING WHICH EES YOURS, MON AMI.
VOILA!
MY PIPE!
EET ARRIVE QUITE SUDDENLY, DURING ZEE STORM... ARE YOU 'UNGRY, MES AMIS?
BEAVER TAIL STEW!
BEAVER TAIL?
DELICIOUS, N'EST PAS? EET EES SO MUCH ZEE FAVORITE WIT' ZEE COUREUR DU BOIS DAT ZEE 'OLY FATHER 'IMSELF 'AS RULE' ZEE BEAVER EES A FISH AN' CAN BE EATEN ON FRIDAY.
A MOS' WISE DECISION!
ESPECIALLY BECAUSE, OUT 'ERE, NO ONE KNOWS WHEN FRIDAY EES.
I AM SURPRISE' TO SEE YOU ALIVE, MONSIEUR LE WOLVERINE!
SLURRP
LEGEND 'AS YOU DEAD ON ZEE TORTURE STAKE OF ZEE IROQUOIS!
ZEE FIVE NATIONS SEARCH FOR YOU MOS' ARDENTLY, NO?

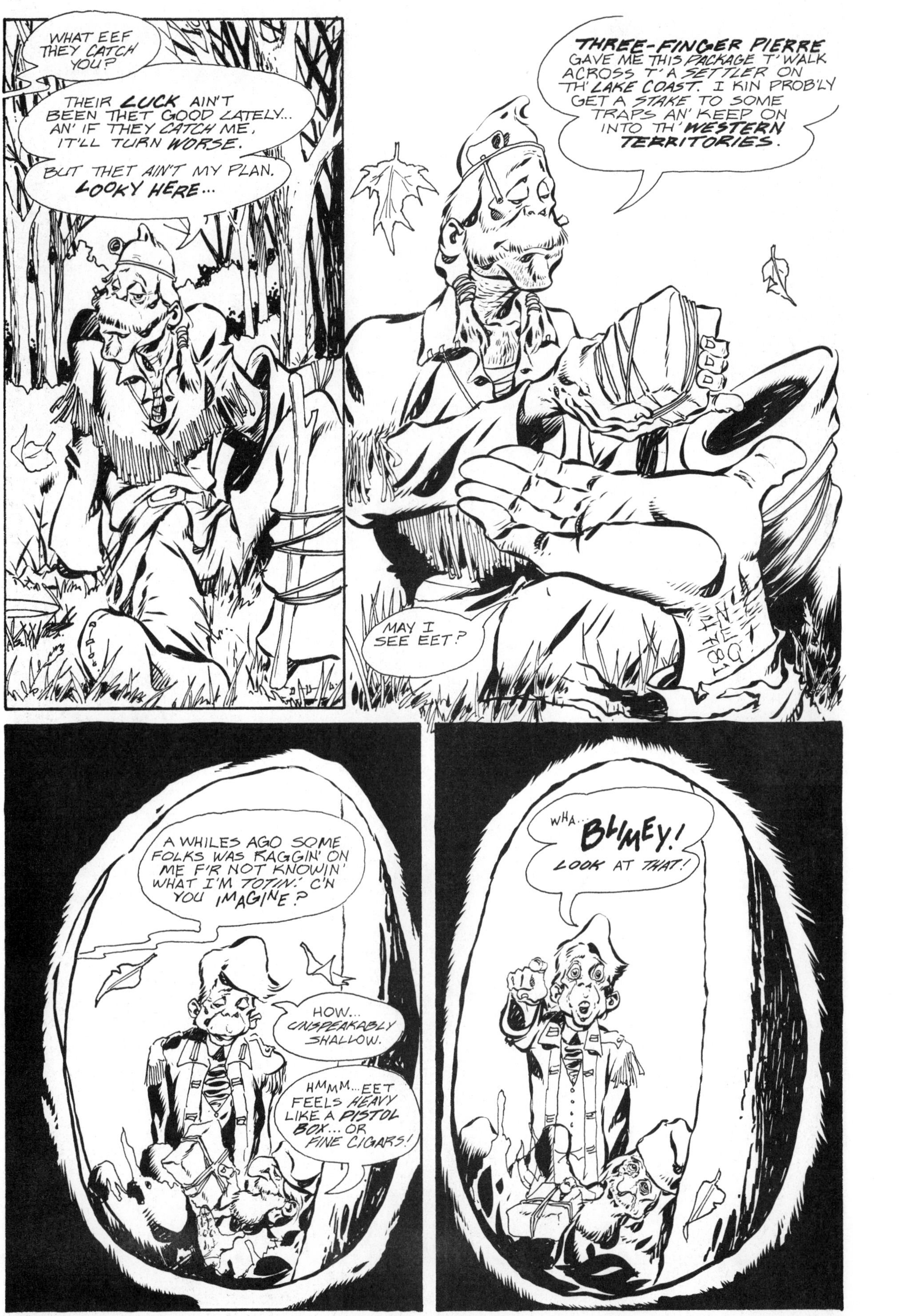

WHAT EEF THEY CATCH YOU?
THEIR LUCK AIN'T BEEN THET GOOD LATELY... AN' IF THEY CATCH ME, IT'LL TURN WORSE.
BUT THET AIN'T MY PLAN. LOOKY HERE...
THREE-FINGER PIERRE GAVE ME THIS PACKAGE T' WALK ACROSS T' A SETTLER ON TH' LAKE COAST. I KIN PROB'LY GET A STAKE TO SOME TRAPS AN' KEEP ON INTO TH' WESTERN TERRITORIES.
MAY I SEE EET?
A WHILES AGO SOME FOLKS WAS RAGGIN' ON ME F'R NOT KNOWIN' WHAT I'M TOTIN.' C'N YOU IMAGINE?
HOW... UNSPEAKABLY SHALLOW.
HMMM... EET FEELS HEAVY LIKE A PISTOL BOX... OR FINE CIGARS!
WHA... BLIMEY! LOOK AT THAT!

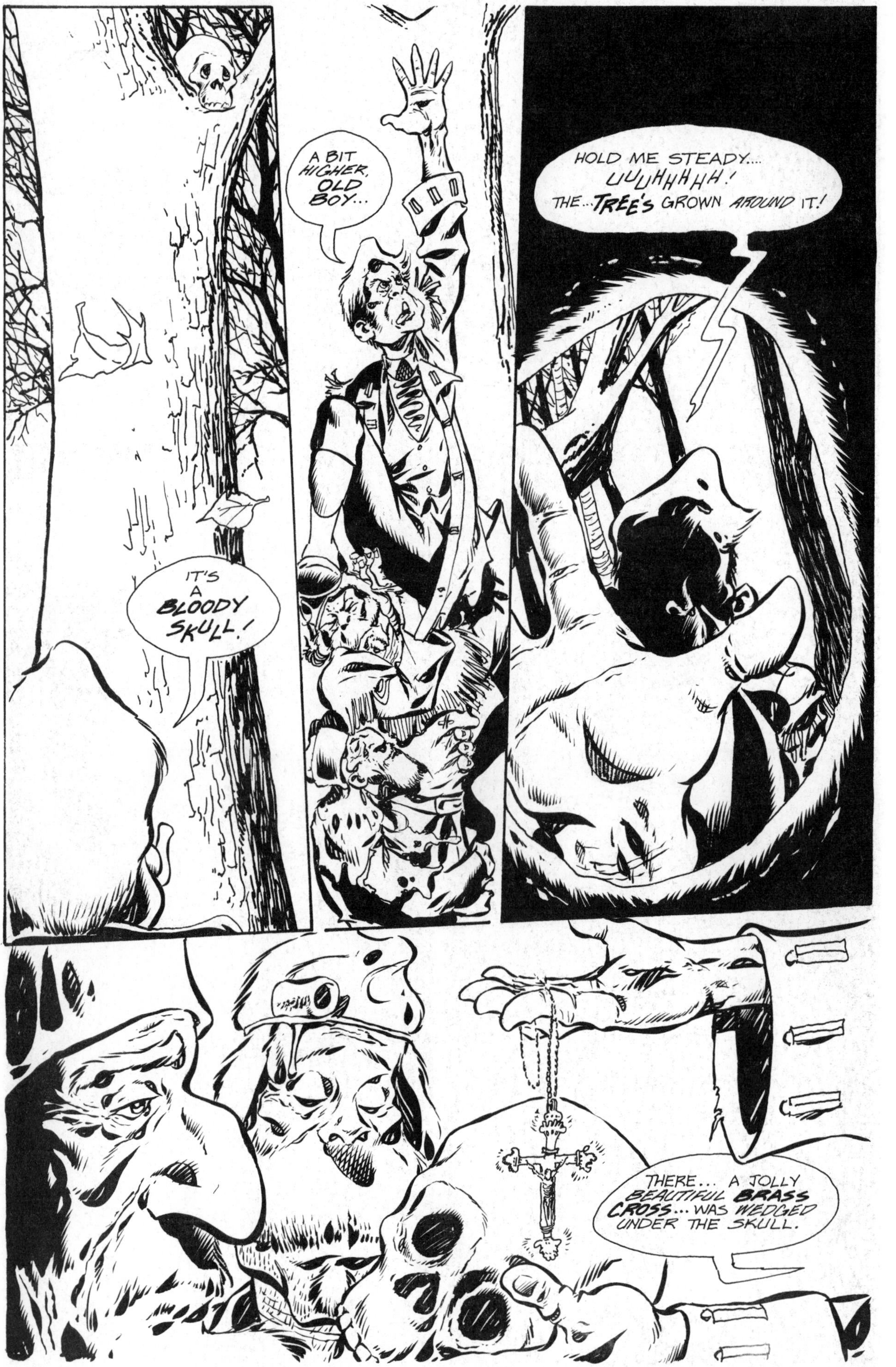
IT'S A BLOODY SKULL!
A BIT HIGHER, OLD BOY...
HOLD ME STEADY.... UUUHHHHH! THE...TREE'S GROWN AROUND IT!
THERE... A JOLLY BEAUTIFUL BRASS CROSS... WAS WEDGED UNDER THE SKULL.

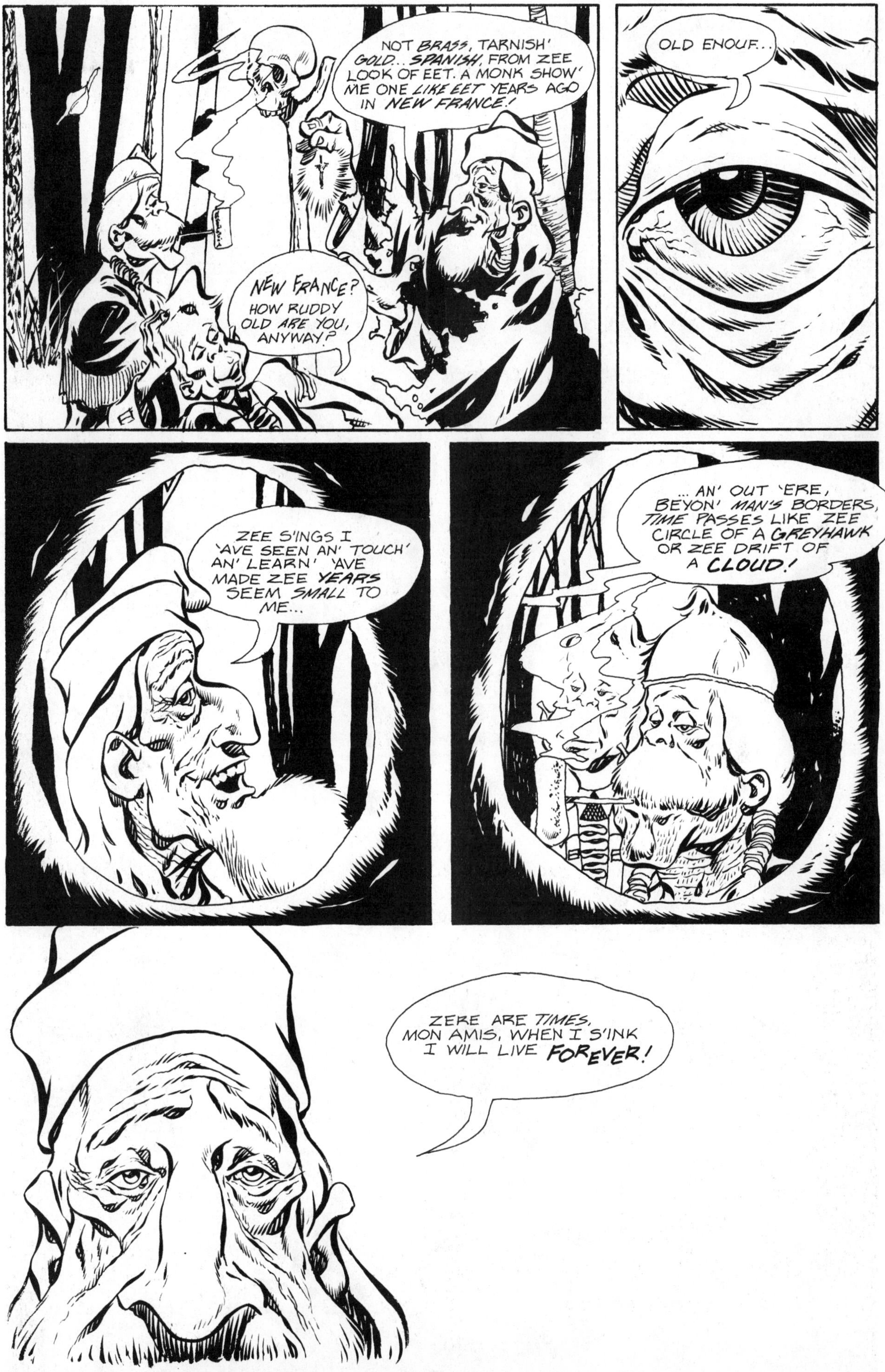
NOT BRASS, TARNISH' GOLD... SPANISH, FROM ZEE LOOK OF EET. A MONK SHOW' ME ONE LIKE EET YEARS AGO IN NEW FRANCE!
NEW FRANCE? HOW RUDDY OLD ARE YOU, ANYWAY?
OLD ENOUF...
ZEE S'INGS I 'AVE SEEN AN' TOUCH' AN' LEARN' 'AVE MADE ZEE YEARS SEEM SMALL TO ME...
... AN' OUT 'ERE, BEYON' MAN'S BORDERS, TIME PASSES LIKE ZEE CIRCLE OF A GREYHAWK OR ZEE DRIFT OF A CLOUD!
ZERE ARE TIMES, MON AMIS, WHEN I S'INK I WILL LIVE FOREVER!

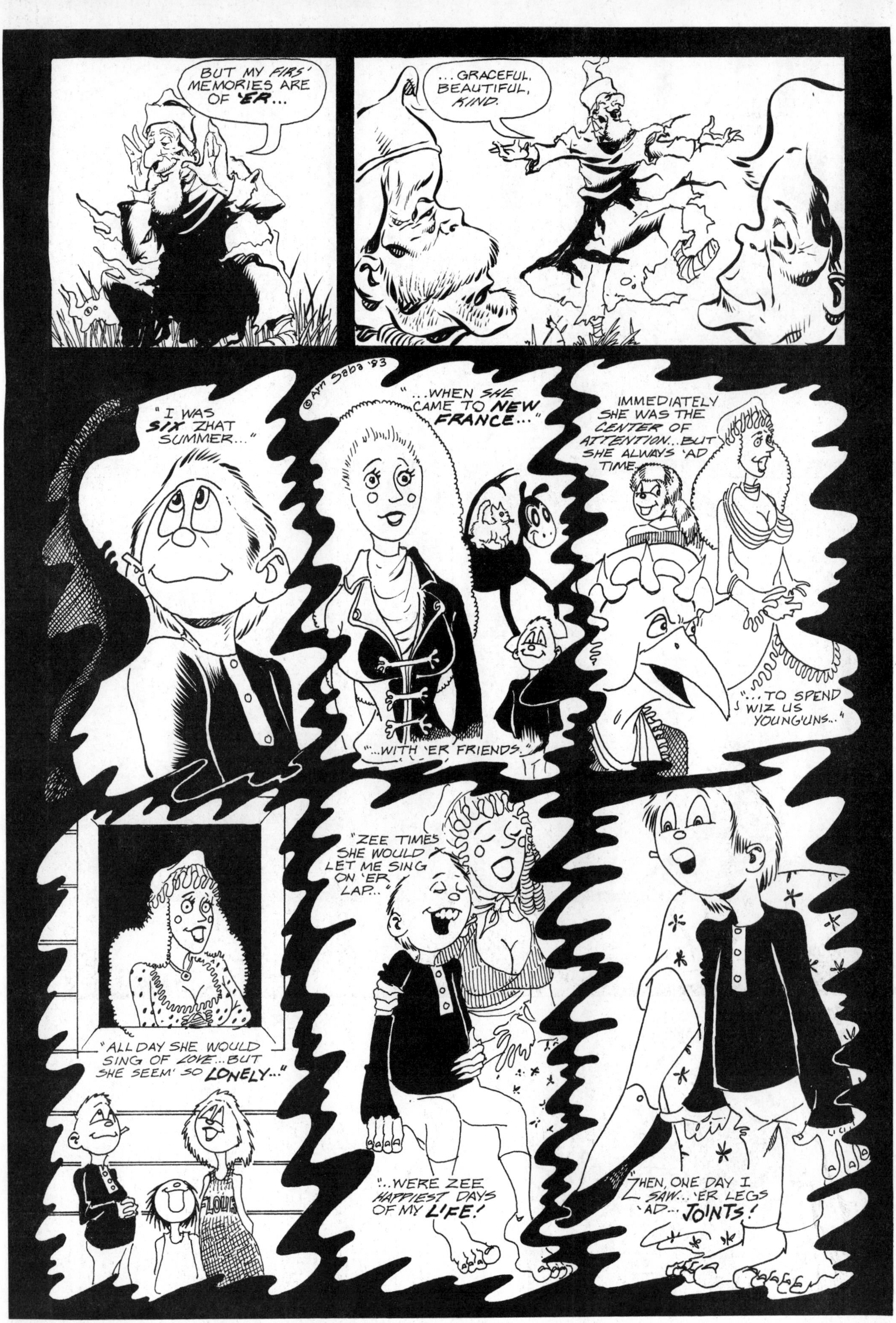
BUT MY FIRS' MEMORIES ARE OF 'ER...
...GRACEFUL, BEAUTIFUL, KIND.
© Ann Saba '83
"I WAS SIX ZHAT SUMMER..."
"...WHEN SHE CAME TO NEW FRANCE..."
"...WITH 'ER FRIENDS."
IMMEDIATELY SHE WAS THE CENTER OF ATTENTION...BUT SHE ALWAYS 'AD TIME...
"...TO SPEND WIZ US YOUNG'UNS..."
"ALL DAY SHE WOULD SING OF LOVE...BUT SHE SEEM' SO LONELY..."
FLOUR
"ZEE TIMES SHE WOULD LET ME SING ON 'ER LAP..."
"...WERE ZEE HAPPIEST DAYS OF MY LIFE!
"ZHEN, ONE DAY I SAW... 'ER LEGS 'AD... JOINTS!

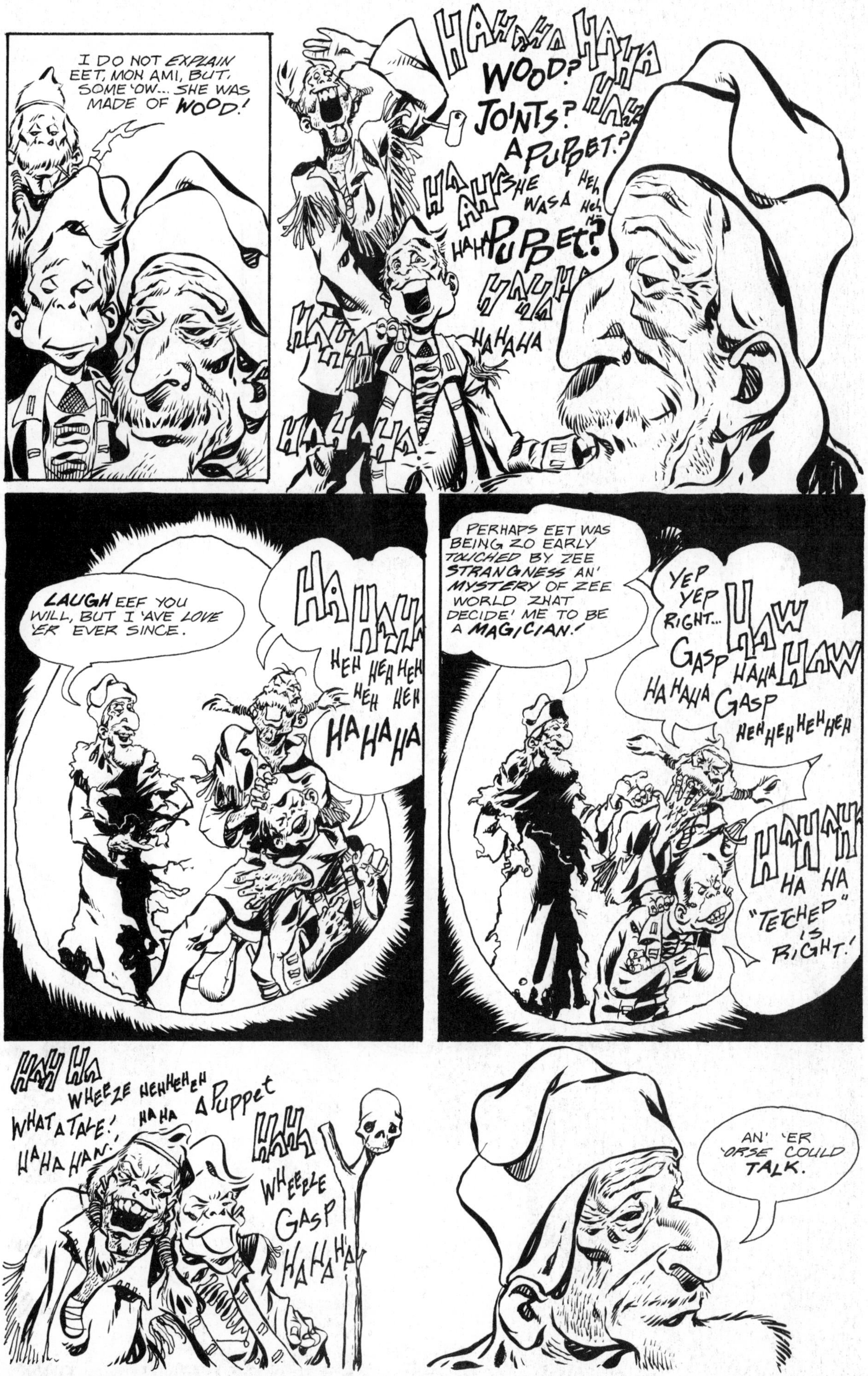
I DO NOT EXPLAIN EET, MON AMI, BUT, SOME 'OW... SHE WAS MADE OF WOOD!
HAHAHA HAHA
WOOD?
JOINTS?
A PUPPET?
HA HAH SHE WAS A PUPPET?
HAHAHA
HAHAHA
LAUGH EEF YOU WILL, BUT I 'AVE LOVE 'ER EVER SINCE.
HA HAH HEH HEH HEH HEH HEH HA HA HA
PERHAPS EET WAS BEING ZO EARLY TOUCHED BY ZEE STRANGNESS AN' MYSTERY OF ZEE WORLD ZHAT DECIDE' ME TO BE A MAGICIAN!
YEP YEP RIGHT... HAW GASP HAHA HAW HA HAHA GASP HEH HEH HEH HEH
HA HA "TETCHED" IS RIGHT!
HAH HA WHEEZE HEH HEH EH WHAT A TALE! HA HA A PUPPET HA HA HAH!
WHEEZE GASP HA HA HA
AN' 'ER 'ORSE COULD TALK.

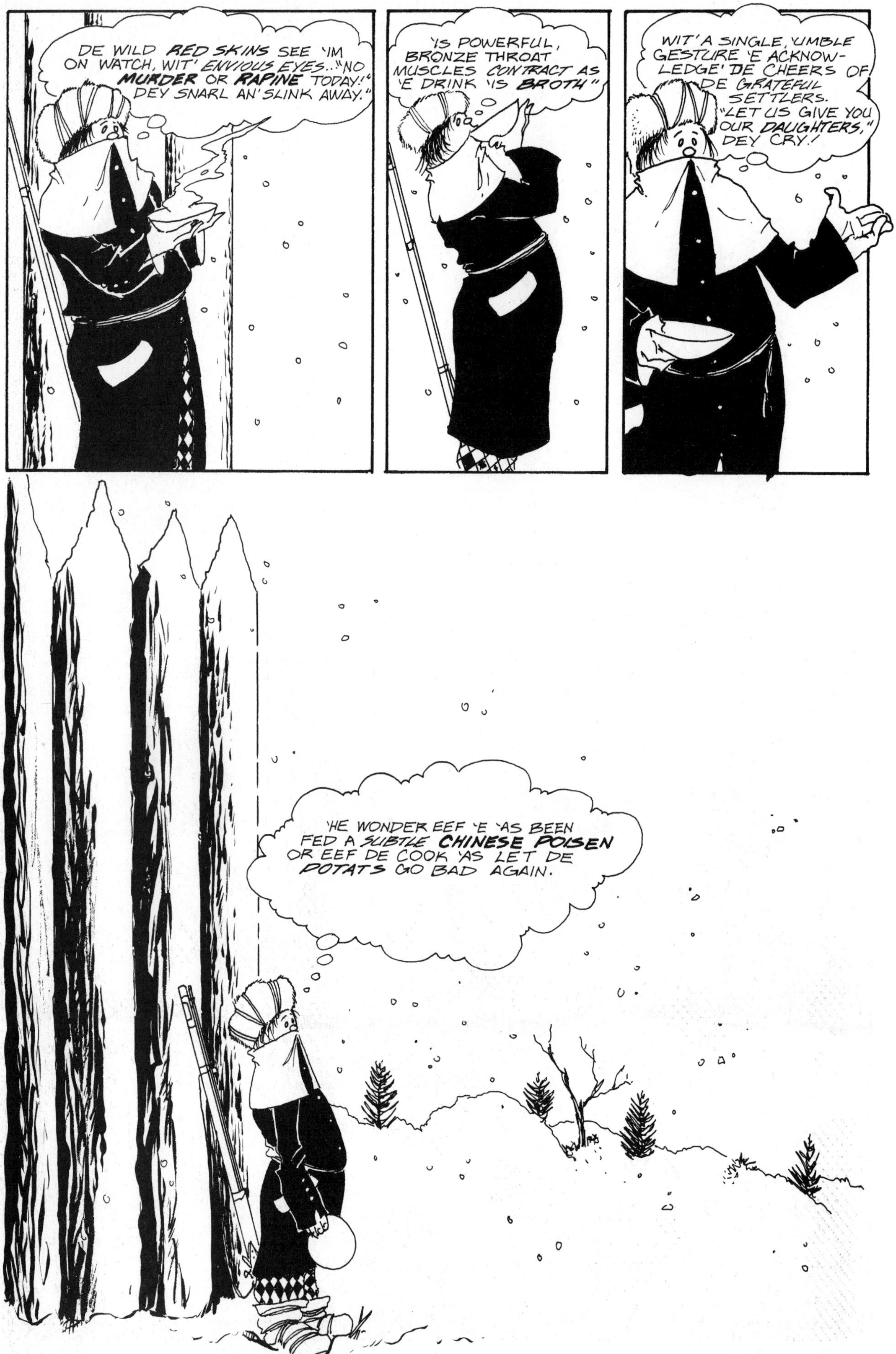
DE WILD RED SKINS SEE 'IM ON WATCH, WIT' ENVIOUS EYES..."NO MURDER OR RAPINE TODAY!" DEY SNARL AN' SLINK AWAY."
'IS POWERFUL, BRONZE THROAT MUSCLES CONTRACT AS 'E DRINK 'IS BROTH"
WIT' A SINGLE, 'UMBLE GESTURE 'E ACKNOWLEDGE' DE CHEERS OF DE GRATEFUL SETTLERS. "LET US GIVE YOU OUR DAUGHTERS," DEY CRY!
'HE WONDER EEF 'E 'AS BEEN FED A SUBTLE CHINESE POISEN OR EEF DE COOK 'AS LET DE POTATS GO BAD AGAIN.

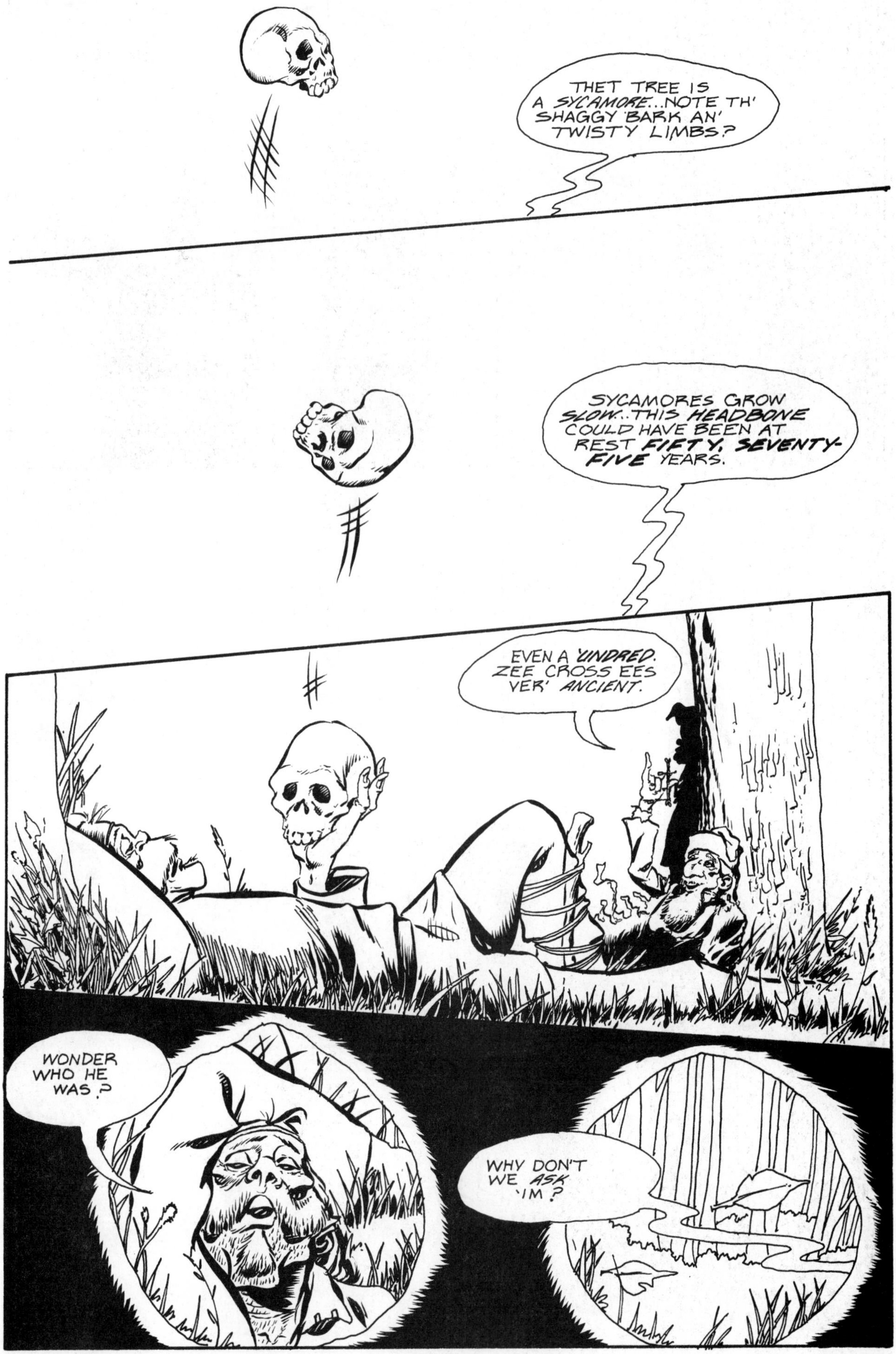
THET TREE IS A SYCAMORE...NOTE TH' SHAGGY BARK AN' TWISTY LIMBS?
SYCAMORES GROW SLOW...THIS HEADBONE COULD HAVE BEEN AT REST FIFTY, SEVENTY-FIVE YEARS.
EVEN A 'UNDRED. ZEE CROSS EES VER' ANCIENT.
WONDER WHO HE WAS?
WHY DON'T WE ASK 'IM?

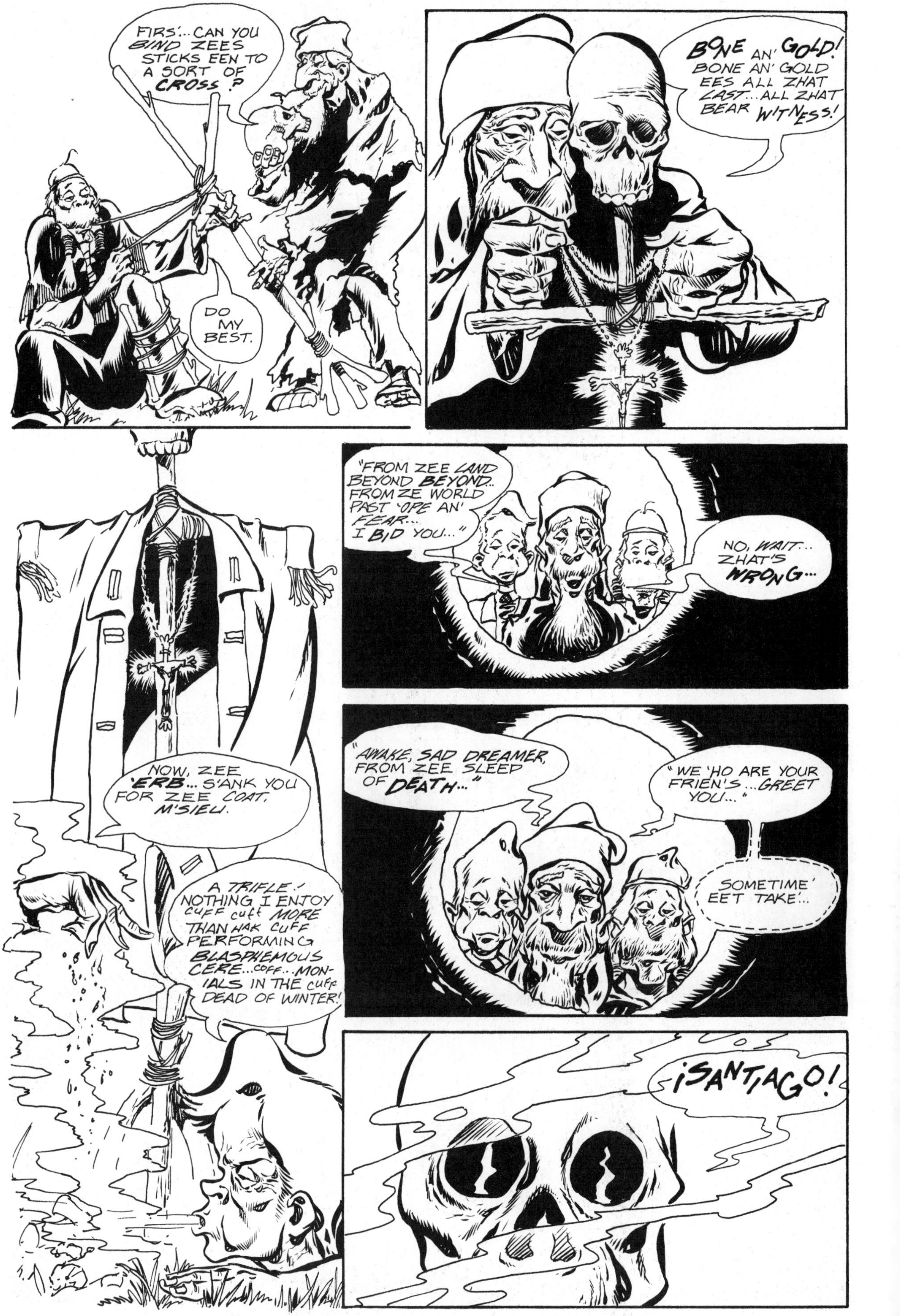

FIRS'... CAN YOU BIND ZEES STICKS EEN TO A SORT OF CROSS ?
DO MY BEST.
BONE AN' GOLD! BONE AN' GOLD EES ALL ZHAT LAST... ALL ZHAT BEAR WITNESS!
NOW, ZEE 'ERB... S'ANK YOU FOR ZEE COAT, M'SIEU.
A TRIFLE! NOTHING I ENJOY cuff cuff MORE THAN HAK CUFF PERFORMING BLASPHEMOUS CERE...COFF... MONIALS IN THE cuff DEAD OF WINTER!
"FROM ZEE LAND BEYOND BEYOND... FROM ZE WORLD PAST 'OPE AN' FEAR... I BID YOU..."
NO, WAIT... ZHAT'S WRONG...
"AWAKE, SAD DREAMER, FROM ZEE SLEEP OF DEATH..."
"WE 'HO ARE YOUR FRIEN'S... GREET YOU..."
SOMETIME' EET TAKE...
¡SANTIAGO!

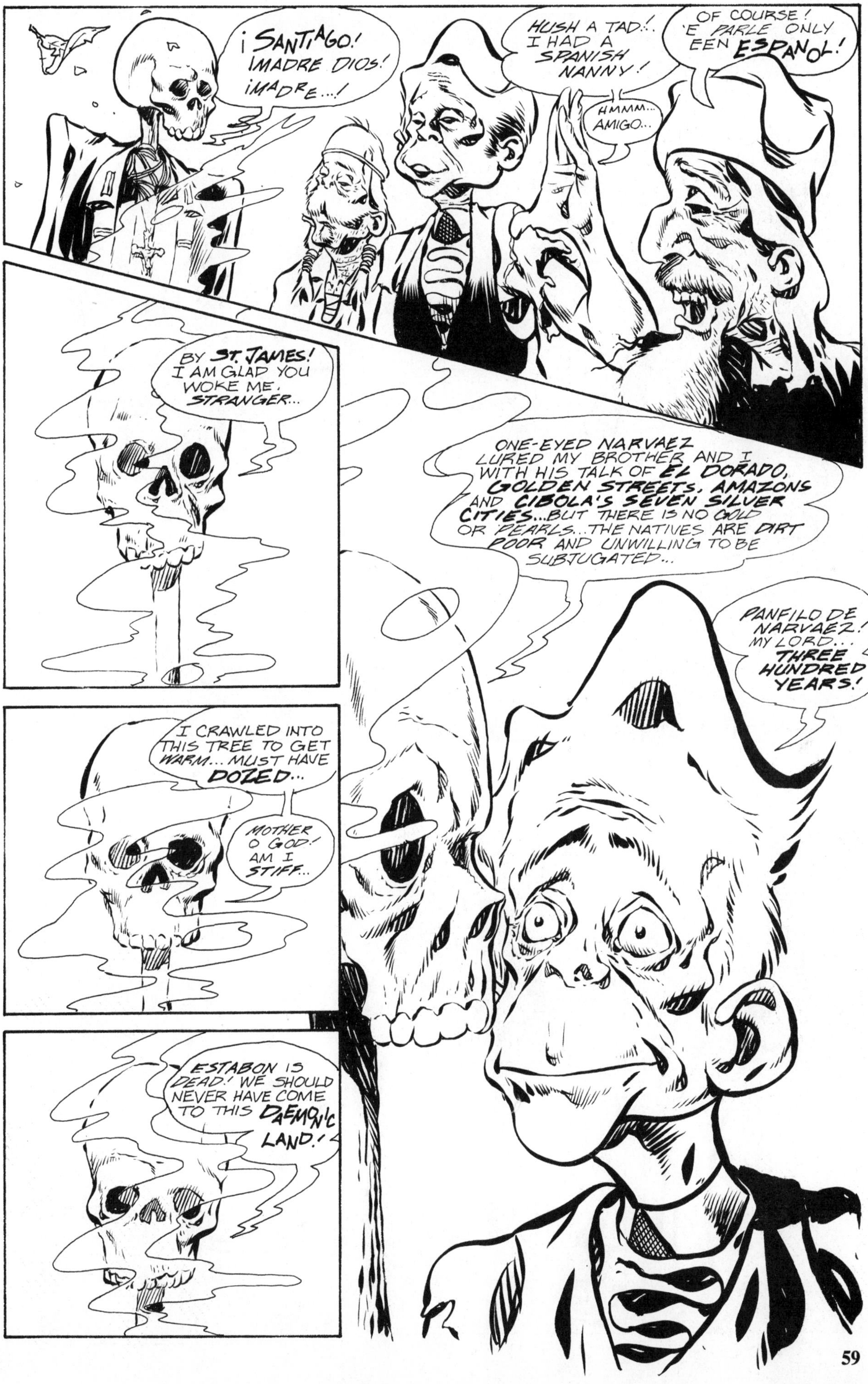
¡SANTIAGO! ¡MADRE DIOS! ¡MADRE...!
HUSH A TAD! I HAD A SPANISH NANNY!
OF COURSE! 'E PARLE ONLY EEN ESPANOL!
HMMM... AMIGO...
BY ST. JAMES! I AM GLAD YOU WOKE ME, STRANGER...
ONE-EYED NARVAEZ LURED MY BROTHER AND I WITH HIS TALK OF EL DORADO, GOLDEN STREETS, AMAZONS AND CIBOLA'S SEVEN SILVER CITIES... BUT THERE IS NO GOLD OR PEARLS... THE NATIVES ARE DIRT POOR AND UNWILLING TO BE SUBJUGATED...
PANFILO DE NARVAEZ! MY LORD... THREE HUNDRED YEARS!
I CRAWLED INTO THIS TREE TO GET WARM... MUST HAVE DOZED...
MOTHER O GOD! AM I STIFF...
ESTABON IS DEAD! WE SHOULD NEVER HAVE COME TO THIS DAEMONIC LAND!

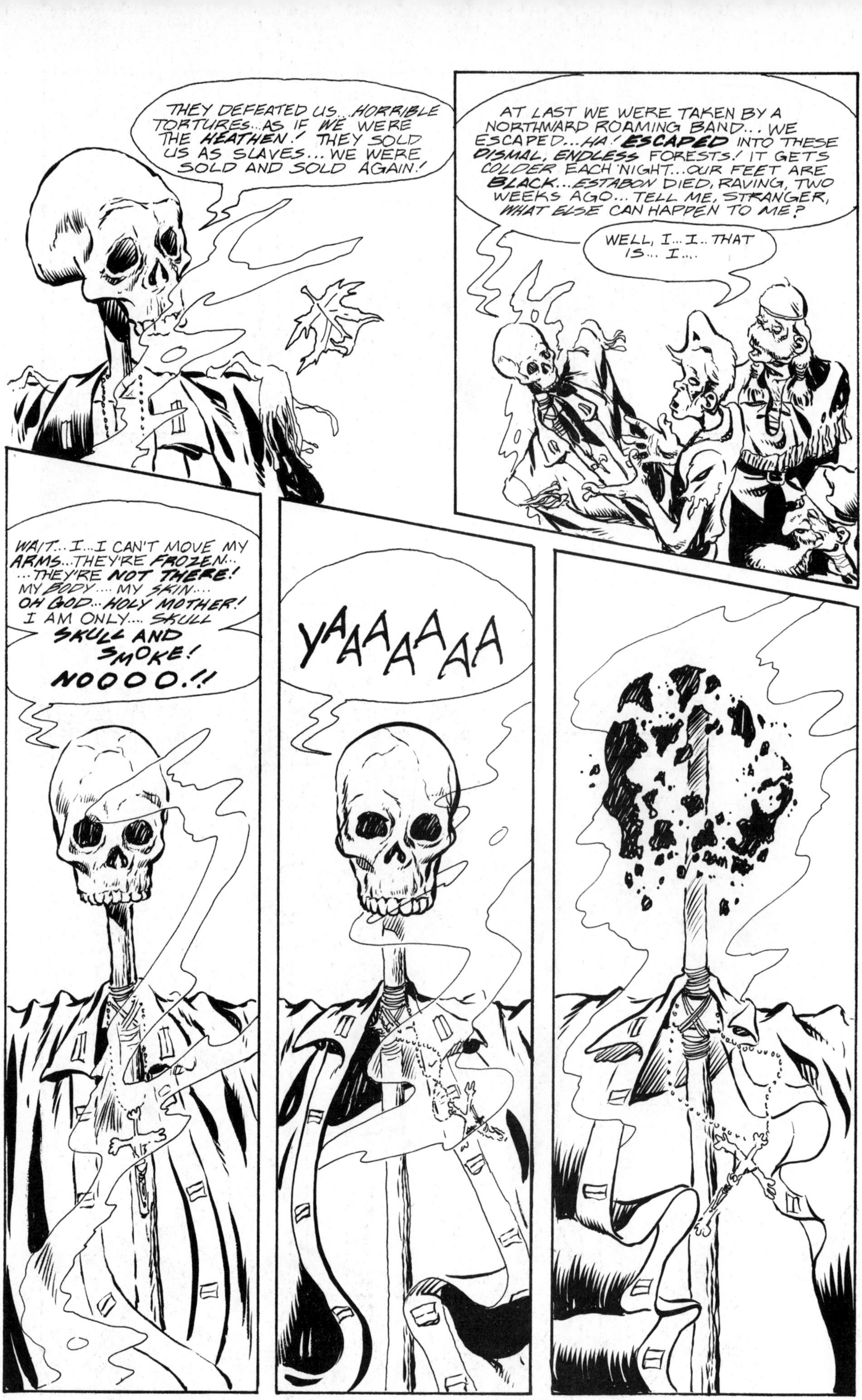
THEY DEFEATED US...HORRIBLE TORTURES...AS IF WE WERE THE HEATHEN! THEY SOLD US AS SLAVES... WE WERE SOLD AND SOLD AGAIN!
AT LAST WE WERE TAKEN BY A NORTHWARD ROAMING BAND... WE ESCAPED...HA! ESCAPED INTO THESE DISMAL, ENDLESS FORESTS! IT GETS COLDER EACH NIGHT...OUR FEET ARE BLACK...ESTABON DIED, RAVING, TWO WEEKS AGO...TELL ME, STRANGER, WHAT ELSE CAN HAPPEN TO ME?
WELL, I...I.. THAT IS... I....
WAIT... I...I CAN'T MOVE MY ARMS...THEY'RE FROZEN... ...THEY'RE NOT THERE! MY BODY... MY SKIN... OH GOD...HOLY MOTHER! I AM ONLY.... SKULL SKULL AND SMOKE! NOOOO.!!
YAAAAAAA

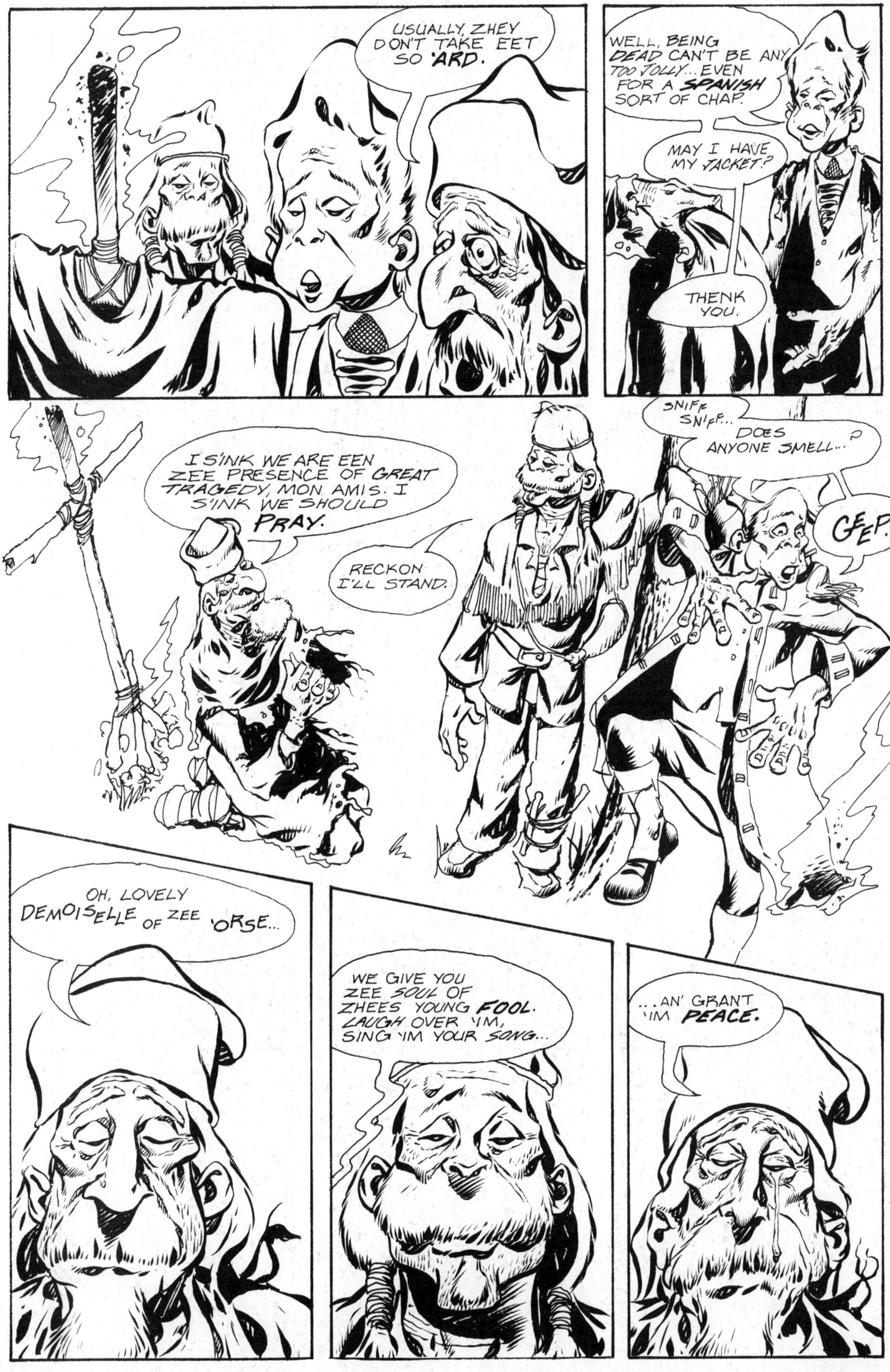
USUALLY, ZHEY DON'T TAKE EET SO 'ARD.
WELL, BEING DEAD CAN'T BE ANY TOO JOLLY... EVEN FOR A SPANISH SORT OF CHAP.
MAY I HAVE MY JACKET?
THENK YOU.
I S'INK WE ARE EEN ZEE PRESENCE OF GREAT TRAGEDY, MON AMIS. I S'INK WE SHOULD PRAY.
RECKON I'LL STAND.
SNIFF SNIFF...
DOES ANYONE SMELL...?
GEEP!
OH, LOVELY DEMOISELLE OF ZEE 'ORSE...
WE GIVE YOU ZEE SOUL OF ZHEES YOUNG FOOL. LAUGH OVER 'IM, SING 'IM YOUR SONG...
...AN' GRANT 'IM PEACE.

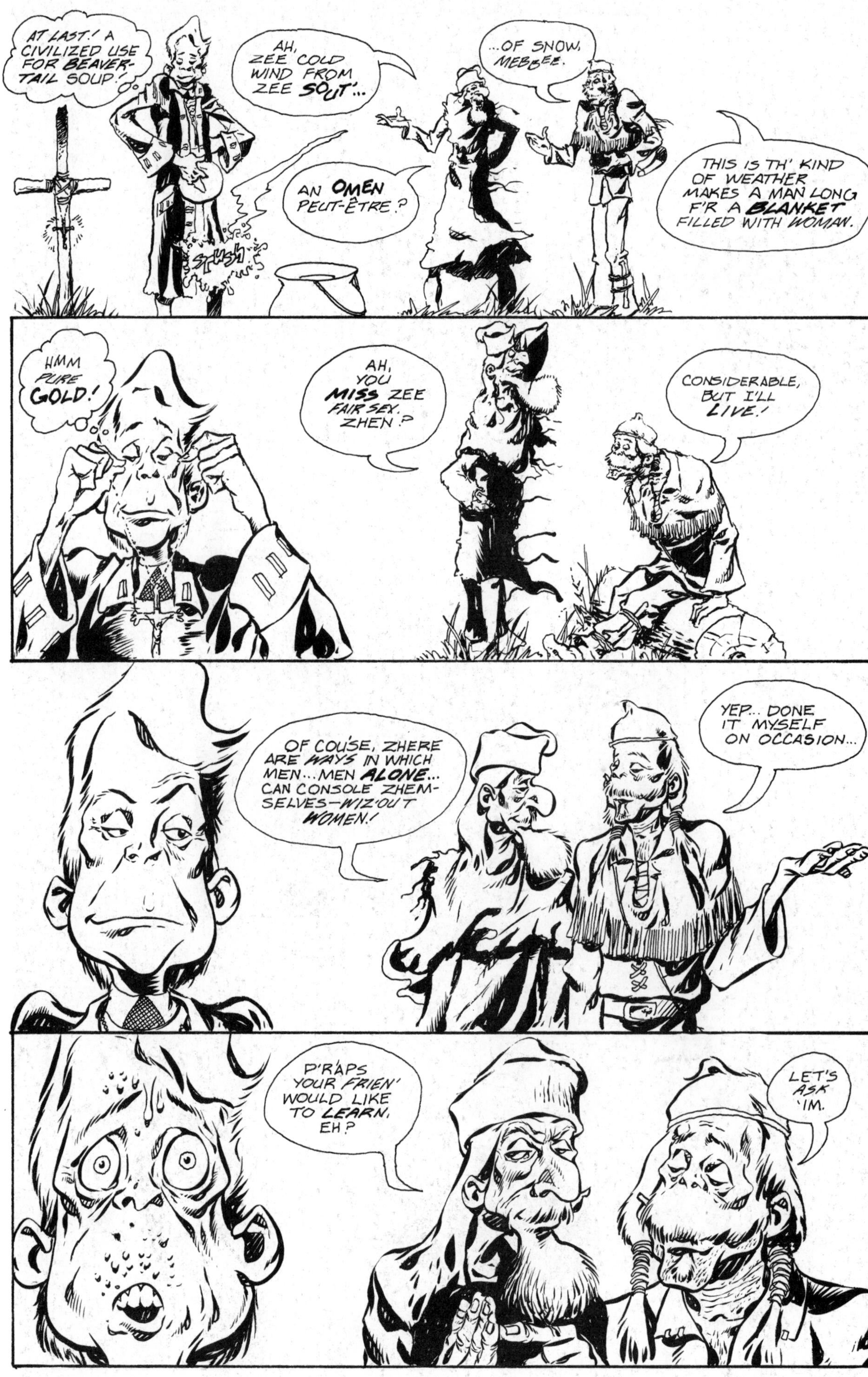
AT LAST! A CIVILIZED USE FOR BEAVER-TAIL SOUP!
AH, ZEE COLD WIND FROM ZEE SOUT'...
...OF SNOW, MEBBEE.
AN OMEN PEUT-ÊTRE?
THIS IS TH' KIND OF WEATHER MAKES A MAN LONG F'R A BLANKET FILLED WITH WOMAN.
HMM PURE GOLD!
AH, YOU MISS ZEE FAIR SEX, ZHEN?
CONSIDERABLE, BUT I'LL LIVE!
OF COU'SE, ZHERE ARE WAYS IN WHICH MEN... MEN ALONE... CAN CONSOLE ZHEM-SELVES—WIZ'OUT WOMEN!
YEP... DONE IT MYSELF ON OCCASION...
P'RAPS YOUR FRIEN' WOULD LIKE TO LEARN, EH?
LET'S ASK 'IM.

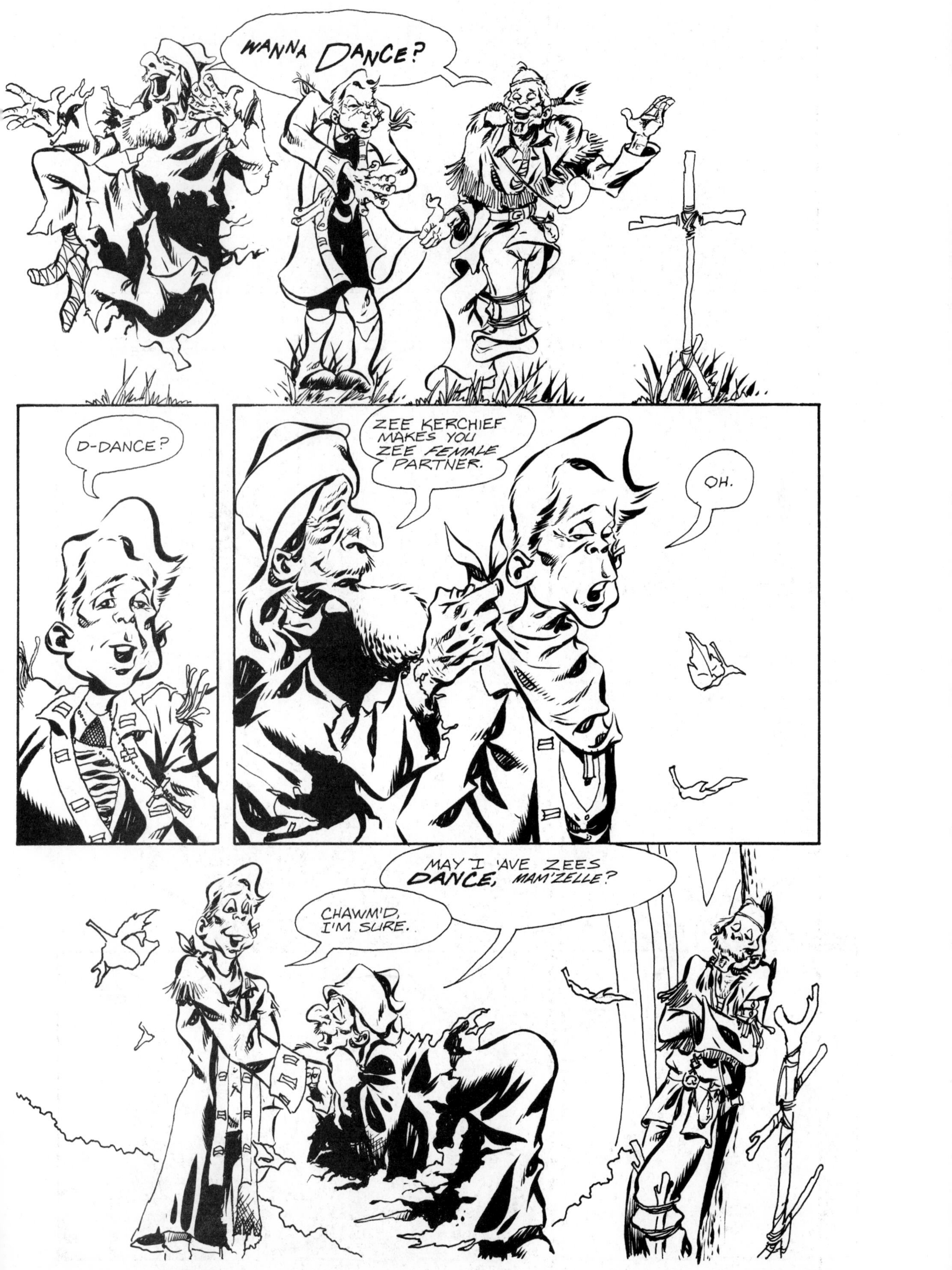
WANNA DANCE?
D-DANCE?
ZEE KERCHIEF MAKES YOU ZEE FEMALE PARTNER.
OH.
MAY I 'AVE ZEES DANCE, MAM'ZELLE?
CHAWM'D, I'M SURE.

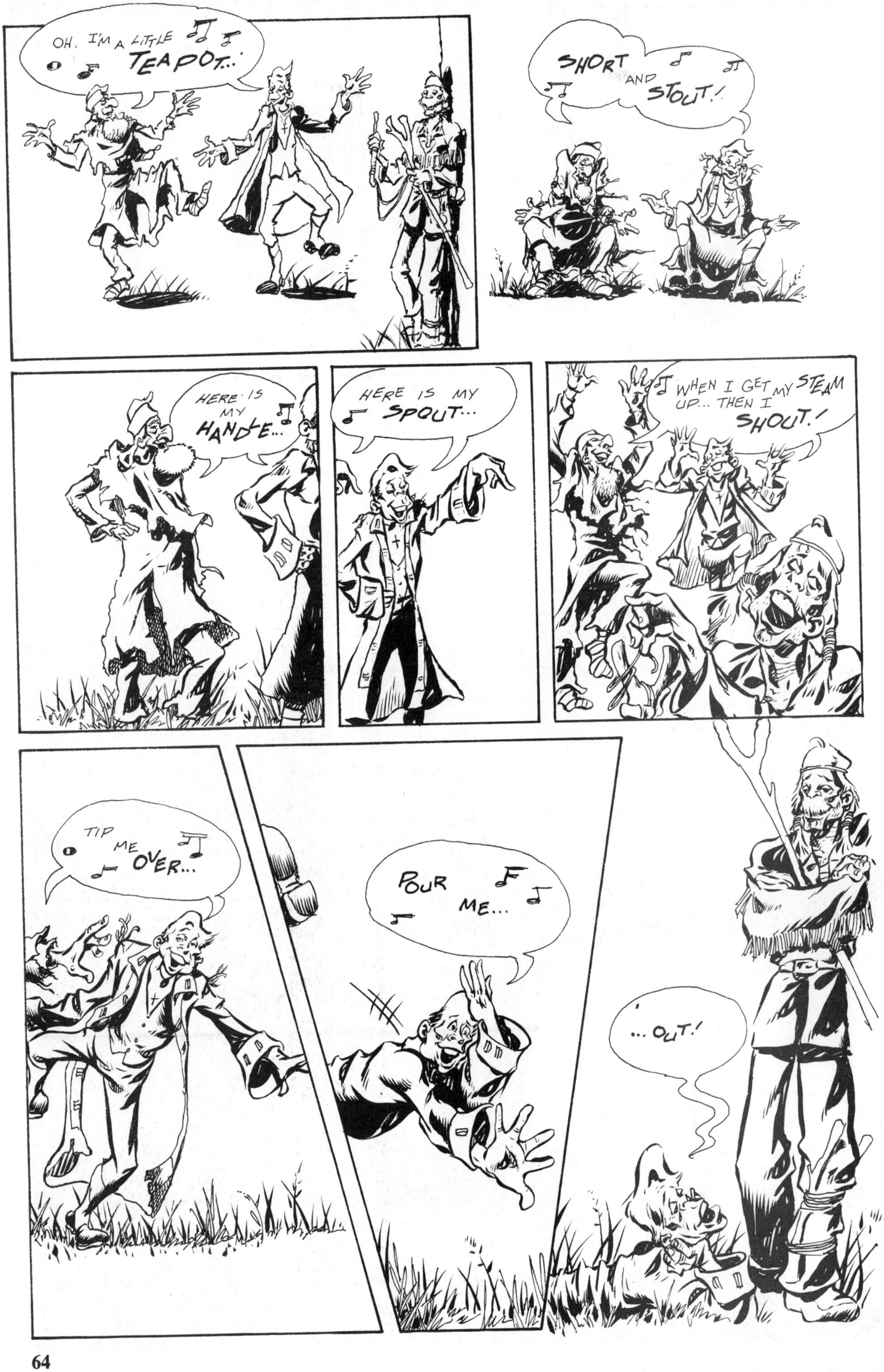
OH, I'M A LITTLE TEAPOT...
SHORT AND STOUT!
HERE IS MY HANDLE...
HERE IS MY SPOUT...
WHEN I GET MY STEAM UP... THEN I SHOUT!
TIP ME OVER...
POUR ME...
...OUT!

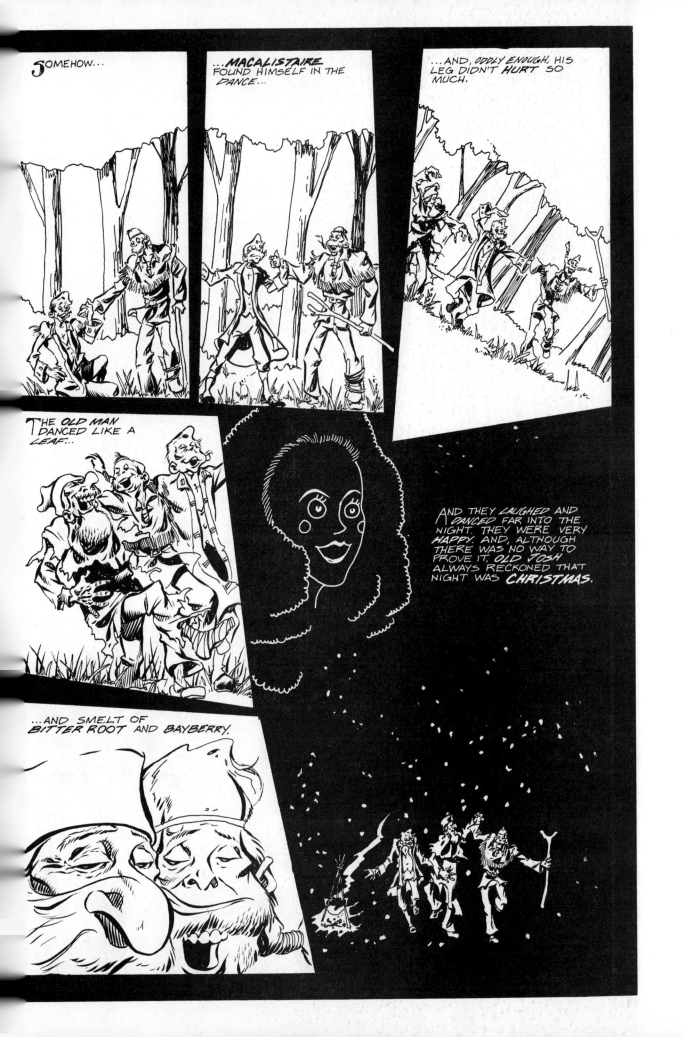

SOMEHOW...

...MACALISTAIRE FOUND HIMSELF IN THE DANCE...

...AND, ODDLY ENOUGH, HIS LEG DIDN'T HURT SO MUCH.

THE OLD MAN DANCED LIKE A LEAF...

...AND SMELT OF BITTER ROOT AND BAYBERRY.

AND THEY LAUGHED AND DANCED FAR INTO THE NIGHT. THEY WERE VERY HAPPY. AND, ALTHOUGH THERE WAS NO WAY TO PROVE IT, OLD JOSH ALWAYS RECKONED THAT NIGHT WAS CHRISTMAS.

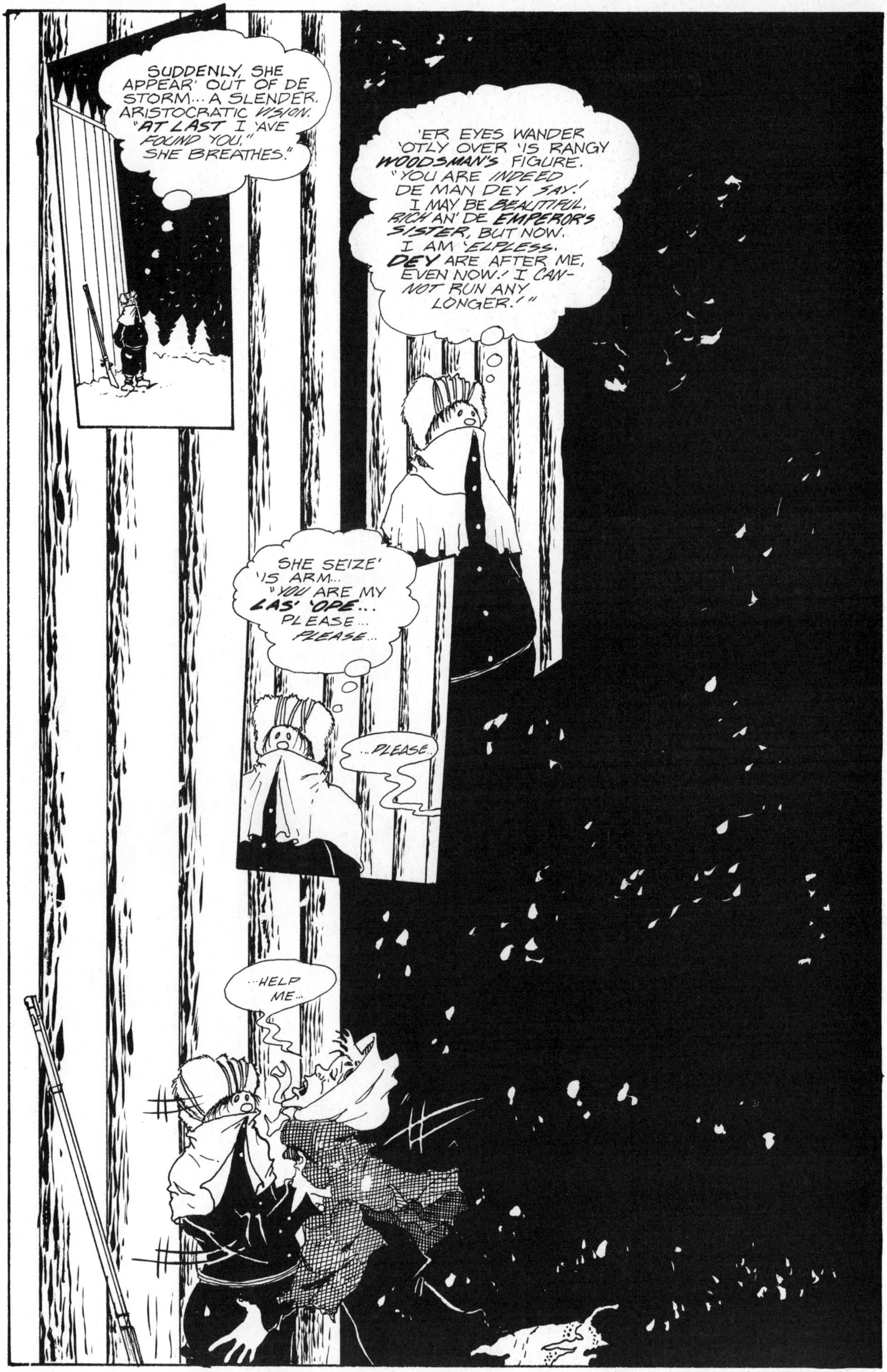
SUDDENLY, SHE APPEAR' OUT OF DE STORM... A SLENDER, ARISTOCRATIC VISION. "AT LAST I 'AVE FOUND YOU," SHE BREATHES."
'ER EYES WANDER 'OTLY OVER 'IS RANGY WOODSMAN'S FIGURE. "YOU ARE INDEED DE MAN DEY SAY! I MAY BE BEAUTIFUL, RICH AN' DE EMPEROR'S SISTER, BUT NOW, I AM 'ELPLESS. DEY ARE AFTER ME, EVEN NOW.! I CAN-NOT RUN ANY LONGER.!"
SHE SEIZE' 'IS ARM... "YOU ARE MY LAS' 'OPE... PLEASE... PLEASE...
...PLEASE...
...HELP ME...

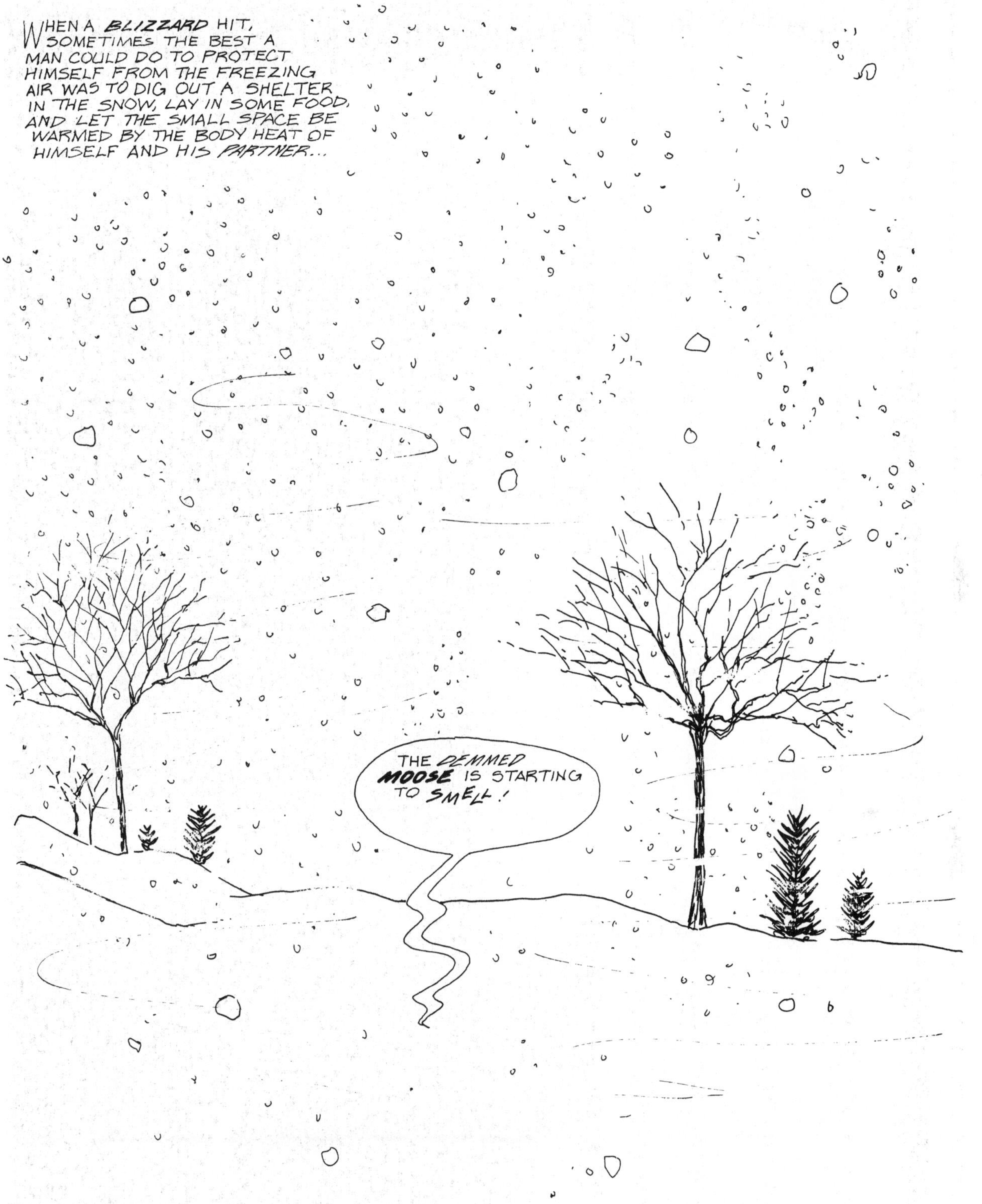
WHEN A BLIZZARD HIT, SOMETIMES THE BEST A MAN COULD DO TO PROTECT HIMSELF FROM THE FREEZING AIR WAS TO DIG OUT A SHELTER IN THE SNOW, LAY IN SOME FOOD, AND LET THE SMALL SPACE BE WARMED BY THE BODY HEAT OF HIMSELF AND HIS PARTNER...
THE DEMMED MOOSE IS STARTING TO SMELL!

Chapter Eight: Partners

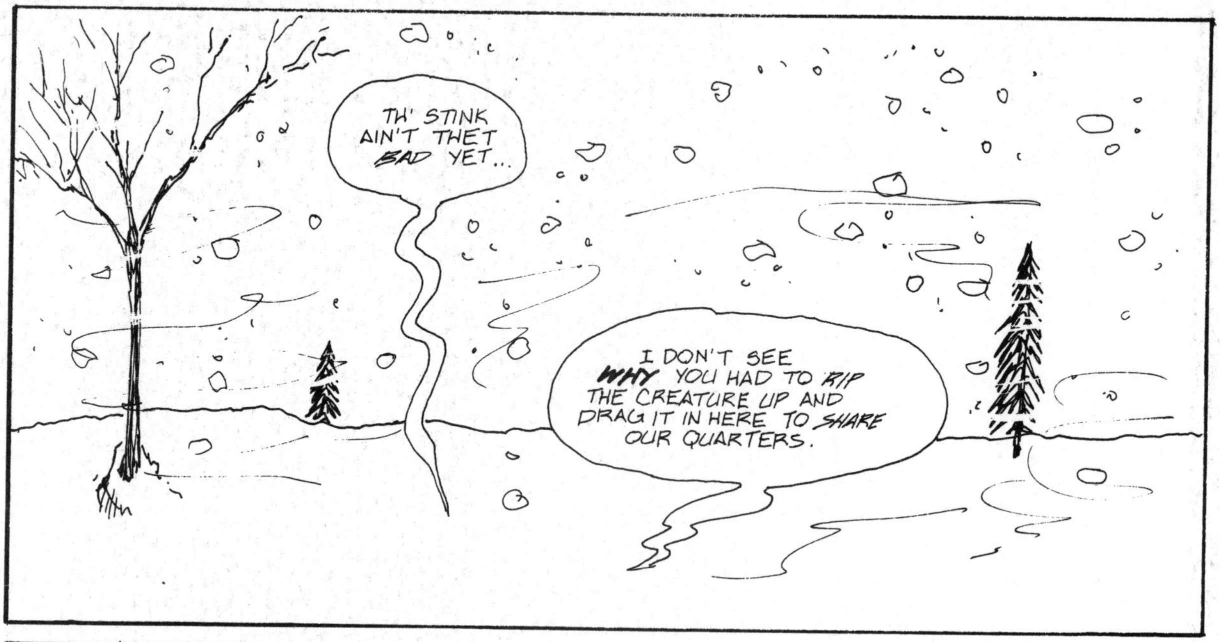
TH' STINK AIN'T THET BAD YET...
I DON'T SEE WHY YOU HAD TO RIP THE CREATURE UP AND DRAG IT IN HERE TO SHARE OUR QUARTERS.

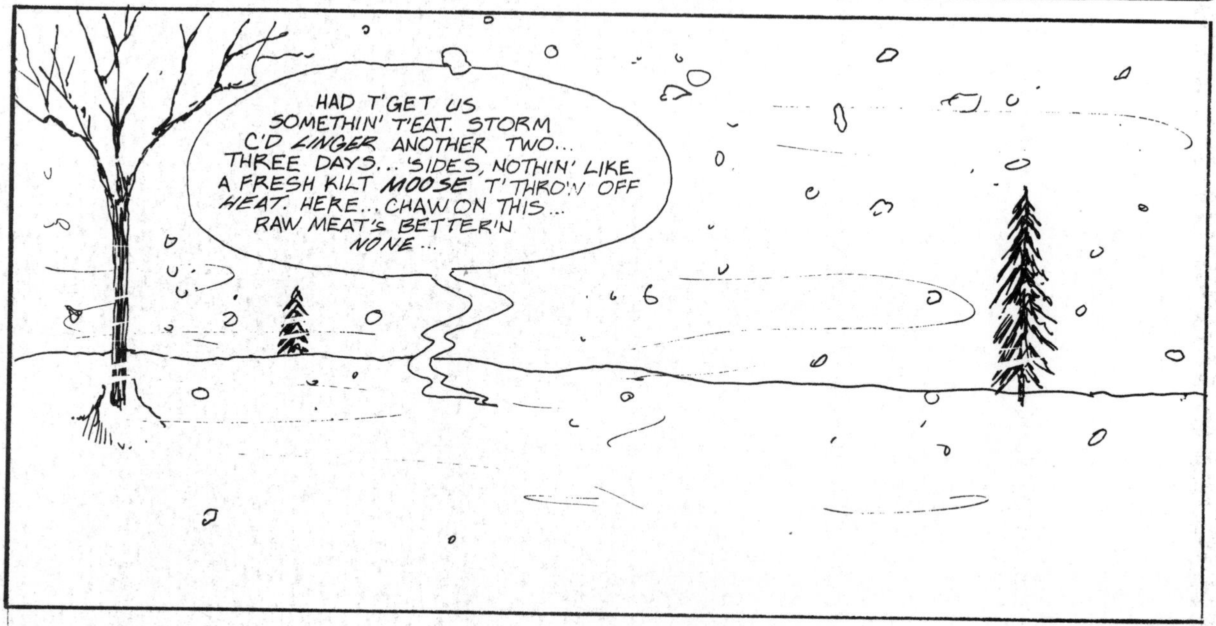
HAD T'GET US SOMETHIN' T'EAT. STORM C'D LINGER ANOTHER TWO... THREE DAYS... 'SIDES, NOTHIN' LIKE A FRESH KILT MOOSE T'THROW OFF HEAT. HERE... CHAW ON THIS... RAW MEAT'S BETTER'N NONE...

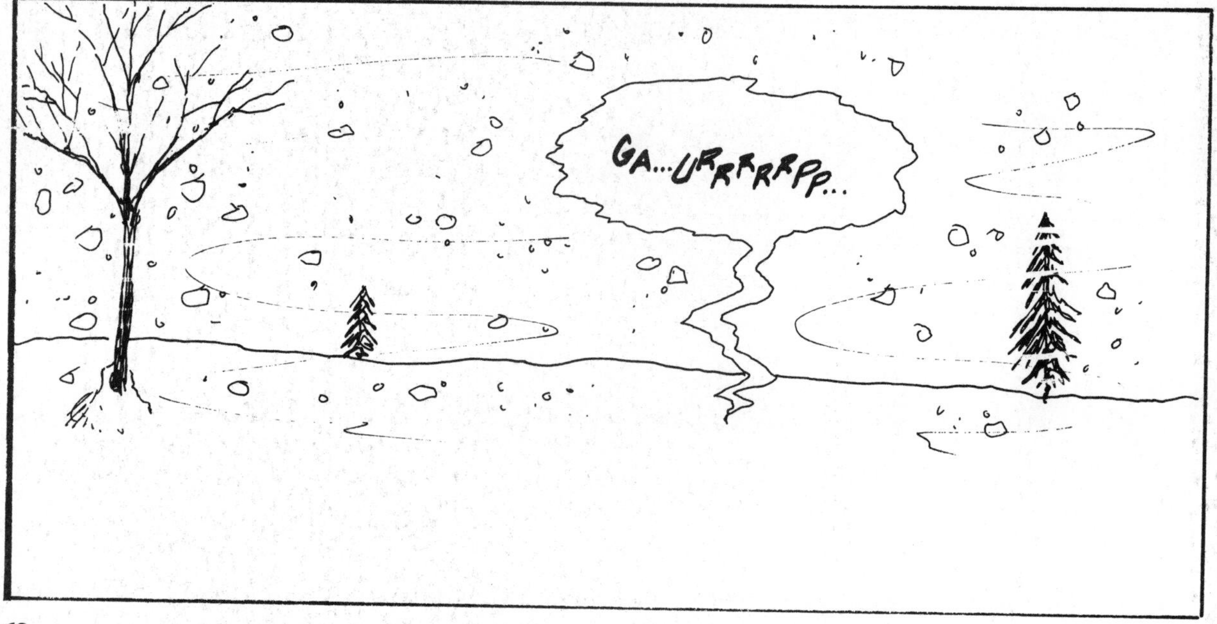
GA...URRRRRPP...

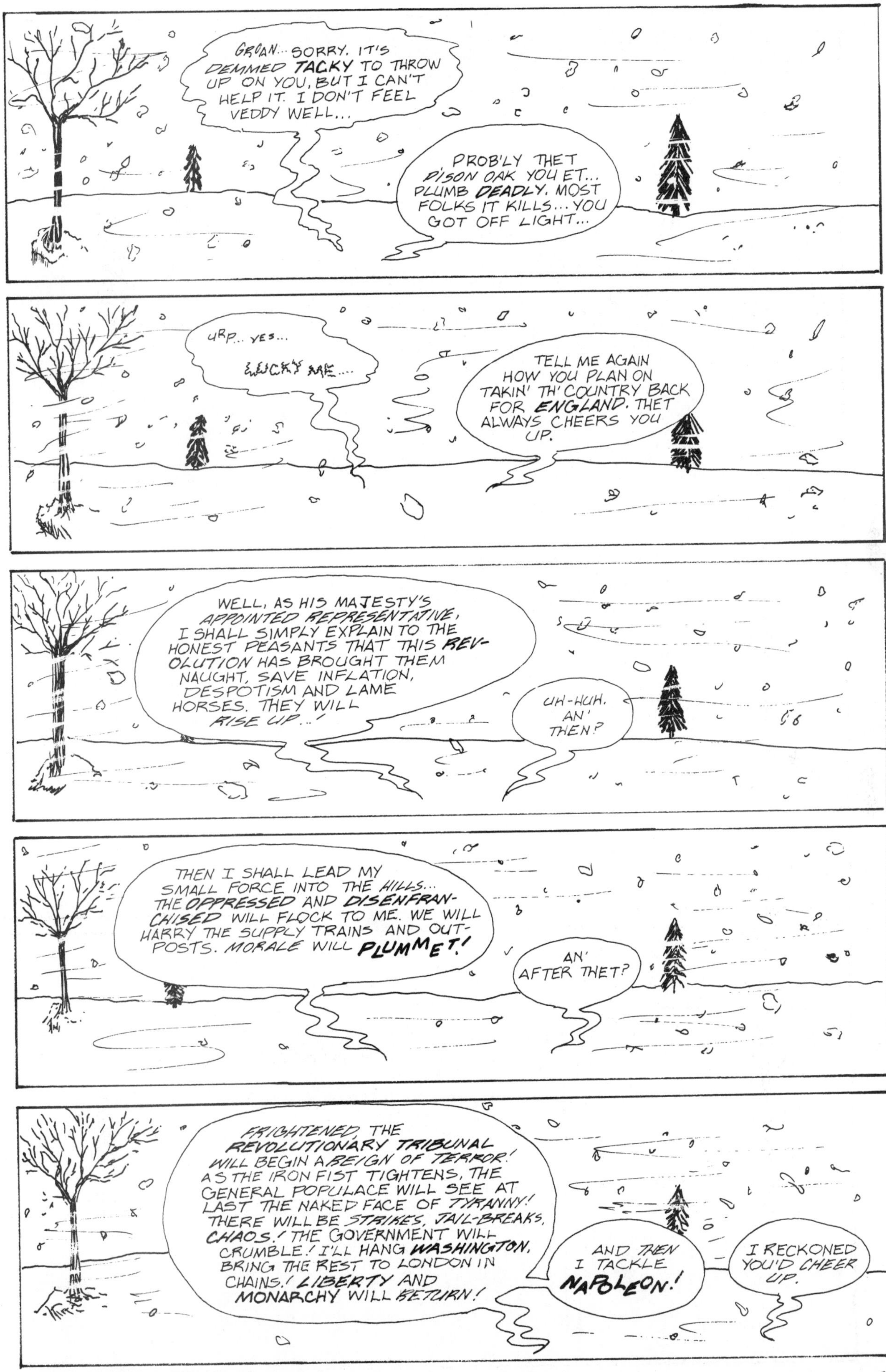
GROAN... SORRY. IT'S DEMMED TACKY TO THROW UP ON YOU, BUT I CAN'T HELP IT. I DON'T FEEL VEDDY WELL...
PROB'LY THET P'ISON OAK YOU ET... PLUMB DEADLY. MOST FOLKS IT KILLS... YOU GOT OFF LIGHT...
URP... YES... LUCKY ME...
TELL ME AGAIN HOW YOU PLAN ON TAKIN' TH' COUNTRY BACK FOR ENGLAND. THET ALWAYS CHEERS YOU UP.
WELL, AS HIS MAJESTY'S APPOINTED REPRESENTATIVE, I SHALL SIMPLY EXPLAIN TO THE HONEST PEASANTS THAT THIS REVOLUTION HAS BROUGHT THEM NAUGHT, SAVE INFLATION, DESPOTISM AND LAME HORSES. THEY WILL RISE UP...!
UH-HUH. AN' THEN?
THEN I SHALL LEAD MY SMALL FORCE INTO THE HILLS... THE OPPRESSED AND DISENFRANCHISED WILL FLOCK TO ME. WE WILL HARRY THE SUPPLY TRAINS AND OUTPOSTS. MORALE WILL PLUMMET!
AN' AFTER THET?
FRIGHTENED, THE REVOLUTIONARY TRIBUNAL WILL BEGIN A REIGN OF TERROR! AS THE IRON FIST TIGHTENS, THE GENERAL POPULACE WILL SEE AT LAST THE NAKED FACE OF TYRANNY! THERE WILL BE STRIKES, JAIL-BREAKS, CHAOS! THE GOVERNMENT WILL CRUMBLE! I'LL HANG WASHINGTON, BRING THE REST TO LONDON IN CHAINS! LIBERTY AND MONARCHY WILL RETURN!
AND THEN I TACKLE NAPOLEON!
I RECKONED YOU'D CHEER UP.

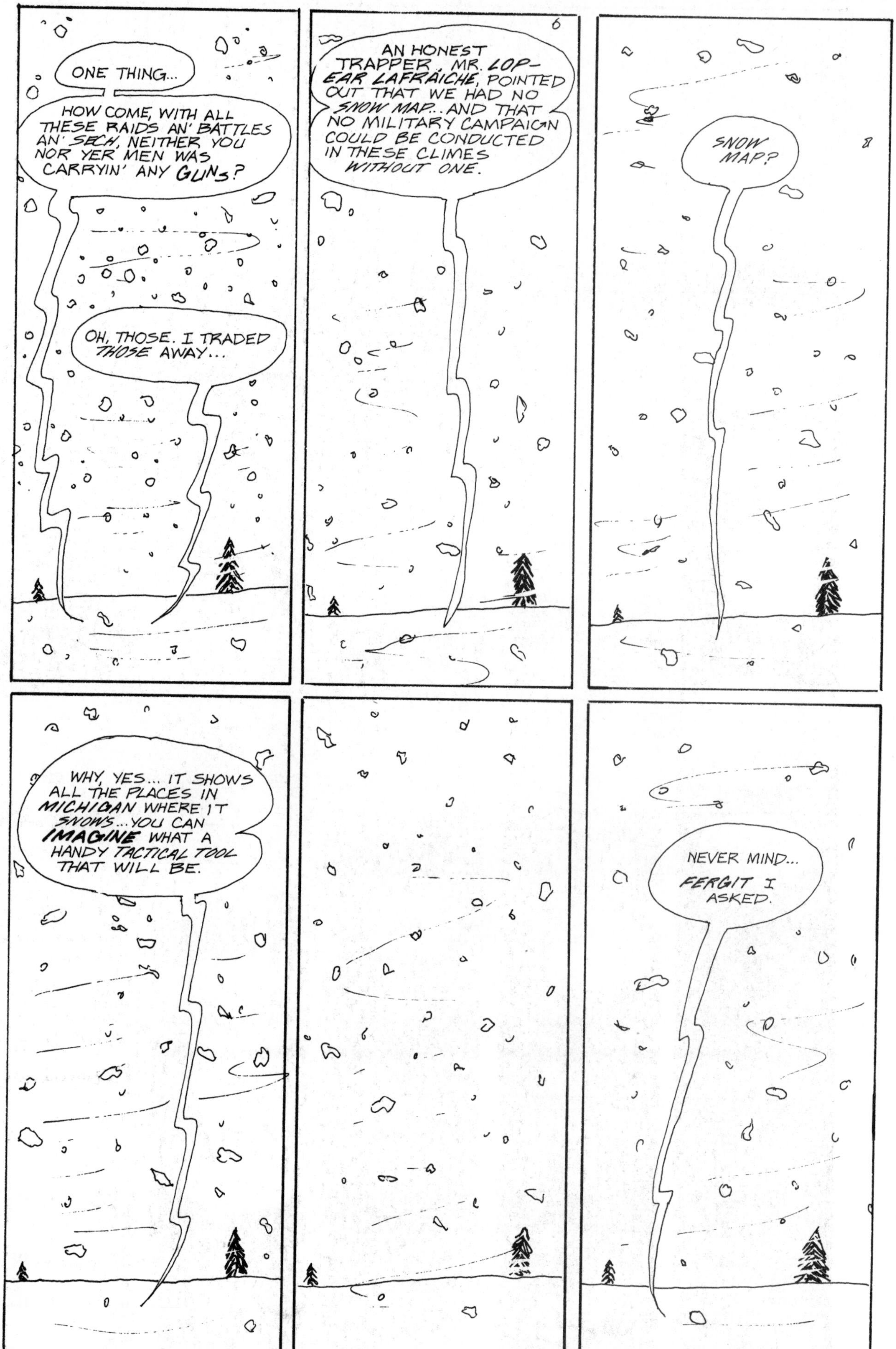
ONE THING...
HOW COME, WITH ALL THESE RAIDS AN' BATTLES AN' SECH, NEITHER YOU NOR YER MEN WAS CARRYIN' ANY GUNS?
OH, THOSE. I TRADED THOSE AWAY...
AN HONEST TRAPPER, MR. LOP-EAR LAFRAICHE, POINTED OUT THAT WE HAD NO SNOW MAP... AND THAT NO MILITARY CAMPAIGN COULD BE CONDUCTED IN THESE CLIMES WITHOUT ONE.
SNOW MAP?
WHY, YES... IT SHOWS ALL THE PLACES IN MICHIGAN WHERE IT SNOWS... YOU CAN IMAGINE WHAT A HANDY TACTICAL TOOL THAT WILL BE.
NEVER MIND... FERGIT I ASKED.

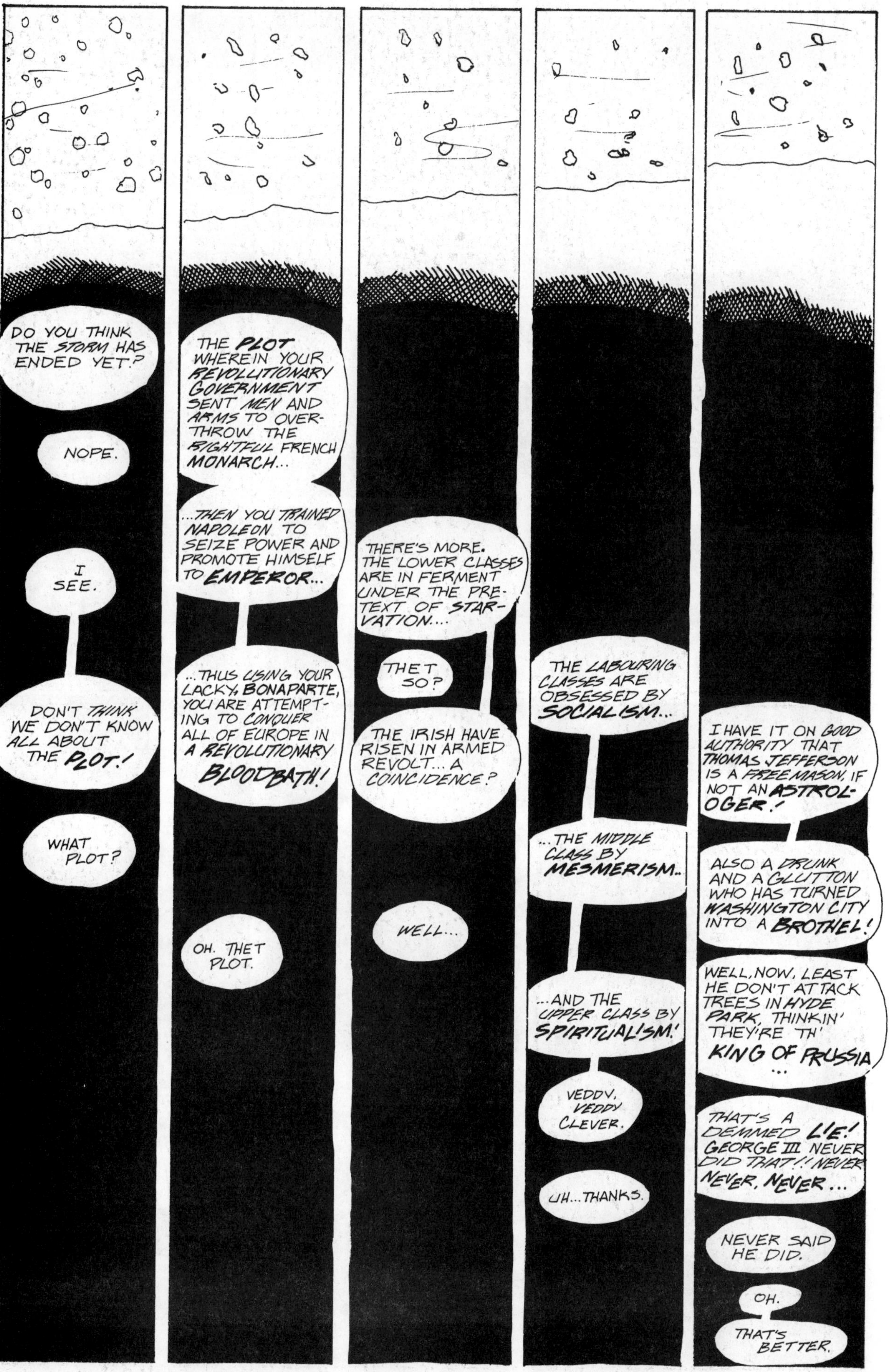
DO YOU THINK THE STORM HAS ENDED YET?
NOPE.
I SEE.
DON'T THINK WE DON'T KNOW ALL ABOUT THE PLOT!
WHAT PLOT?
THE PLOT WHEREIN YOUR REVOLUTIONARY GOVERNMENT SENT MEN AND ARMS TO OVERTHROW THE RIGHTFUL FRENCH MONARCH...
...THEN YOU TRAINED NAPOLEON TO SEIZE POWER AND PROMOTE HIMSELF TO EMPEROR...
...THUS USING YOUR LACKY, BONAPARTE, YOU ARE ATTEMPTING TO CONQUER ALL OF EUROPE IN A REVOLUTIONARY BLOODBATH!
OH. THET PLOT.
THERE'S MORE. THE LOWER CLASSES ARE IN FERMENT UNDER THE PRETEXT OF STARVATION...
THET SO?
THE IRISH HAVE RISEN IN ARMED REVOLT... A COINCIDENCE?
WELL...
THE LABOURING CLASSES ARE OBSESSED BY SOCIALISM...
...THE MIDDLE CLASS BY MESMERISM...
...AND THE UPPER CLASS BY SPIRITUALISM!
VEDDY, VEDDY CLEVER.
UH... THANKS.
I HAVE IT ON GOOD AUTHORITY THAT THOMAS JEFFERSON IS A FREEMASON, IF NOT AN ASTROLOGER!
ALSO A DRUNK AND A GLUTTON WHO HAS TURNED WASHINGTON CITY INTO A BROTHEL!
WELL, NOW, LEAST HE DON'T ATTACK TREES IN HYDE PARK, THINKIN' THEY'RE TH' KING OF PRUSSIA ...
THAT'S A DEMMED LIE! GEORGE III NEVER DID THAT!! NEVER NEVER, NEVER...
NEVER SAID HE DID.
OH.
THAT'S BETTER.

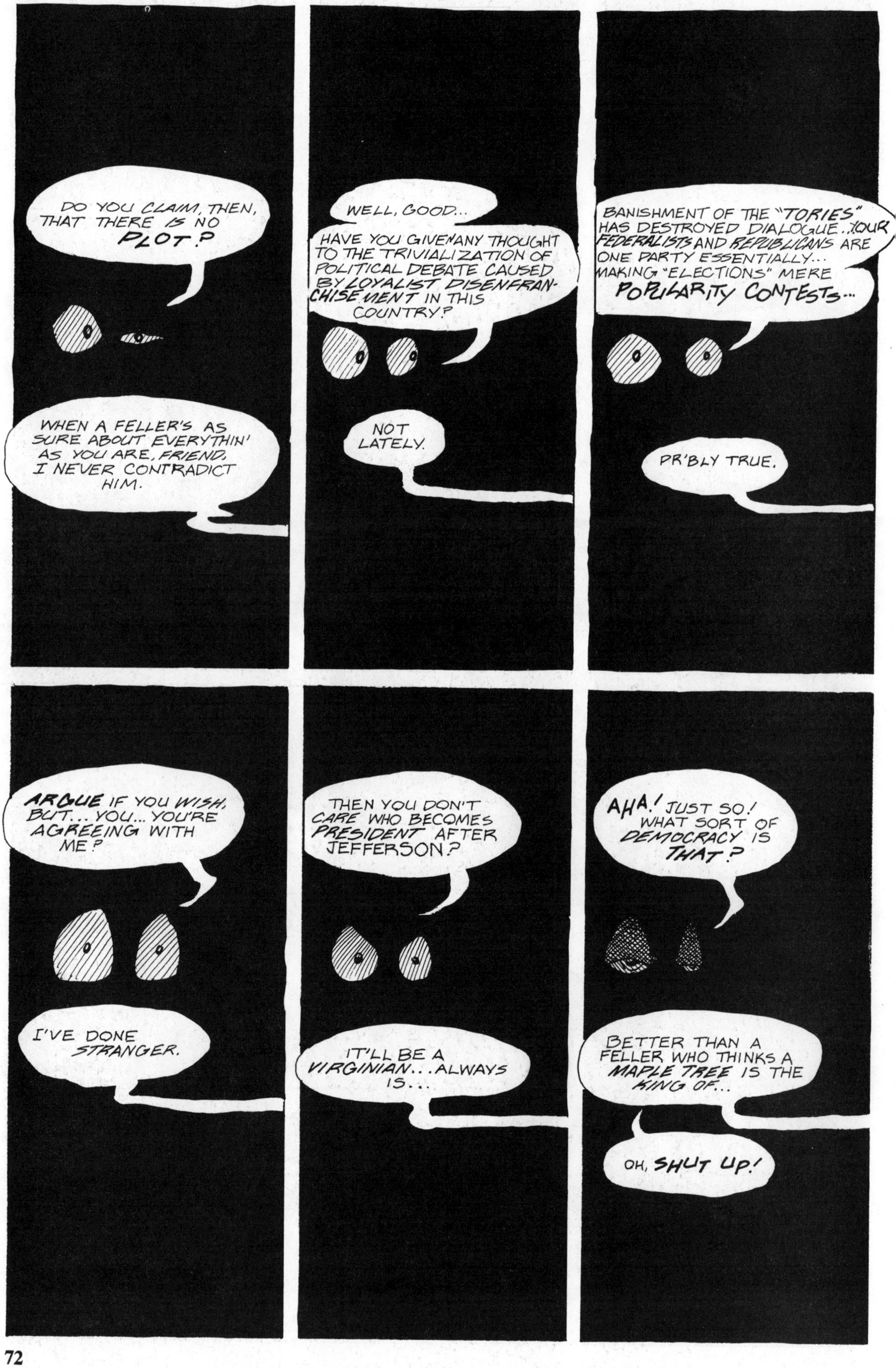
DO YOU CLAIM, THEN, THAT THERE IS NO PLOT?
WHEN A FELLER'S AS SURE ABOUT EVERYTHIN' AS YOU ARE, FRIEND, I NEVER CONTRADICT HIM.
WELL, GOOD...
HAVE YOU GIVEN ANY THOUGHT TO THE TRIVIALIZATION OF POLITICAL DEBATE CAUSED BY LOYALIST DISENFRANCHISEMENT IN THIS COUNTRY?
NOT LATELY.
BANISHMENT OF THE "TORIES" HAS DESTROYED DIALOGUE...YOUR FEDERALISTS AND REPUBLICANS ARE ONE PARTY ESSENTIALLY... MAKING "ELECTIONS" MERE POPULARITY CONTESTS...
PR'BLY TRUE.
ARGUE IF YOU WISH. BUT... YOU... YOU'RE AGREEING WITH ME?
I'VE DONE STRANGER.
THEN YOU DON'T CARE WHO BECOMES PRESIDENT AFTER JEFFERSON?
IT'LL BE A VIRGINIAN...ALWAYS IS...
AHA! JUST SO! WHAT SORT OF DEMOCRACY IS THAT?
BETTER THAN A FELLER WHO THINKS A MAPLE TREE IS THE KING OF...
OH, SHUT UP!

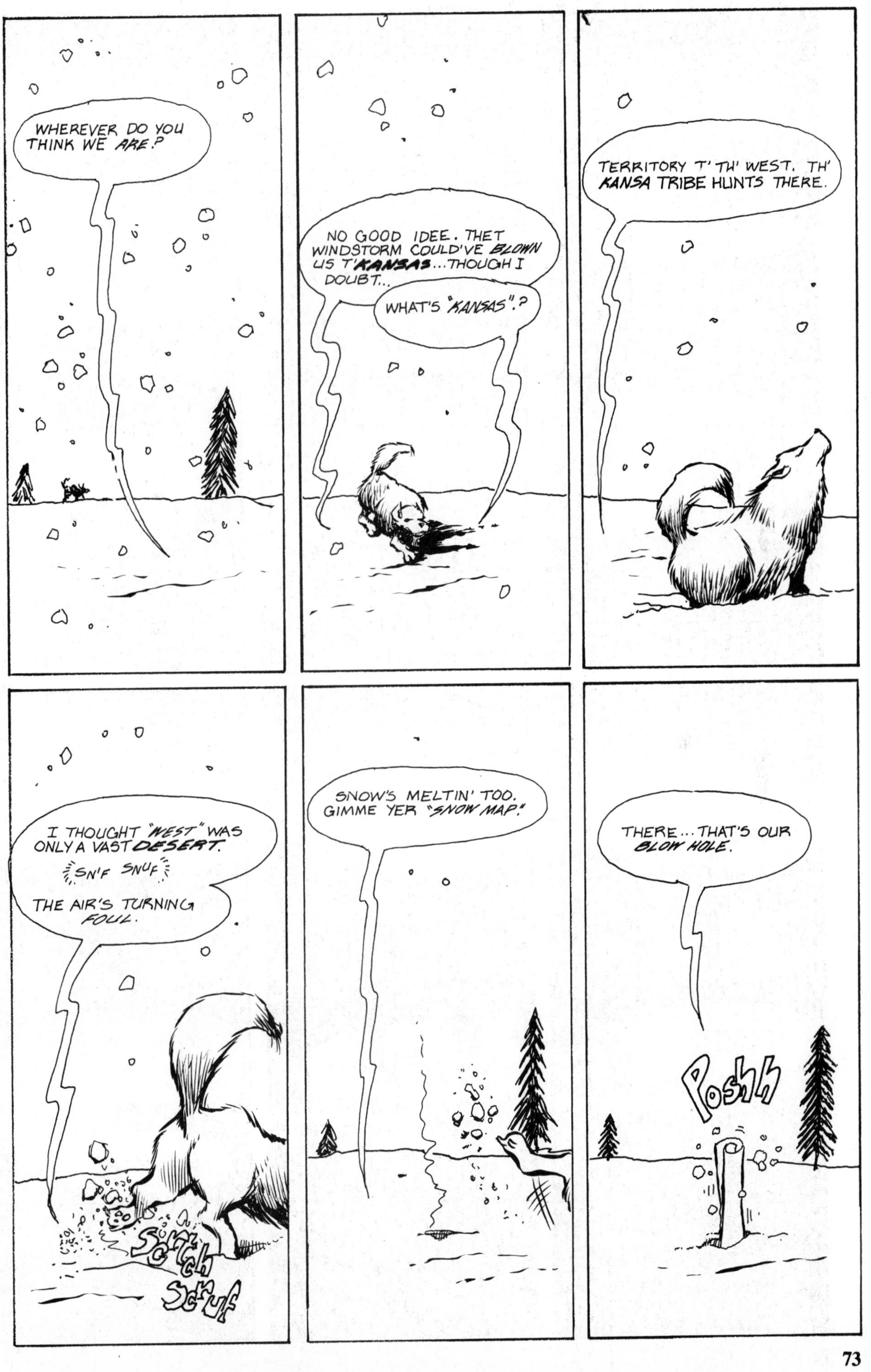
WHEREVER DO YOU THINK WE ARE?
NO GOOD IDEE. THET WINDSTORM COULD'VE BLOWN US T'KANSAS...THOUGH I DOUBT...
WHAT'S "KANSAS"?
TERRITORY T' TH' WEST. TH' KANSA TRIBE HUNTS THERE.
I THOUGHT "WEST" WAS ONLY A VAST DESERT.
SN'F SNUF
THE AIR'S TURNING FOUL.
Scrtch
Scruf
SNOW'S MELTIN' TOO. GIMME YER "SNOW MAP."
THERE... THAT'S OUR BLOW HOLE.
Poshh

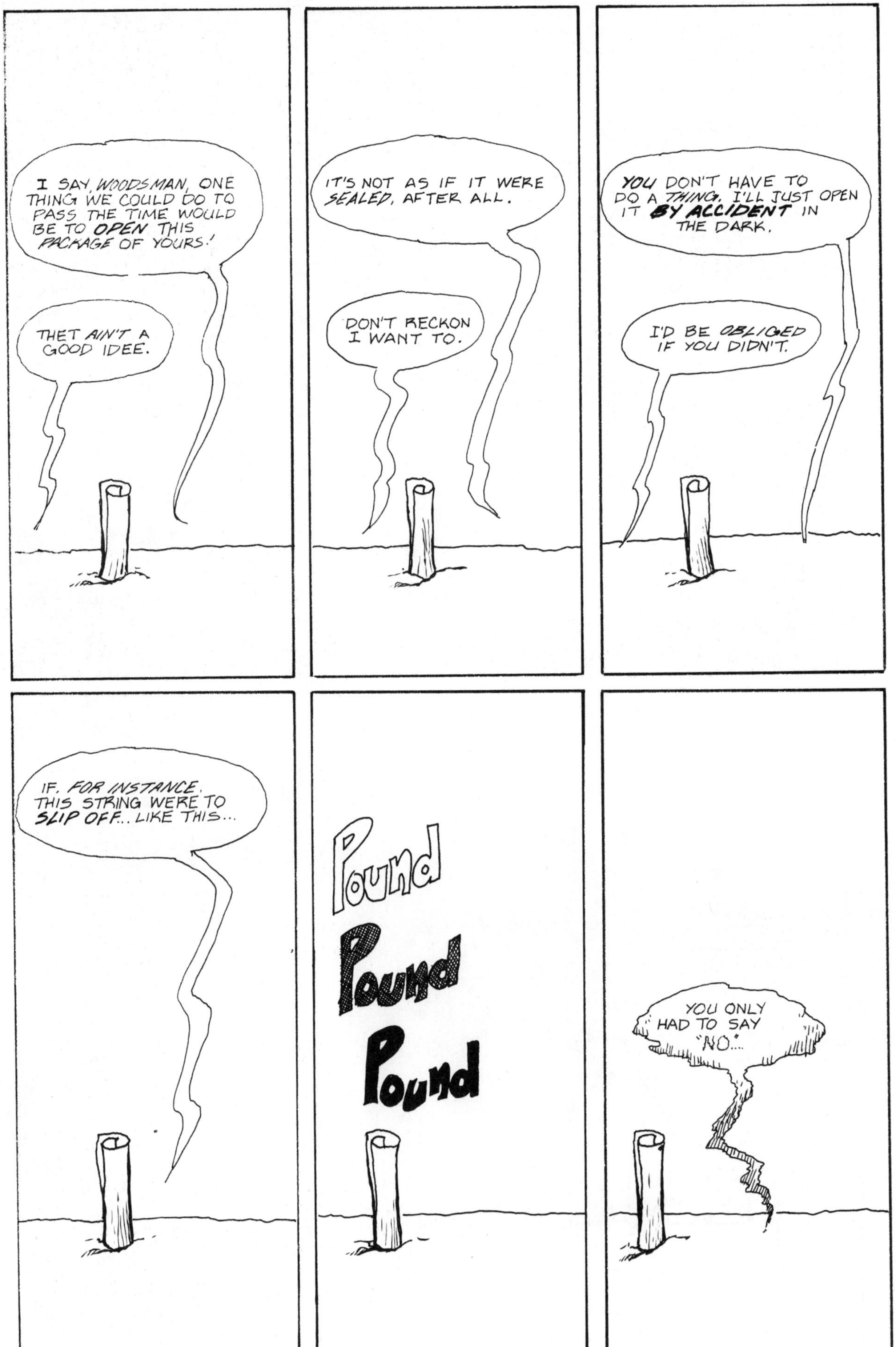
I SAY, WOODSMAN, ONE THING WE COULD DO TO PASS THE TIME WOULD BE TO OPEN THIS PACKAGE OF YOURS!
THET AIN'T A GOOD IDEE.
IT'S NOT AS IF IT WERE SEALED, AFTER ALL.
DON'T RECKON I WANT TO.
YOU DON'T HAVE TO DO A THING. I'LL JUST OPEN IT BY ACCIDENT IN THE DARK.
I'D BE OBLIGED IF YOU DIDN'T.
IF, FOR INSTANCE, THIS STRING WERE TO SLIP OFF... LIKE THIS...
Pound
Pound
Pound
YOU ONLY HAD TO SAY "NO"...

NOW *HERE'S* A BIT OF A *JOLLY* NOTION! WITH A *CHIMNEY* LIKE THAT WE CAN BUILD A TOASTY *FIRE!*

FORTUNATELY I HAVE MY *FLINT* AND *STEEL!*

...MEBBEE, IF WE KEEP IT *SMALL*...

tskt tst

NATURALLY.

AH, THERE IT GOES... FORTUNATELY I HAVE SOME *DRY* TWIGS...

VEDDY NICE... I BELIEVE I HAVE AN *OLD LETTER* OR SOMETHING TO FEED IT WITH...

OOPS... DIDN'T MEAN TO SET YOUR *HAT* AFIRE, OLD SPORT...

OH... AND *GOOD LORD,* YOUR *BLANKET ROLL* TOO... WHO'D THINK COF WOOL COULD *BURN* SO COF COF QUICKLY?

THERE COF HACK THAT'S *DONE* IT... YOU'LL COF COF *HARDLY* NOTICE THAT COF SPOT.... HAK COF

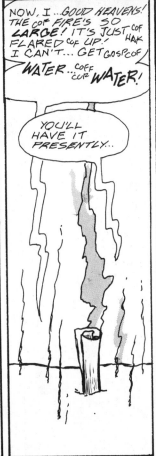

NOW, I... COF *GOOD HEAVENS!* THE COF FIRE'S SO *LARGE!* IT'S JUST COF FLARED COF UP! HAK I CAN'T... GET GOSP COF *WATER*... COFF COF *WATER!*

YOU'LL HAVE IT *PRESENTLY*...

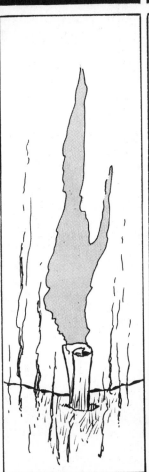

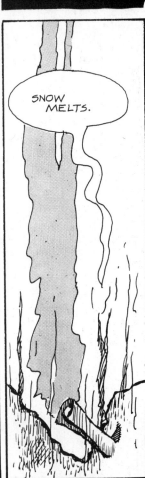

SNOW MELTS.

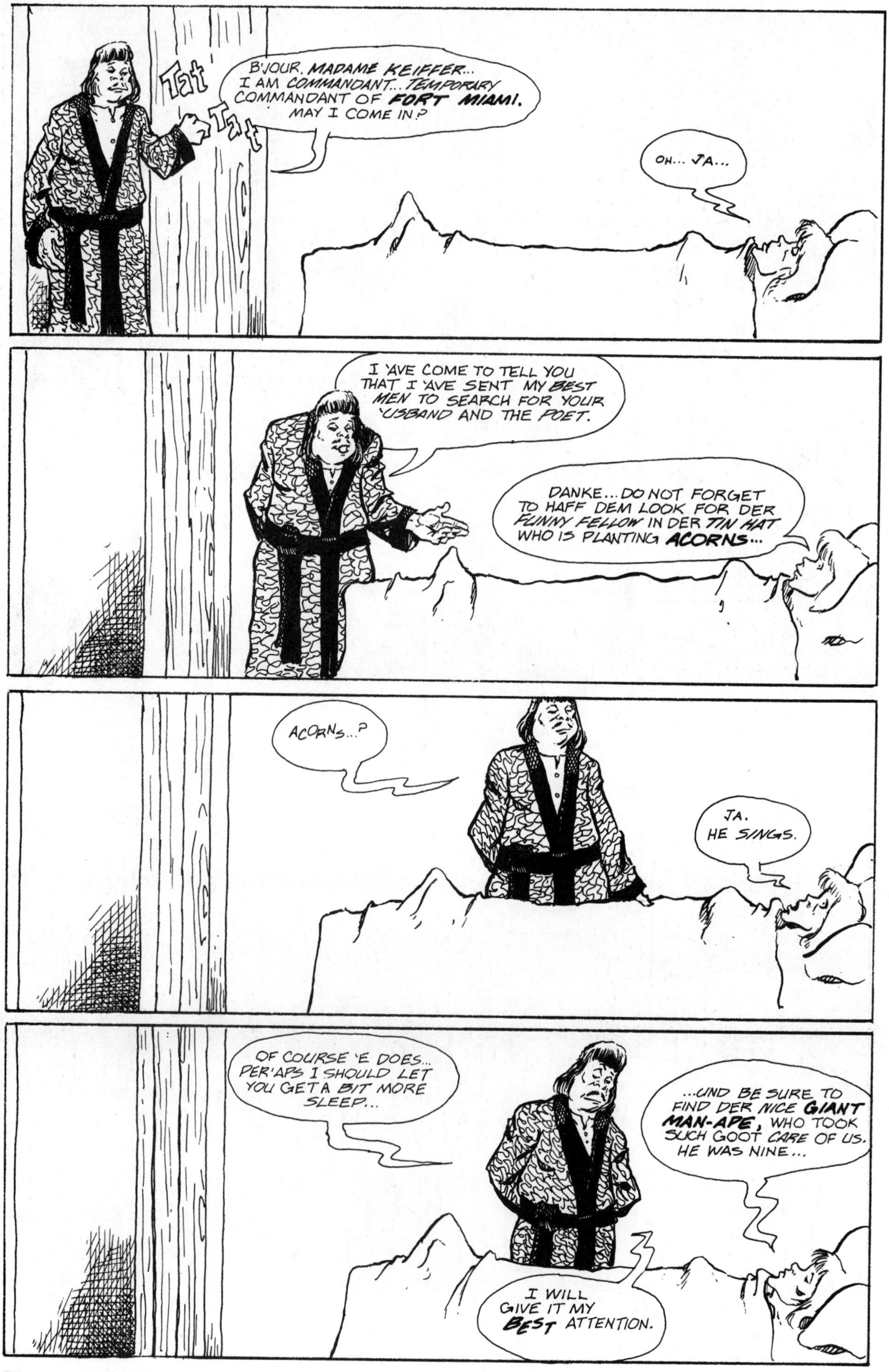
Tat Tat
B'JOUR, MADAME KEIFFER... I AM COMMANDANT... TEMPORARY COMMANDANT OF FORT MIAMI. MAY I COME IN?
OH... JA...
I 'AVE COME TO TELL YOU THAT I 'AVE SENT MY BEST MEN TO SEARCH FOR YOUR 'USBAND AND THE POET.
DANKE... DO NOT FORGET TO HAFF DEM LOOK FOR DER FUNNY FELLOW IN DER TIN HAT WHO IS PLANTING ACORNS...
ACORNS...?
JA. HE SINGS.
OF COURSE 'E DOES... PER'APS I SHOULD LET YOU GET A BIT MORE SLEEP...
...UND BE SURE TO FIND DER NICE GIANT MAN-APE, WHO TOOK SUCH GOOT CARE OF US. HE WAS NINE...
I WILL GIVE IT MY BEST ATTENTION.

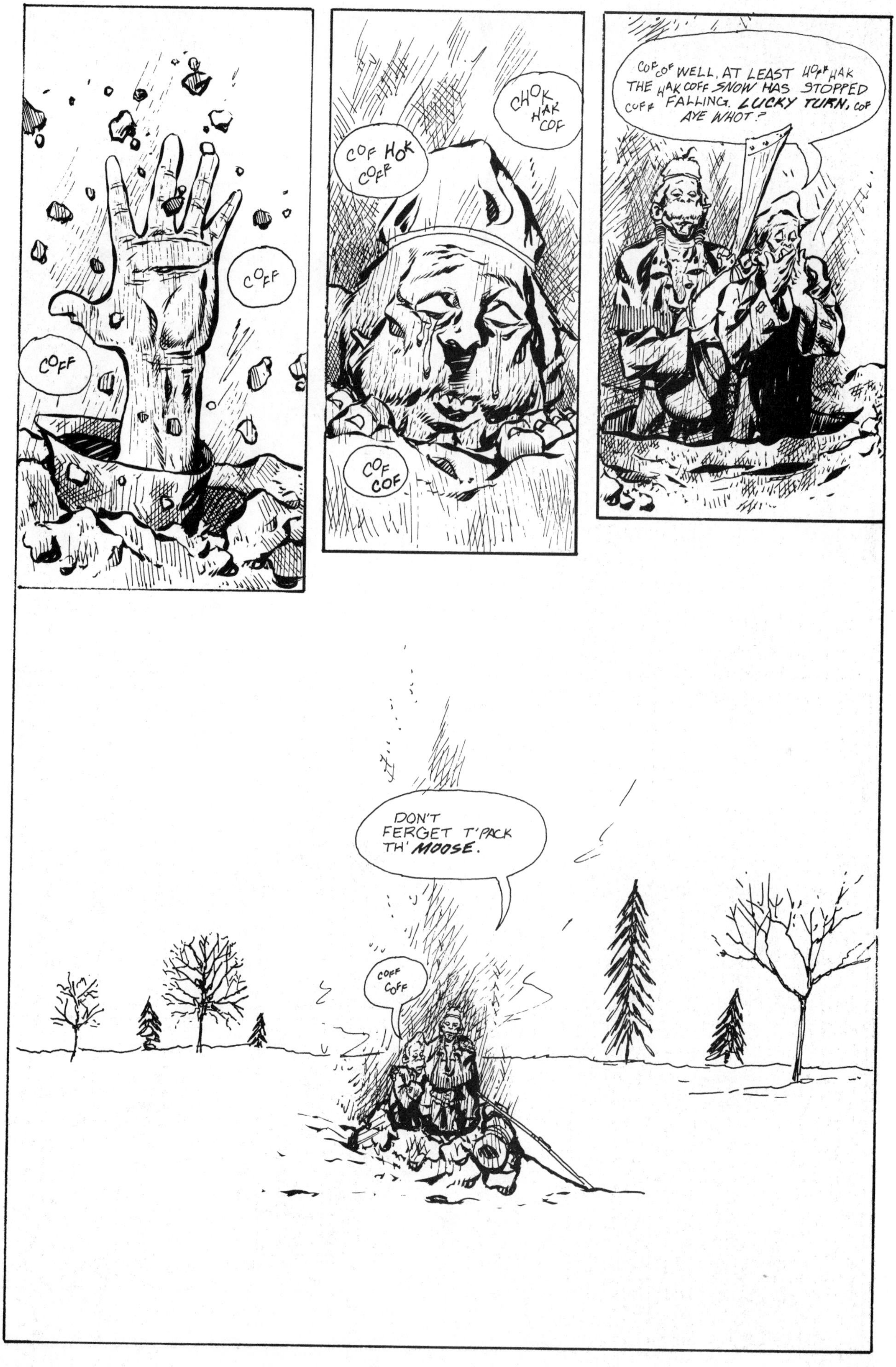
COFF
COFF
COF HOK COFF
CHOK HAK COF
COF COF
COF COF WELL, AT LEAST HOFF HAK THE HAK COFF SNOW HAS STOPPED COFF FALLING. LUCKY TURN, COF AYE WHOT?
DON'T FERGET T'PACK TH' MOOSE.
COFF COFF

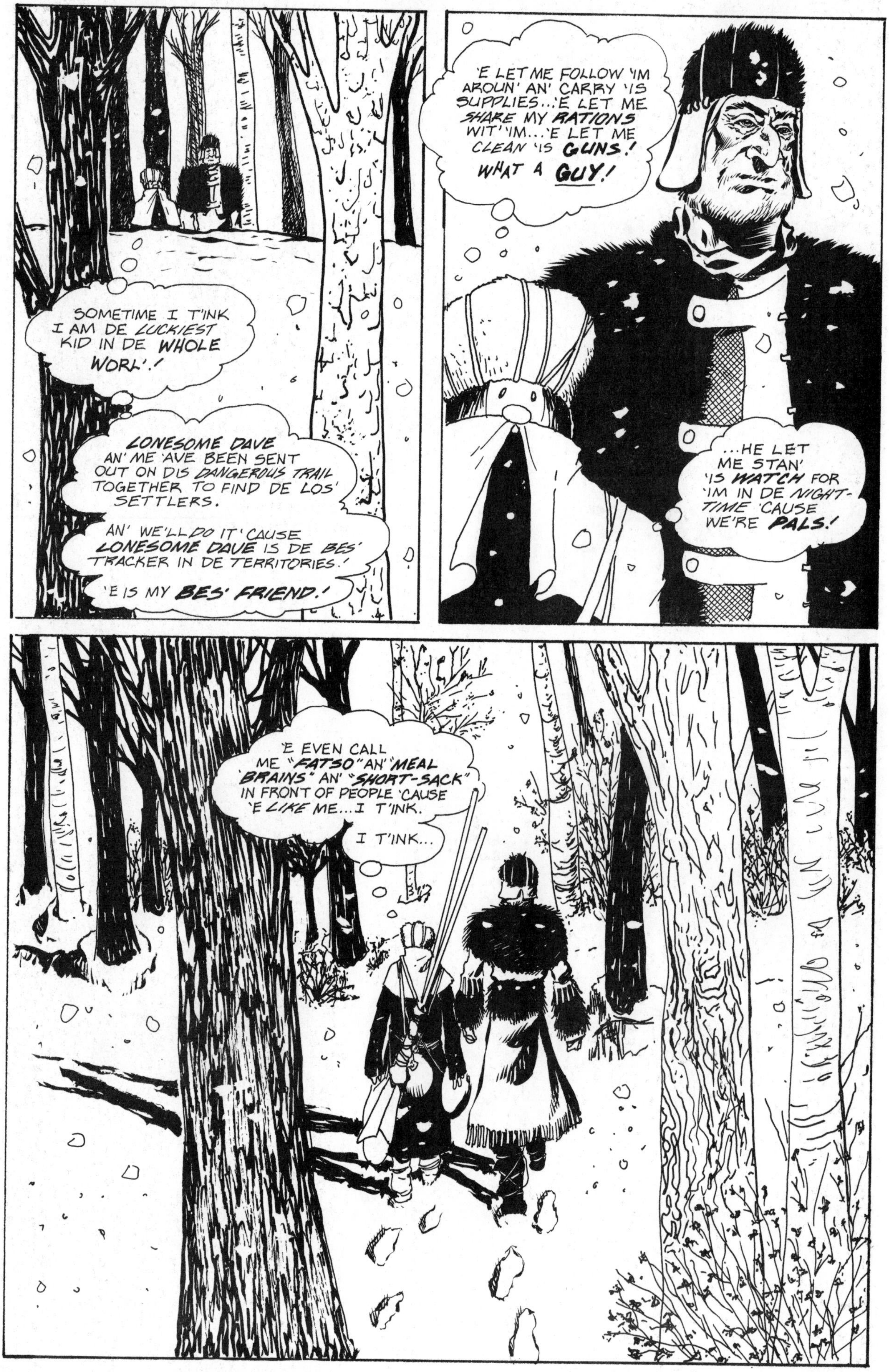
SOMETIME I T'INK I AM DE LUCKIEST KID IN DE WHOLE WORL'.!
LONESOME DAVE AN' ME 'AVE BEEN SENT OUT ON DIS DANGEROUS TRAIL TOGETHER TO FIND DE LOS' SETTLERS.
AN' WE'LL DO IT 'CAUSE LONESOME DAVE IS DE BES' TRACKER IN DE TERRITORIES.'
'E IS MY BES' FRIEND.!
'E LET ME FOLLOW 'IM AROUN' AN' CARRY 'IS SUPPLIES...'E LET ME SHARE MY RATIONS WIT' 'IM...'E LET ME CLEAN 'IS GUNS!
WHAT A GUY!
...HE LET ME STAN' 'IS WATCH FOR 'IM IN DE NIGHT-TIME 'CAUSE WE'RE PALS!
'E EVEN CALL ME "FATSO" AN' "MEAL BRAINS" AN' "SHORT-SACK" IN FRONT OF PEOPLE 'CAUSE 'E LIKE ME...I T'INK.
I T'INK...

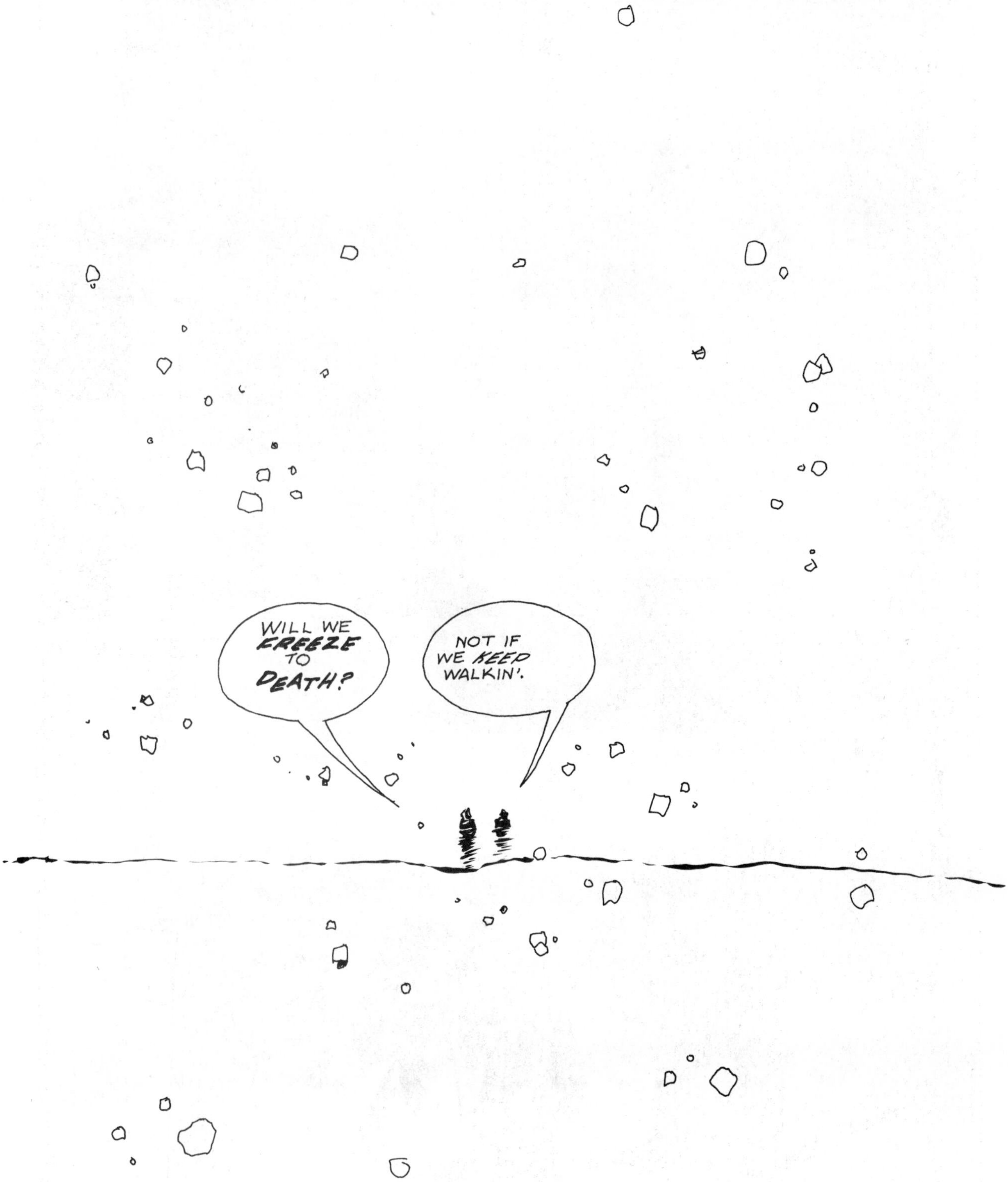
WILL WE FREEZE TO DEATH?
NOT IF WE KEEP WALKIN'.

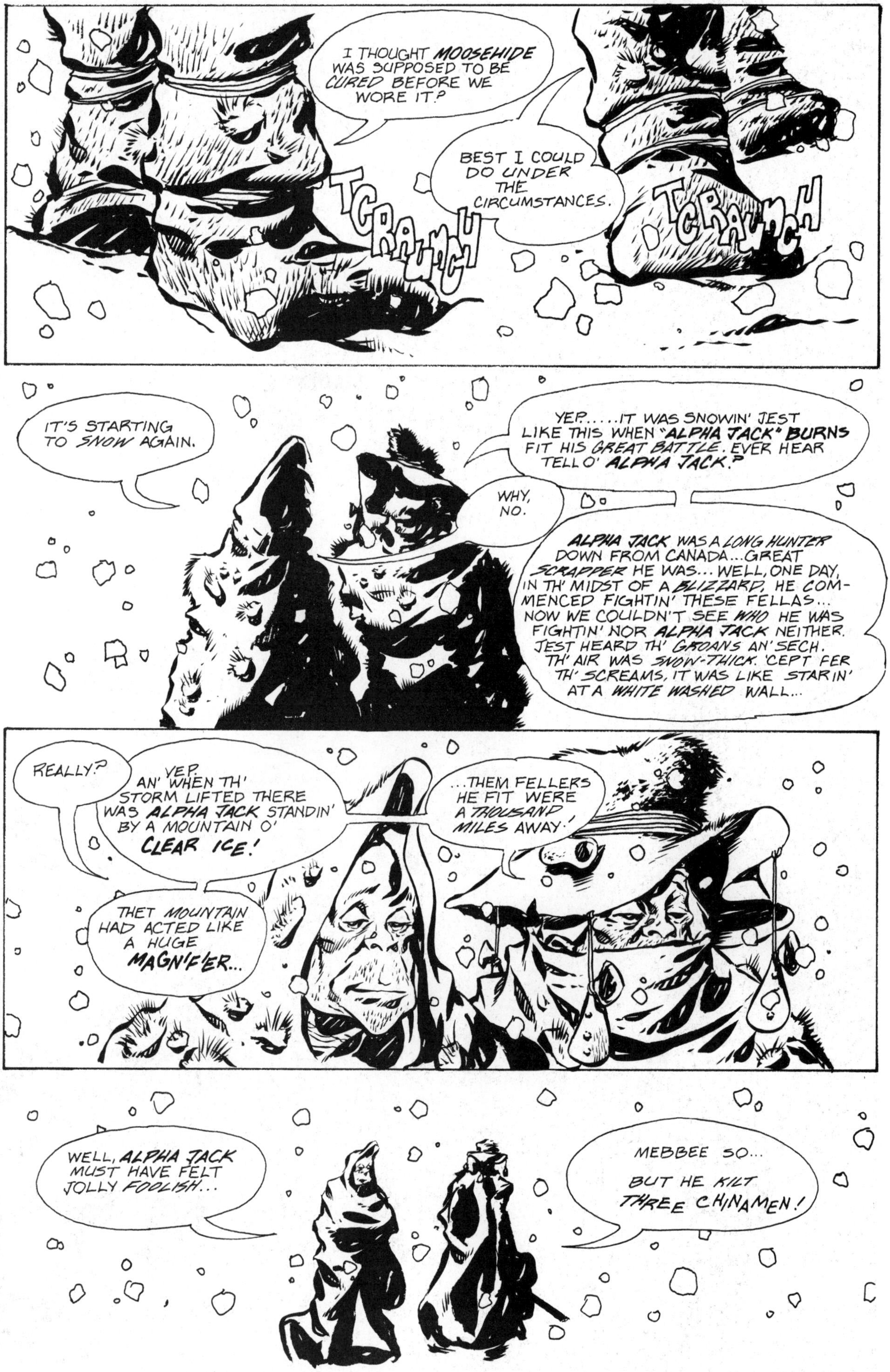

I THOUGHT MOOSEHIDE WAS SUPPOSED TO BE CURED BEFORE WE WORE IT?
BEST I COULD DO UNDER THE CIRCUMSTANCES.
TCRAUNCH
TCRAUNCH
IT'S STARTING TO SNOW AGAIN.
YEP.....IT WAS SNOWIN' JEST LIKE THIS WHEN "ALPHA JACK" BURNS FIT HIS GREAT BATTLE. EVER HEAR TELL O' ALPHA JACK?
WHY, NO.
ALPHA JACK WAS A LONG HUNTER DOWN FROM CANADA...GREAT SCRAPPER HE WAS... WELL, ONE DAY, IN TH' MIDST OF A BLIZZARD, HE COMMENCED FIGHTIN' THESE FELLAS... NOW WE COULDN'T SEE WHO HE WAS FIGHTIN' NOR ALPHA JACK NEITHER. JEST HEARD TH' GROANS AN' SECH. TH' AIR WAS SNOW-THICK. 'CEPT FER TH' SCREAMS, IT WAS LIKE STARIN' AT A WHITE WASHED WALL...
REALLY?
YEP. AN' WHEN TH' STORM LIFTED THERE WAS ALPHA JACK STANDIN' BY A MOUNTAIN O' CLEAR ICE!
THET MOUNTAIN HAD ACTED LIKE A HUGE MAGNI'FI'ER...
...THEM FELLERS HE FIT WERE A THOUSAND MILES AWAY!
WELL, ALPHA JACK MUST HAVE FELT JOLLY FOOLISH...
MEBBEE SO... BUT HE KILT THREE CHINAMEN!

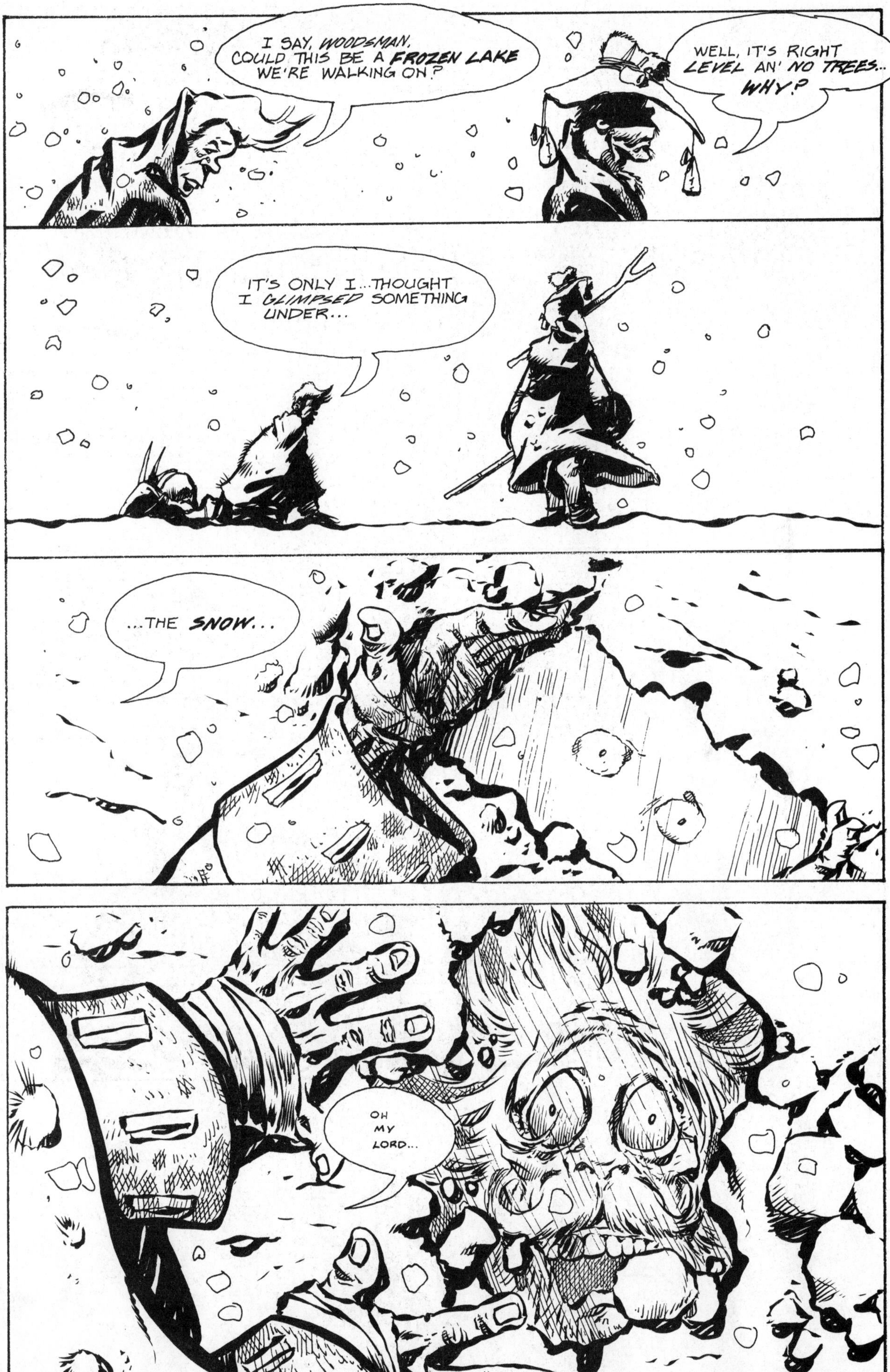
I SAY, WOODSMAN, COULD THIS BE A FROZEN LAKE WE'RE WALKING ON?
WELL, IT'S RIGHT LEVEL AN' NO TREES... WHY?
IT'S ONLY I... THOUGHT I GLIMPSED SOMETHING UNDER...
...THE SNOW...
OH MY LORD...

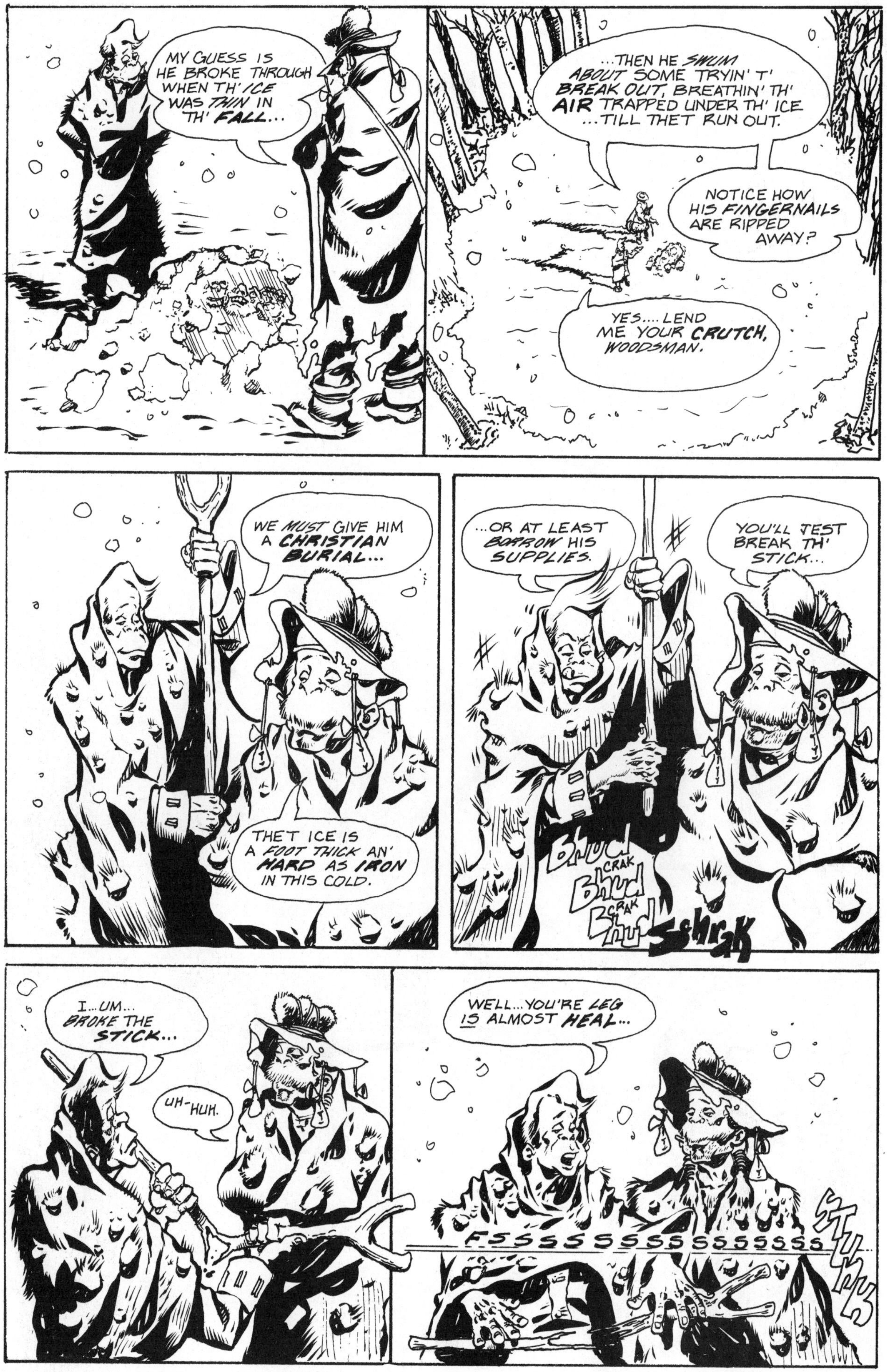
MY GUESS IS HE BROKE THROUGH WHEN TH' ICE WAS THIN IN TH' FALL...
...THEN HE SWUM ABOUT SOME TRYIN' T' BREAK OUT, BREATHIN' TH' AIR TRAPPED UNDER TH' ICE ...TILL THET RUN OUT.
NOTICE HOW HIS FINGERNAILS ARE RIPPED AWAY?
YES.... LEND ME YOUR CRUTCH, WOODSMAN.
WE MUST GIVE HIM A CHRISTIAN BURIAL...
THET ICE IS A FOOT THICK AN' HARD AS IRON IN THIS COLD.
...OR AT LEAST BORROW HIS SUPPLIES.
YOU'LL JEST BREAK TH' STICK...
Bhud
CRAK
Bhud
CRAK
Bhud
SCHRAK
I...UM... BROKE THE STICK...
UH-HUH.
WELL...YOU'RE LEG IS ALMOST HEAL...
FSSSSSSSSSSSSSSSSSS
STUMP

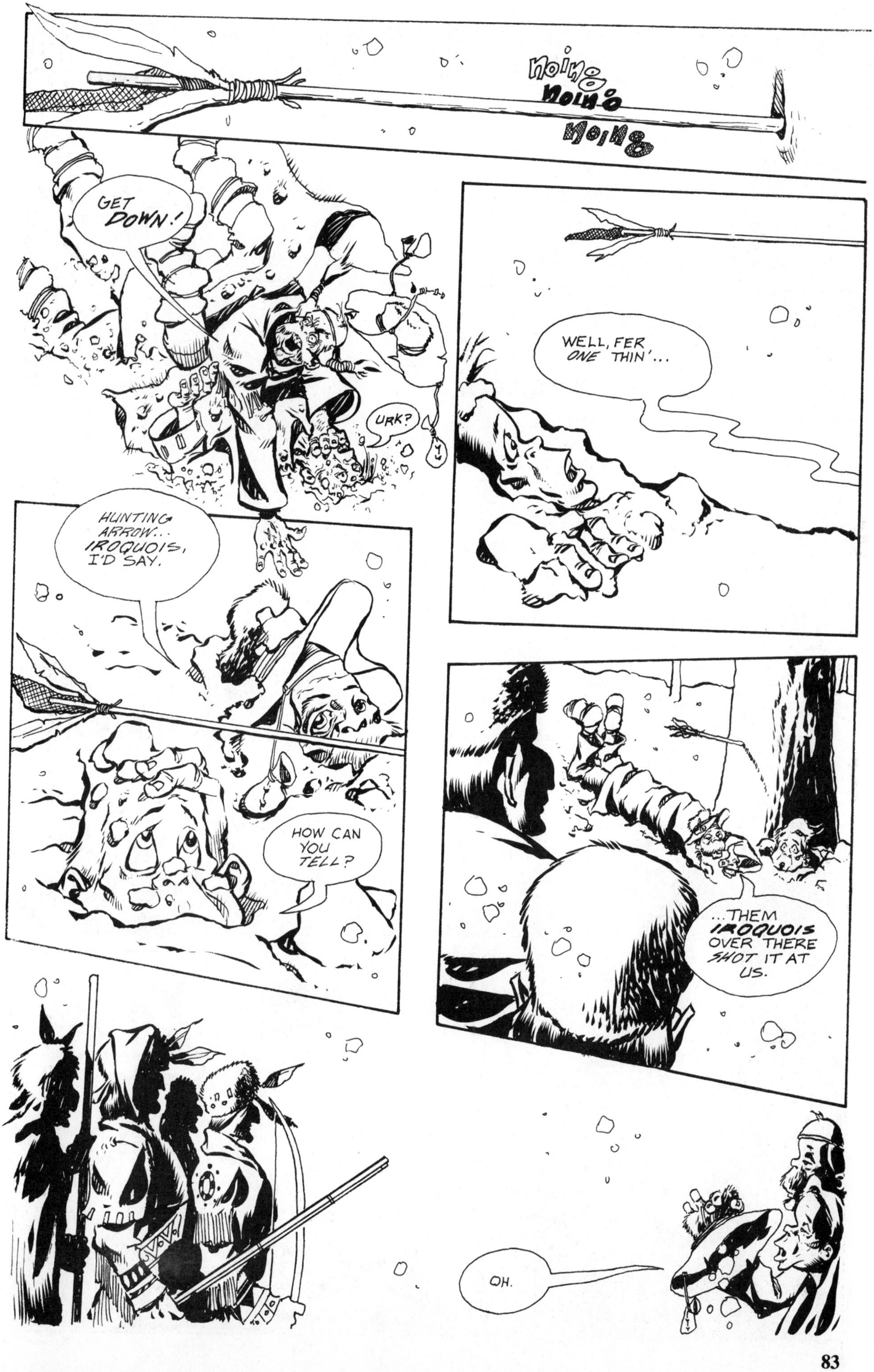
NOING NOING NOING
GET DOWN!
URK?
WELL, FER ONE THIN'...
HUNTING ARROW... IROQUOIS, I'D SAY.
HOW CAN YOU TELL?
...THEM IROQUOIS OVER THERE SHOT IT AT US.
OH.

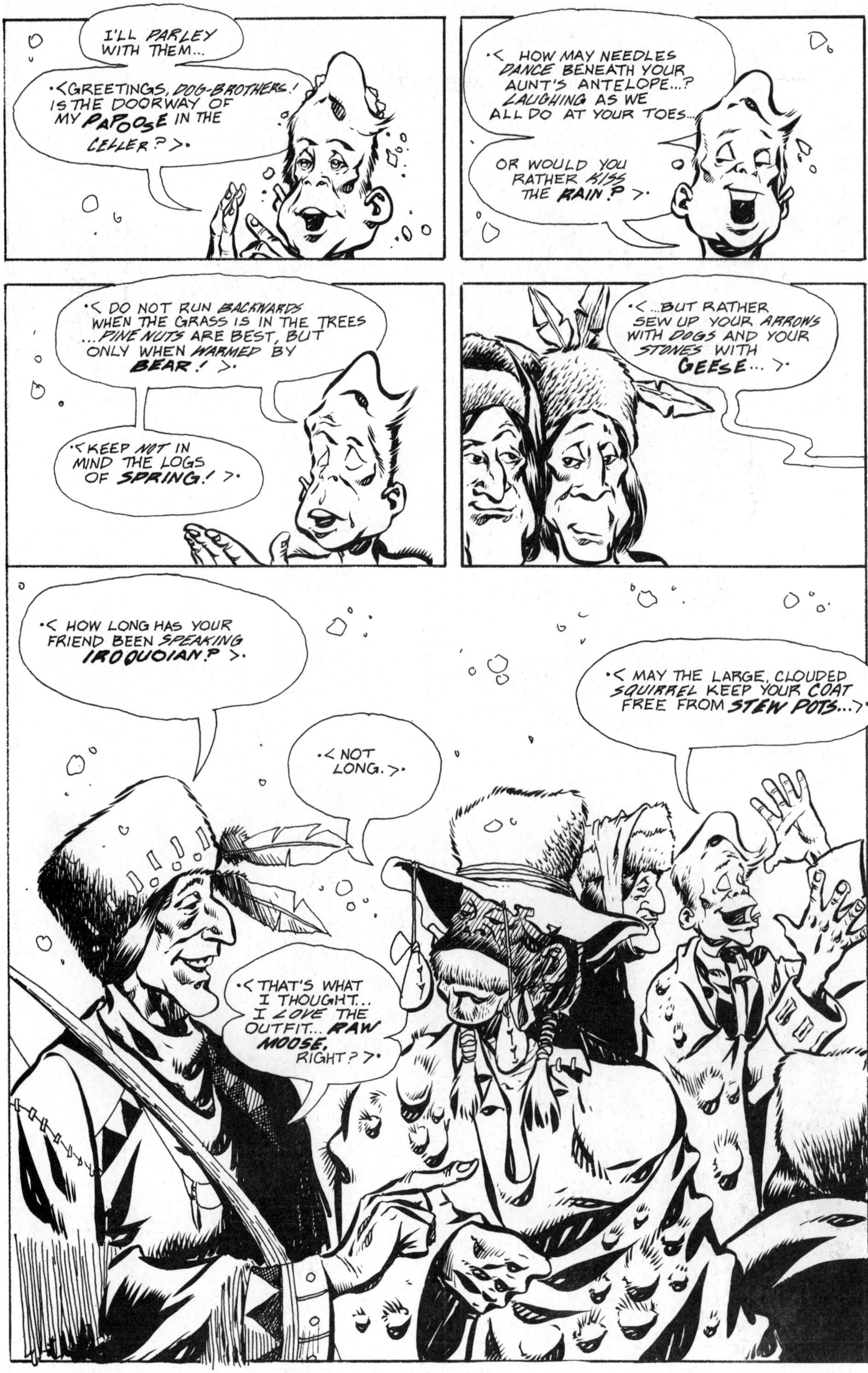
I'LL PARLEY WITH THEM...
•<GREETINGS, DOG-BROTHERS! IS THE DOORWAY OF MY PAPOOSE IN THE CELLER?>•
•< HOW MAY NEEDLES DANCE BENEATH YOUR AUNT'S ANTELOPE...? LAUGHING AS WE ALL DO AT YOUR TOES...
OR WOULD YOU RATHER KISS THE RAIN? >•
•< DO NOT RUN BACKWARDS WHEN THE GRASS IS IN THE TREES ...PINE NUTS ARE BEST, BUT ONLY WHEN WARMED BY BEAR! >•
•<KEEP NOT IN MIND THE LOGS OF SPRING! >•
•< ...BUT RATHER SEW UP YOUR ARROWS WITH DOGS AND YOUR STONES WITH GEESE... >•
•< HOW LONG HAS YOUR FRIEND BEEN SPEAKING IROQUOIAN? >•
•< NOT LONG. >•
•< MAY THE LARGE, CLOUDED SQUIRREL KEEP YOUR COAT FREE FROM STEW POTS...>•
•< THAT'S WHAT I THOUGHT... I LOVE THE OUTFIT... RAW MOOSE, RIGHT? >•

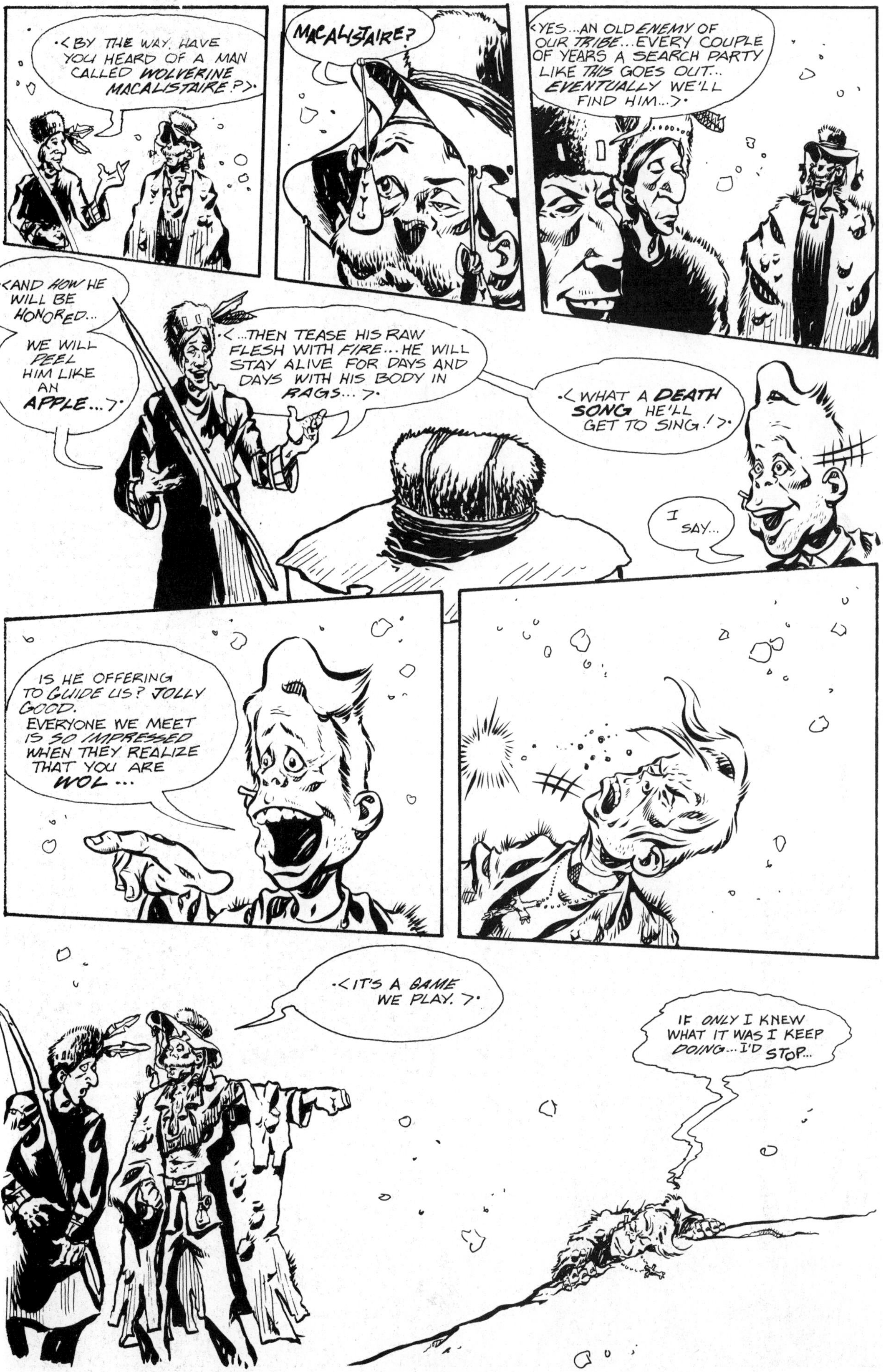
<BY THE WAY, HAVE YOU HEARD OF A MAN CALLED WOLVERINE MACALISTAIRE?>
MACALISTAIRE?
<YES... AN OLD ENEMY OF OUR TRIBE... EVERY COUPLE OF YEARS A SEARCH PARTY LIKE THIS GOES OUT... EVENTUALLY WE'LL FIND HIM...>
<AND HOW HE WILL BE HONORED...
WE WILL PEEL HIM LIKE AN APPLE...>
<...THEN TEASE HIS RAW FLESH WITH FIRE... HE WILL STAY ALIVE FOR DAYS AND DAYS WITH HIS BODY IN RAGS...>
<WHAT A DEATH SONG HE'LL GET TO SING!>
I SAY...
IS HE OFFERING TO GUIDE US? JOLLY GOOD. EVERYONE WE MEET IS SO IMPRESSED WHEN THEY REALIZE THAT YOU ARE WOL...
<IT'S A GAME WE PLAY.>
IF ONLY I KNEW WHAT IT WAS I KEEP DOING... I'D STOP...

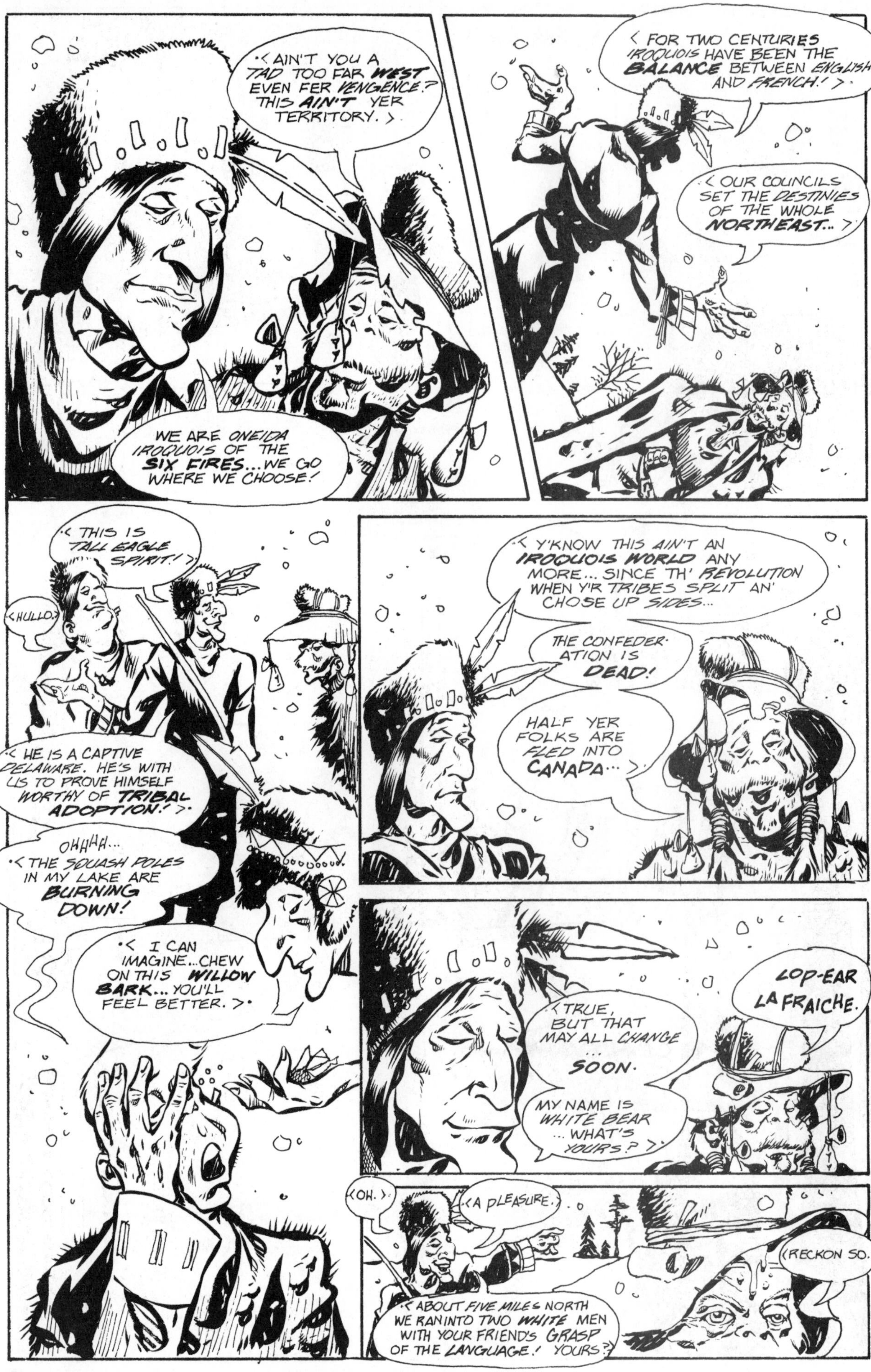

< AIN'T YOU A TAD TOO FAR WEST EVEN FER VENGENCE? THIS AIN'T YER TERRITORY. >
WE ARE ONEIDA IROQUOIS OF THE SIX FIRES... WE GO WHERE WE CHOOSE!
< FOR TWO CENTURIES IROQUOIS HAVE BEEN THE BALANCE BETWEEN ENGLISH AND FRENCH! >
< OUR COUNCILS SET THE DESTINIES OF THE WHOLE NORTHEAST... >
< THIS IS TALL EAGLE SPIRIT! >
<HULLO.>
< HE IS A CAPTIVE DELAWARE. HE'S WITH US TO PROVE HIMSELF WORTHY OF TRIBAL ADOPTION! >
OHHHH...
< THE SQUASH POLES IN MY LAKE ARE BURNING DOWN!
< I CAN IMAGINE... CHEW ON THIS WILLOW BARK... YOU'LL FEEL BETTER. >
< Y'KNOW THIS AIN'T AN IROQUOIS WORLD ANY MORE... SINCE TH' REVOLUTION WHEN Y'R TRIBES SPLIT AN' CHOSE UP SIDES...
THE CONFEDERATION IS DEAD!
HALF YER FOLKS ARE FLED INTO CANADA... >
< TRUE, BUT THAT MAY ALL CHANGE ... SOON.
MY NAME IS WHITE BEAR ... WHAT'S YOURS? >
LOP-EAR LA FRAICHE.
< OH. >
< A PLEASURE. >
< RECKON SO. >
< ABOUT FIVE MILES NORTH WE RAN INTO TWO WHITE MEN WITH YOUR FRIEND'S GRASP OF THE LANGUAGE! YOURS? >

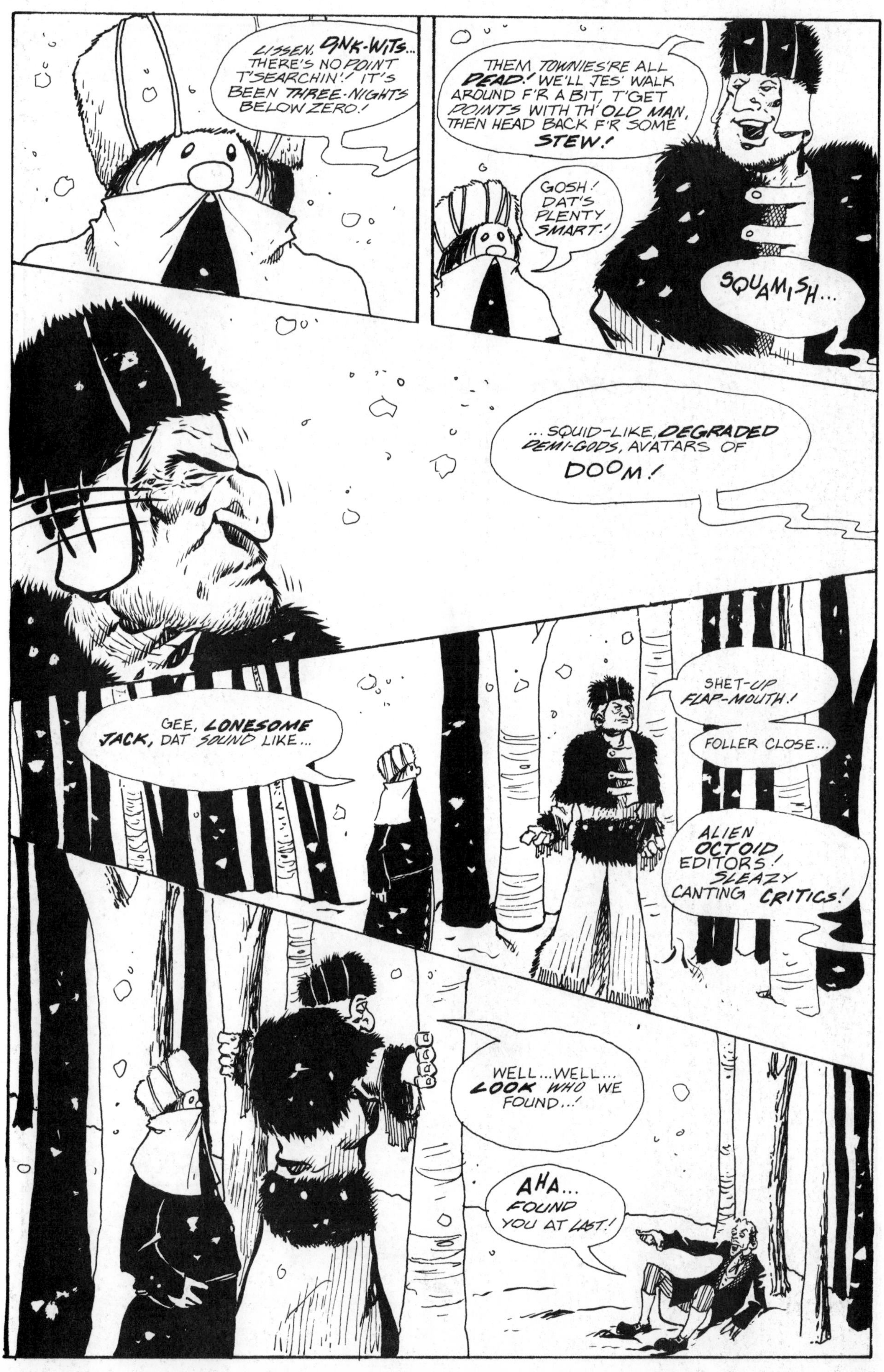
LISSEN, DINK-WITS... THERE'S NO POINT T'SEARCHIN'! IT'S BEEN THREE-NIGHTS BELOW ZERO!
THEM TOWNIES'RE ALL DEAD! WE'LL JES' WALK AROUND F'R A BIT, T'GET POINTS WITH TH' OLD MAN, THEN HEAD BACK F'R SOME STEW!
GOSH! DAT'S PLENTY SMART!
SQUAMISH...
...SQUID-LIKE, DEGRADED DEMI-GODS, AVATARS OF DOOM!
GEE, LONESOME JACK, DAT SOUND LIKE...
SHET-UP FLAP-MOUTH!
FOLLER CLOSE...
ALIEN OCTOID EDITORS! SLEAZY CANTING CRITICS!
WELL...WELL... LOOK WHO WE FOUND...!
AHA... FOUND YOU AT LAST!

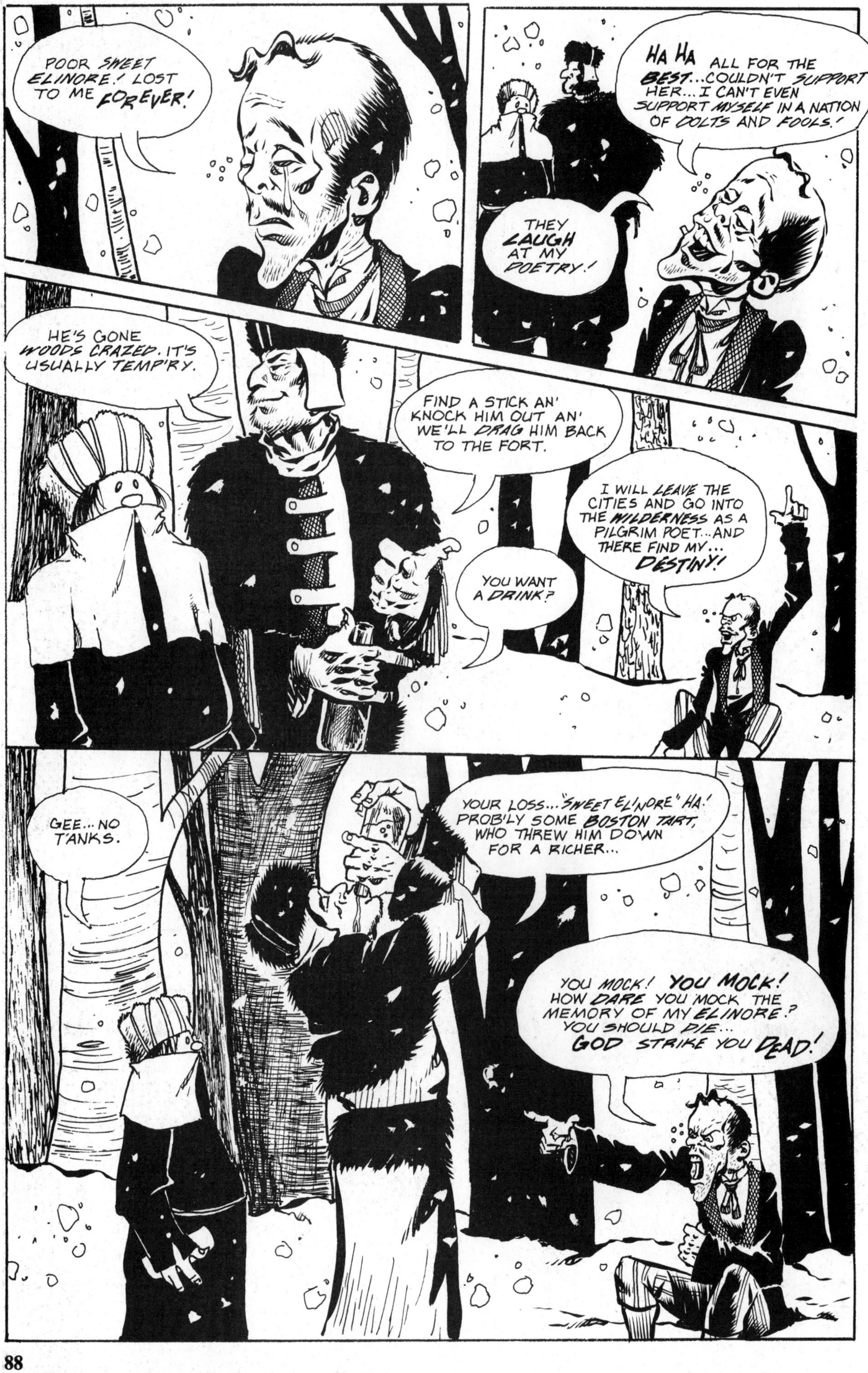
POOR SWEET ELINORE! LOST TO ME FOREVER!
HA HA ALL FOR THE BEST...COULDN'T SUPPORT HER...I CAN'T EVEN SUPPORT MYSELF IN A NATION OF DOLTS AND FOOLS!
THEY LAUGH AT MY POETRY!
HE'S GONE WOODS CRAZED. IT'S USUALLY TEMP'RY.
FIND A STICK AN' KNOCK HIM OUT AN' WE'LL DRAG HIM BACK TO THE FORT.
I WILL LEAVE THE CITIES AND GO INTO THE WILDERNESS AS A PILGRIM POET...AND THERE FIND MY... DESTINY!
YOU WANT A DRINK?
GEE...NO TANKS.
YOUR LOSS..."SWEET EL'NORE" HA! PROB'LY SOME BOSTON TART, WHO THREW HIM DOWN FOR A RICHER...
YOU MOCK! YOU MOCK! HOW DARE YOU MOCK THE MEMORY OF MY ELINORE? YOU SHOULD DIE... GOD STRIKE YOU DEAD!

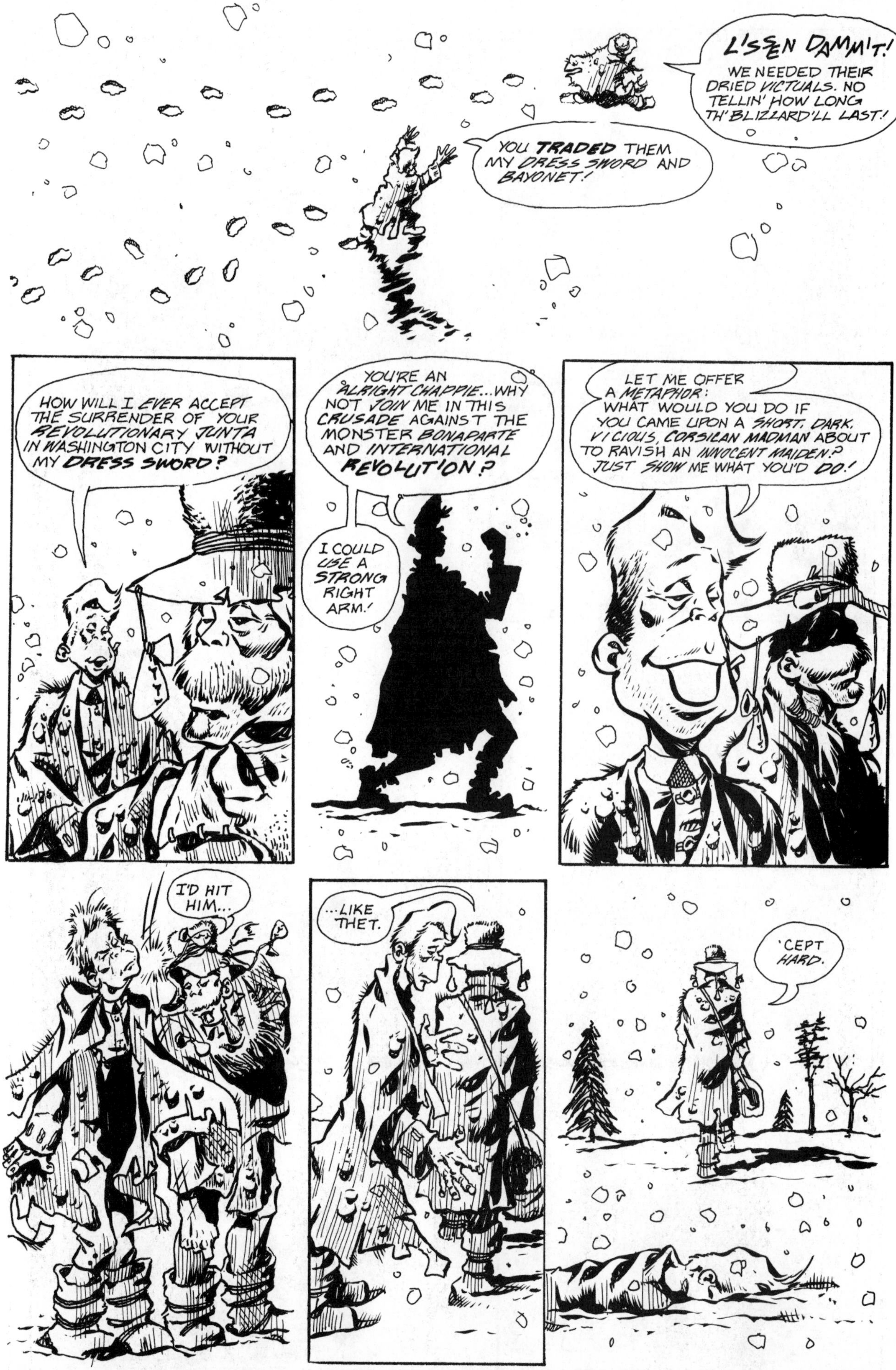
L'ISSEN DAMMIT!
WE NEEDED THEIR DRIED VICTUALS. NO TELLIN' HOW LONG TH' BLIZZARD'LL LAST!
YOU TRADED THEM MY DRESS SWORD AND BAYONET!
HOW WILL I EVER ACCEPT THE SURRENDER OF YOUR REVOLUTIONARY JUNTA IN WASHINGTON CITY WITHOUT MY DRESS SWORD?
YOU'RE AN ALRIGHT CHAPPIE...WHY NOT JOIN ME IN THIS CRUSADE AGAINST THE MONSTER BONAPARTE AND INTERNATIONAL REVOLUTION?
I COULD USE A STRONG RIGHT ARM!
LET ME OFFER A METAPHOR: WHAT WOULD YOU DO IF YOU CAME UPON A SHORT, DARK, VICIOUS, CORSICAN MADMAN ABOUT TO RAVISH AN INNOCENT MAIDEN? JUST SHOW ME WHAT YOU'D DO!
I'D HIT HIM...
...LIKE THET.
'CEPT HARD.

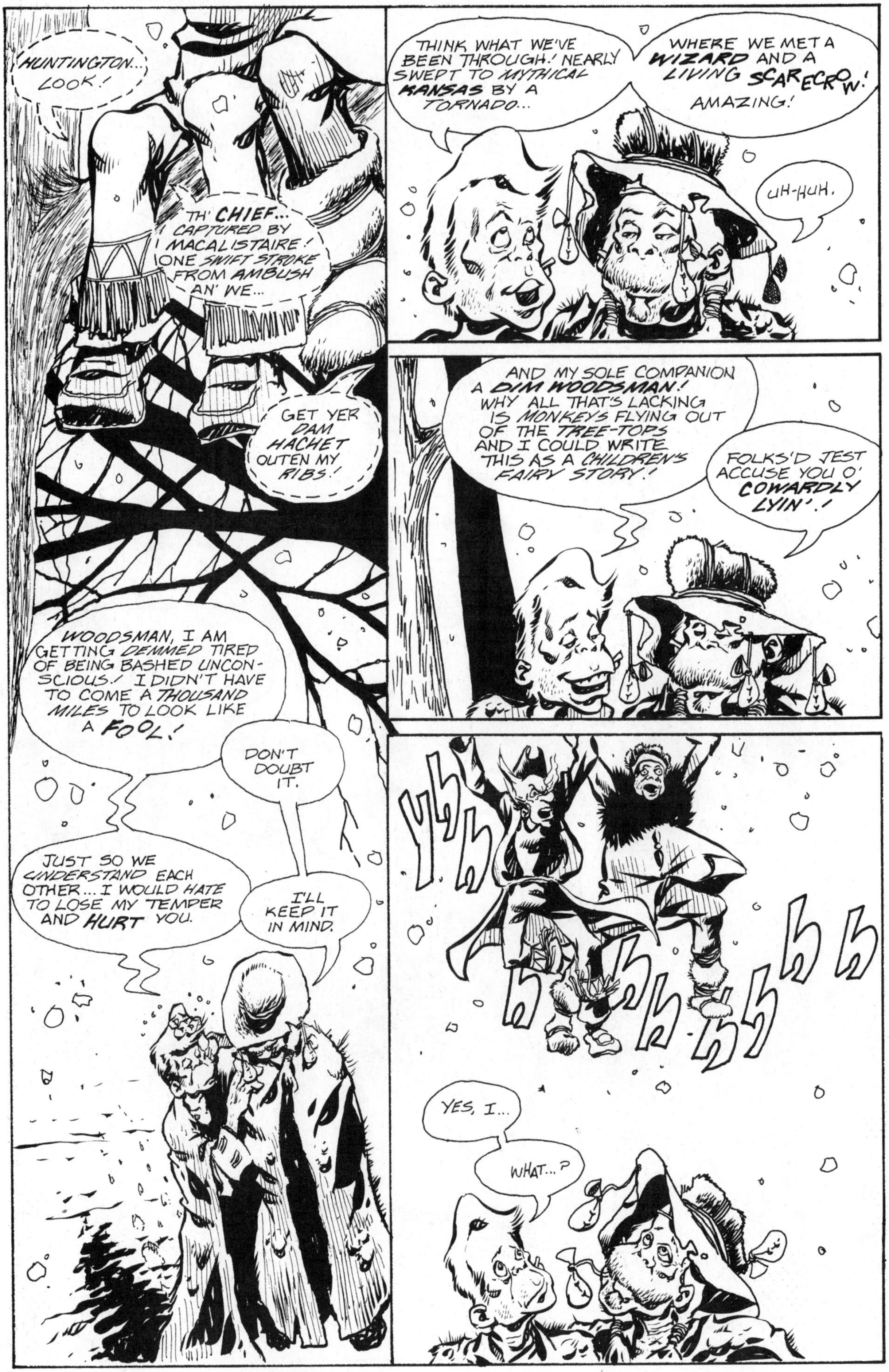

HUNTINGTON... LOOK!
TH' CHIEF... CAPTURED BY MACALISTAIRE! ONE SWIFT STROKE FROM AMBUSH AN' WE...
GET YER DAM HACHET OUTEN MY RIBS!
THINK WHAT WE'VE BEEN THROUGH! NEARLY SWEPT TO MYTHICAL KANSAS BY A TORNADO...
WHERE WE MET A WIZARD AND A LIVING SCARECROW! AMAZING!
UH-HUH.
AND MY SOLE COMPANION A DIM WOODSMAN! WHY ALL THAT'S LACKING IS MONKEYS FLYING OUT OF THE TREE-TOPS AND I COULD WRITE THIS AS A CHILDREN'S FAIRY STORY!
FOLKS'D JEST ACCUSE YOU O' COWARDLY LYIN'!
WOODSMAN, I AM GETTING DEMMED TIRED OF BEING BASHED UNCONSCIOUS! I DIDN'T HAVE TO COME A THOUSAND MILES TO LOOK LIKE A FOOL!
DON'T DOUBT IT.
JUST SO WE UNDERSTAND EACH OTHER... I WOULD HATE TO LOSE MY TEMPER AND HURT YOU.
I'LL KEEP IT IN MIND.
YES, I...
WHAT...?

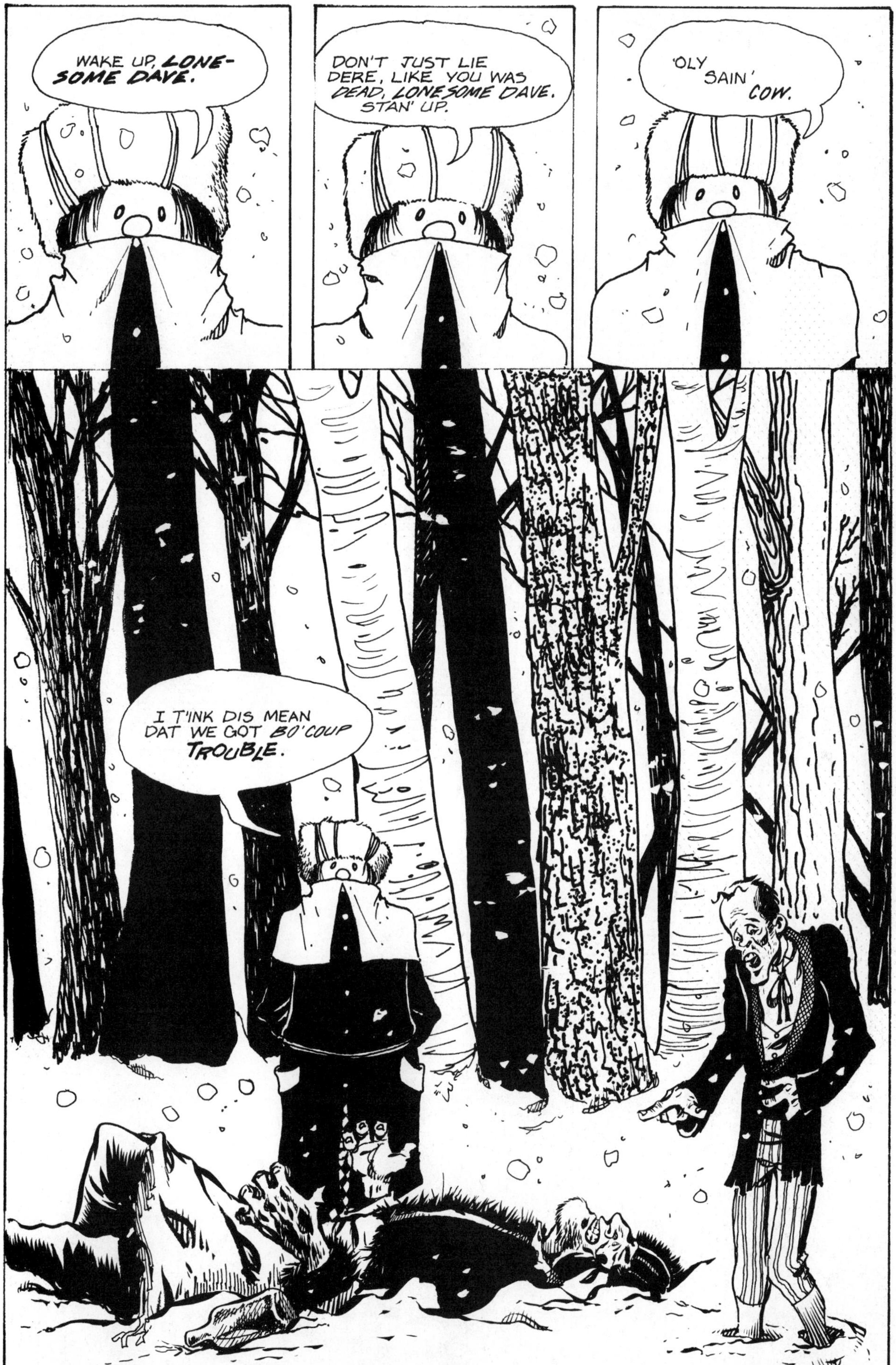
WAKE UP, LONE-SOME DAVE.
DON'T JUST LIE DERE, LIKE YOU WAS DEAD, LONESOME DAVE. STAN' UP.
'OLY SAIN' COW.
I T'INK DIS MEAN DAT WE GOT BO'COUP TROUBLE.

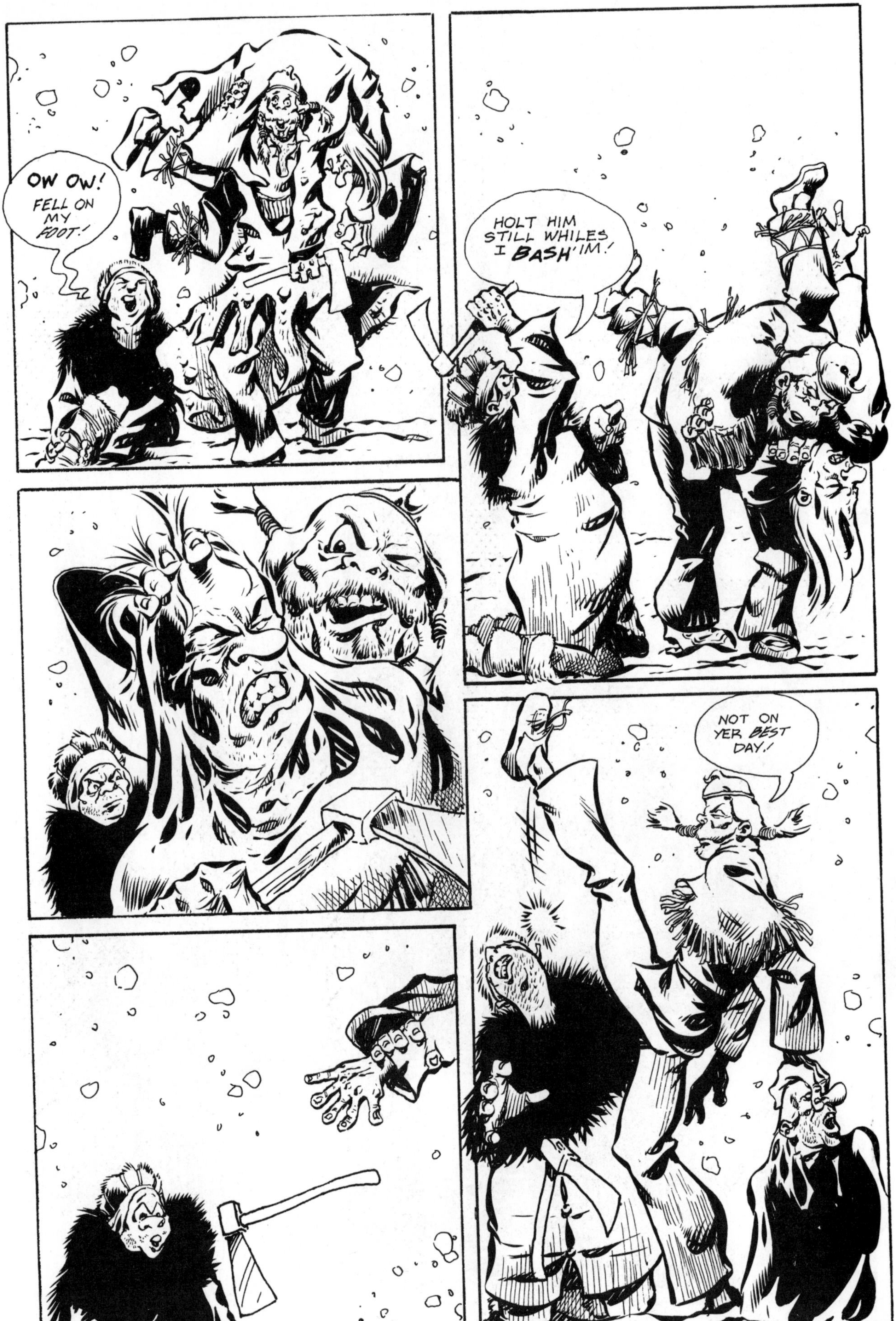
OW OW! FELL ON MY FOOT!
HOLT HIM STILL WHILES I BASH'IM!
NOT ON YER BEST DAY!

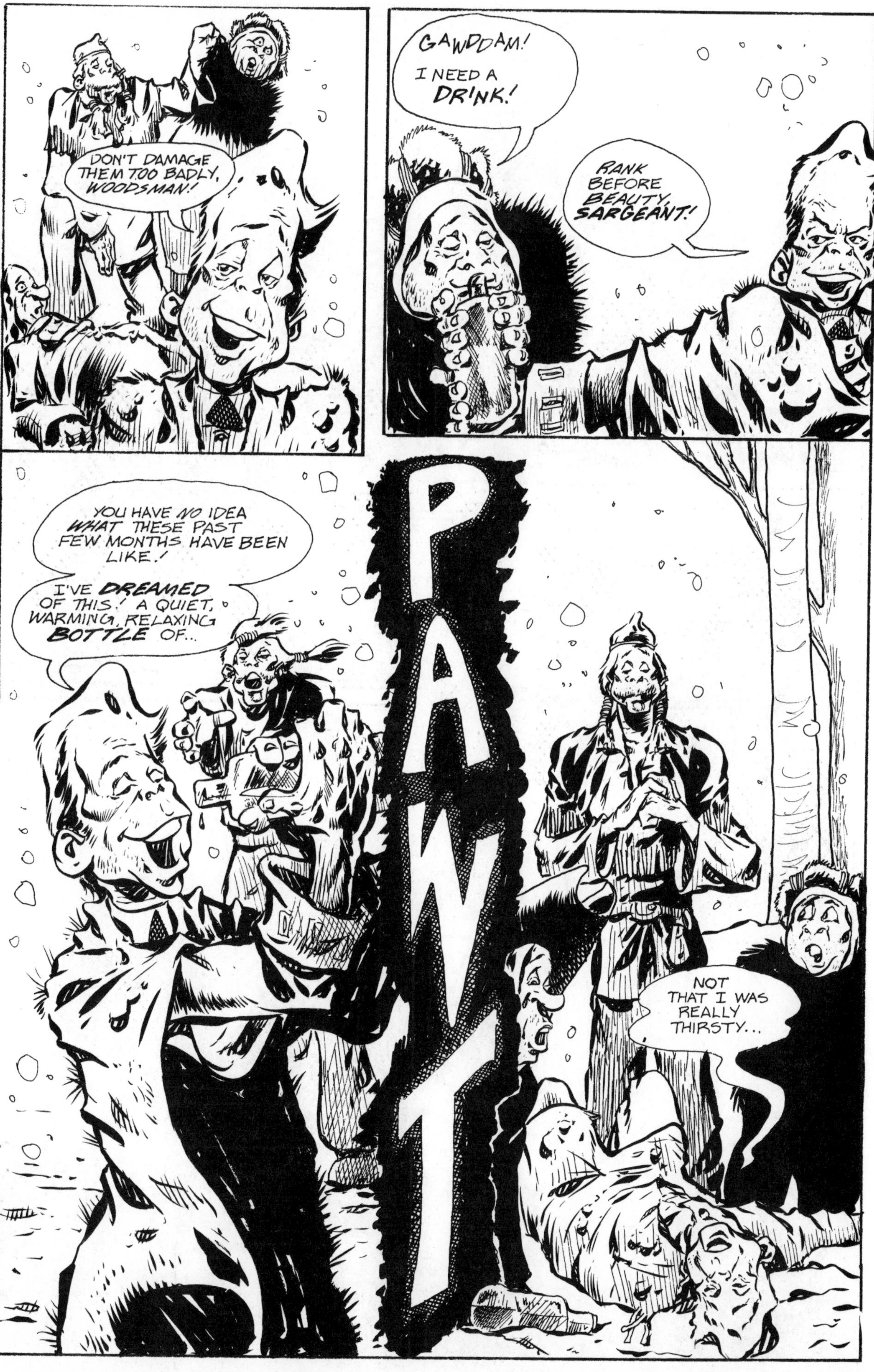
DON'T DAMAGE THEM TOO BADLY, WOODSMAN!
GAWDDAM!
I NEED A DRINK!
RANK BEFORE BEAUTY, SARGEANT!
YOU HAVE NO IDEA WHAT THESE PAST FEW MONTHS HAVE BEEN LIKE!
I'VE DREAMED OF THIS! A QUIET, WARMING, RELAXING BOTTLE OF...
PAWT
NOT THAT I WAS REALLY THIRSTY...

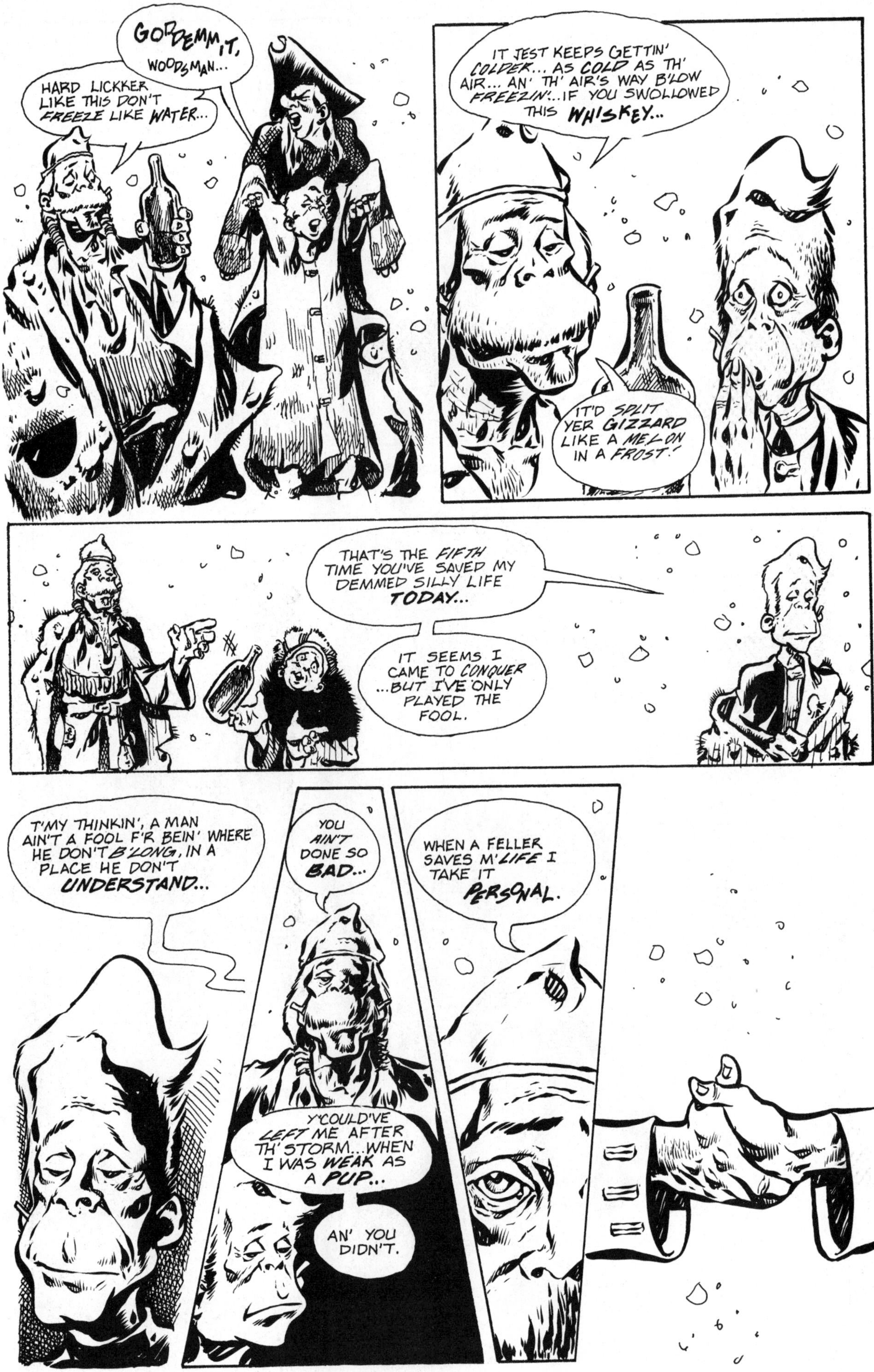
HARD LICKKER LIKE THIS DON'T FREEZE LIKE WATER...
GODDEMMIT, WOODSMAN...
IT JEST KEEPS GETTIN' COLDER... AS COLD AS TH' AIR... AN' TH' AIR'S WAY B'LOW FREEZIN'... IF YOU SWOLLOWED THIS WHISKEY...
IT'D SPLIT YER GIZZARD LIKE A MELON IN A FROST!
THAT'S THE FIFTH TIME YOU'VE SAVED MY DEMMED SILLY LIFE TODAY...
IT SEEMS I CAME TO CONQUER ...BUT I'VE ONLY PLAYED THE FOOL.
T'MY THINKIN', A MAN AIN'T A FOOL F'R BEIN' WHERE HE DON'T B'LONG, IN A PLACE HE DON'T UNDERSTAND...
YOU AIN'T DONE SO BAD...
Y'COULD'VE LEFT ME AFTER TH' STORM... WHEN I WAS WEAK AS A PUP...
AN' YOU DIDN'T.
WHEN A FELLER SAVES M'LIFE I TAKE IT PERSONAL.

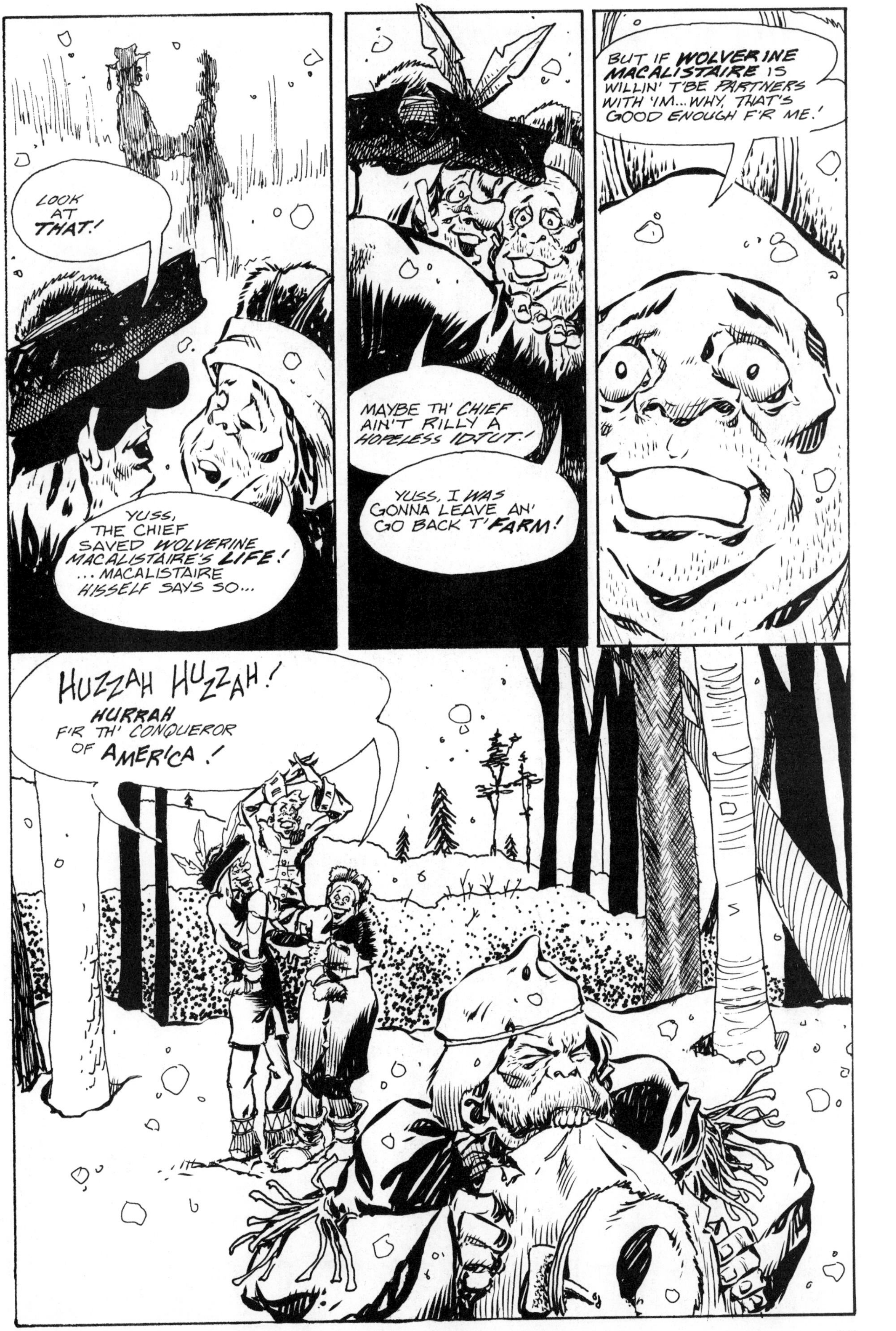
LOOK AT THAT!
YUSS, THE CHIEF SAVED WOLVERINE MACALISTAIRE'S LIFE! ...MACALISTAIRE HISSELF SAYS SO...
MAYBE TH' CHIEF AIN'T RILLY A HOPELESS IDJUT!
YUSS, I WAS GONNA LEAVE AN' GO BACK T' FARM!
BUT IF WOLVERINE MACALISTAIRE IS WILLIN' T'BE PARTNERS WITH 'IM... WHY, THAT'S GOOD ENOUGH F'R ME!
HUZZAH HUZZAH! HURRAH F'R TH' CONQUEROR OF AMERICA!

EPILOGUE... Chapter Nine "Partners."

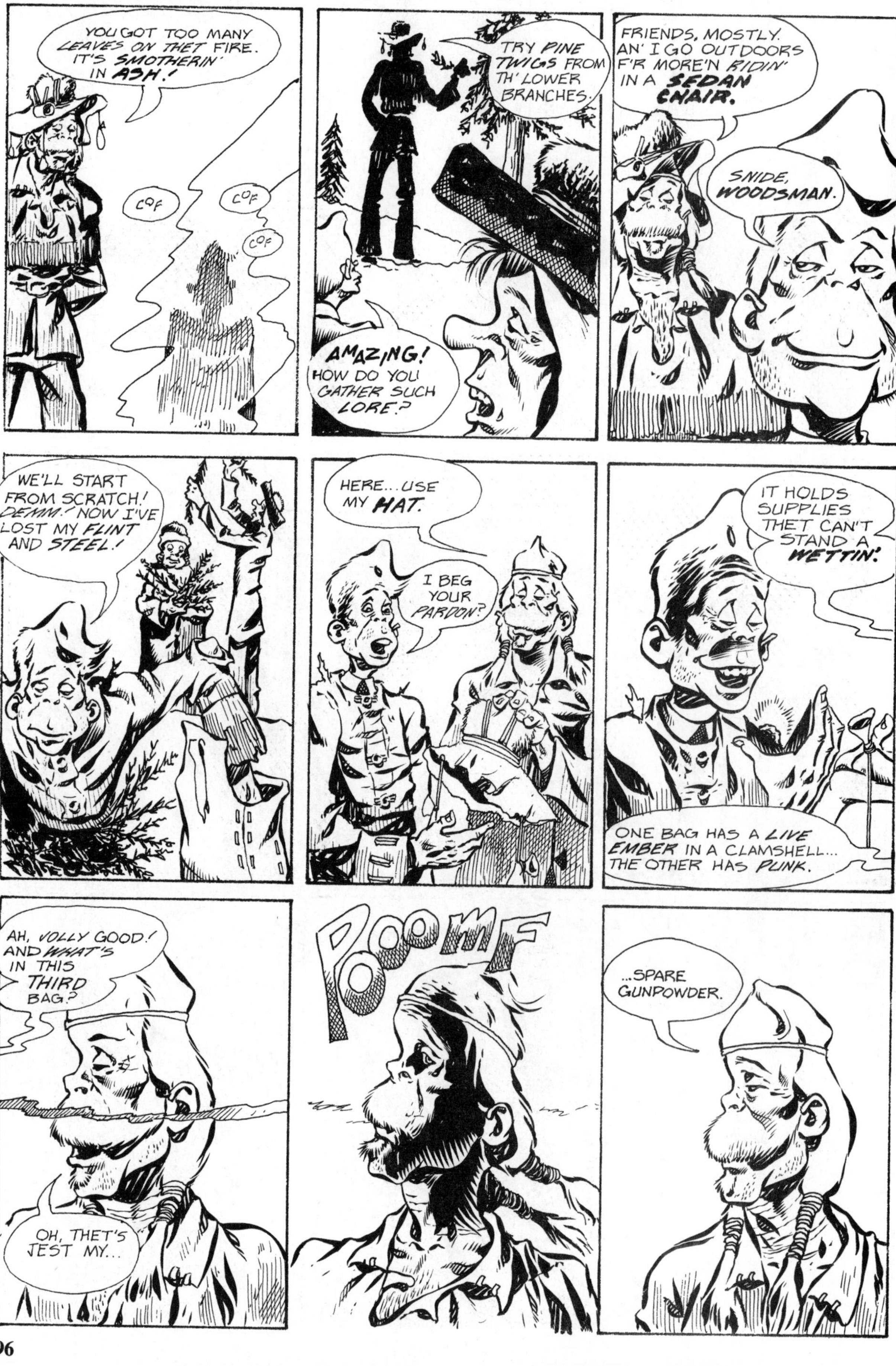

YOU GOT TOO MANY LEAVES ON THET FIRE. IT'S SMOTHERIN' IN ASH!
COF
COF
COF
TRY PINE TWIGS FROM TH' LOWER BRANCHES.
AMAZING! HOW DO YOU GATHER SUCH LORE?
FRIENDS, MOSTLY. AN' I GO OUTDOORS F'R MORE'N RIDIN' IN A SEDAN CHAIR.
SNIDE, WOODSMAN.
WE'LL START FROM SCRATCH! DEMM! NOW I'VE LOST MY FLINT AND STEEL!
HERE... USE MY HAT.
I BEG YOUR PARDON?
IT HOLDS SUPPLIES THET CAN'T STAND A WETTIN'.
ONE BAG HAS A LIVE EMBER IN A CLAMSHELL... THE OTHER HAS PUNK.
AH, VOLLY GOOD! AND WHAT'S IN THIS THIRD BAG?
OH, THET'S JEST MY...
POOOMF
...SPARE GUNPOWDER.

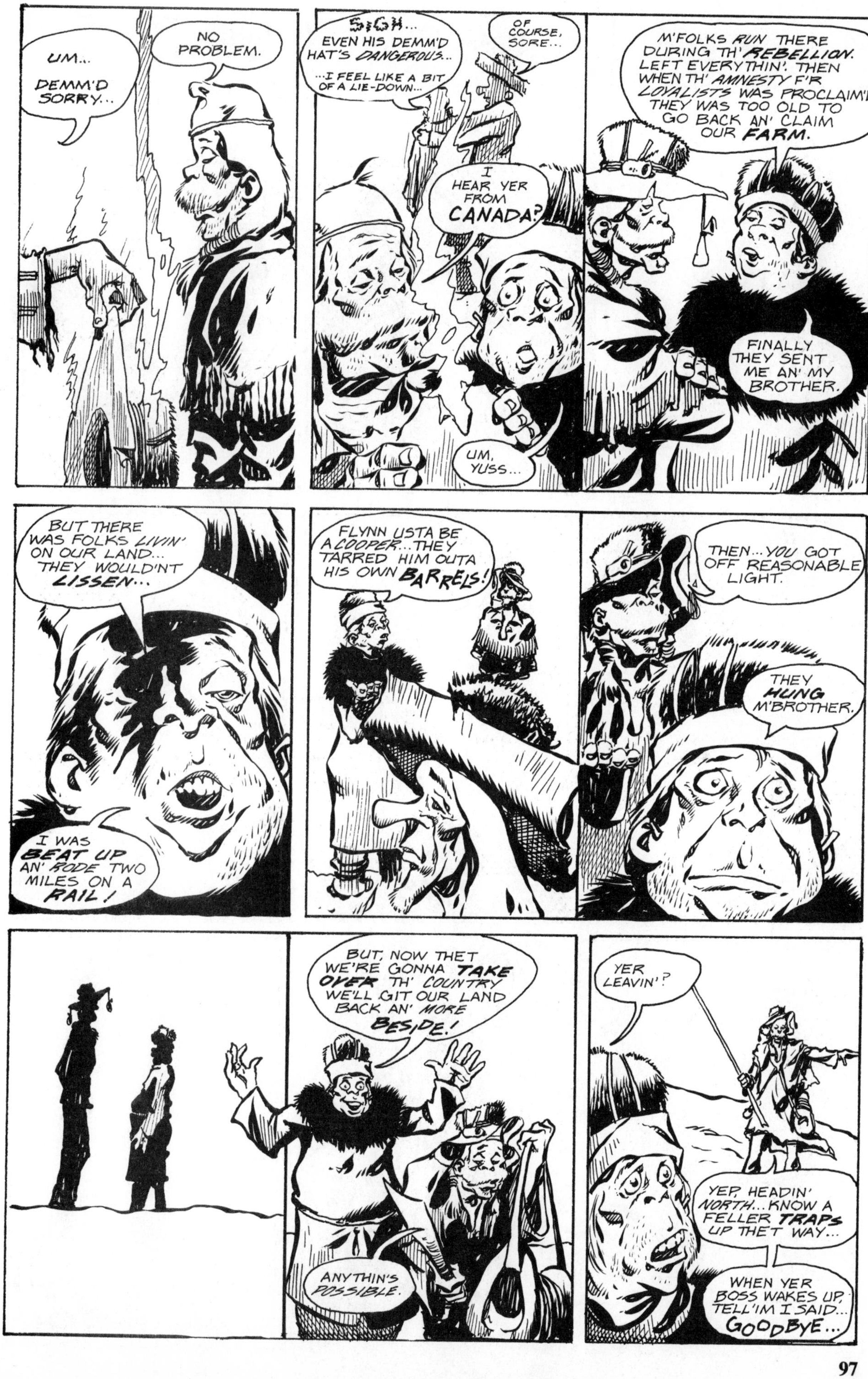
UM... DEMM'D SORRY...
NO PROBLEM.
SIGH... EVEN HIS DEMM'D HAT'S DANGEROUS...
...I FEEL LIKE A BIT OF A LIE-DOWN...
OF COURSE, SORE...
I HEAR YER FROM CANADA?
UM, YUSS...
M'FOLKS RUN THERE DURING TH' REBELLION. LEFT EVERYTHIN'. THEN WHEN TH' AMNESTY F'R LOYALISTS WAS PROCLAIM'D THEY WAS TOO OLD TO GO BACK AN' CLAIM OUR FARM.
FINALLY THEY SENT ME AN' MY BROTHER.
BUT THERE WAS FOLKS LIVIN' ON OUR LAND... THEY WOULDN'T LISSEN...
I WAS BEAT UP AN' RODE TWO MILES ON A RAIL!
FLYNN USTA BE A COOPER... THEY TARRED HIM OUTA HIS OWN BARRELS!
THEN... YOU GOT OFF REASONABLE LIGHT.
THEY HUNG M'BROTHER.
BUT, NOW THET WE'RE GONNA TAKE OVER TH' COUNTRY WE'LL GIT OUR LAND BACK AN' MORE BESIDE!
ANYTHIN'S POSSIBLE.
YER LEAVIN'?
YEP, HEADIN' NORTH... KNOW A FELLER TRAPS UP THET WAY...
WHEN YER BOSS WAKES UP, TELL'IM I SAID... GOODBYE...

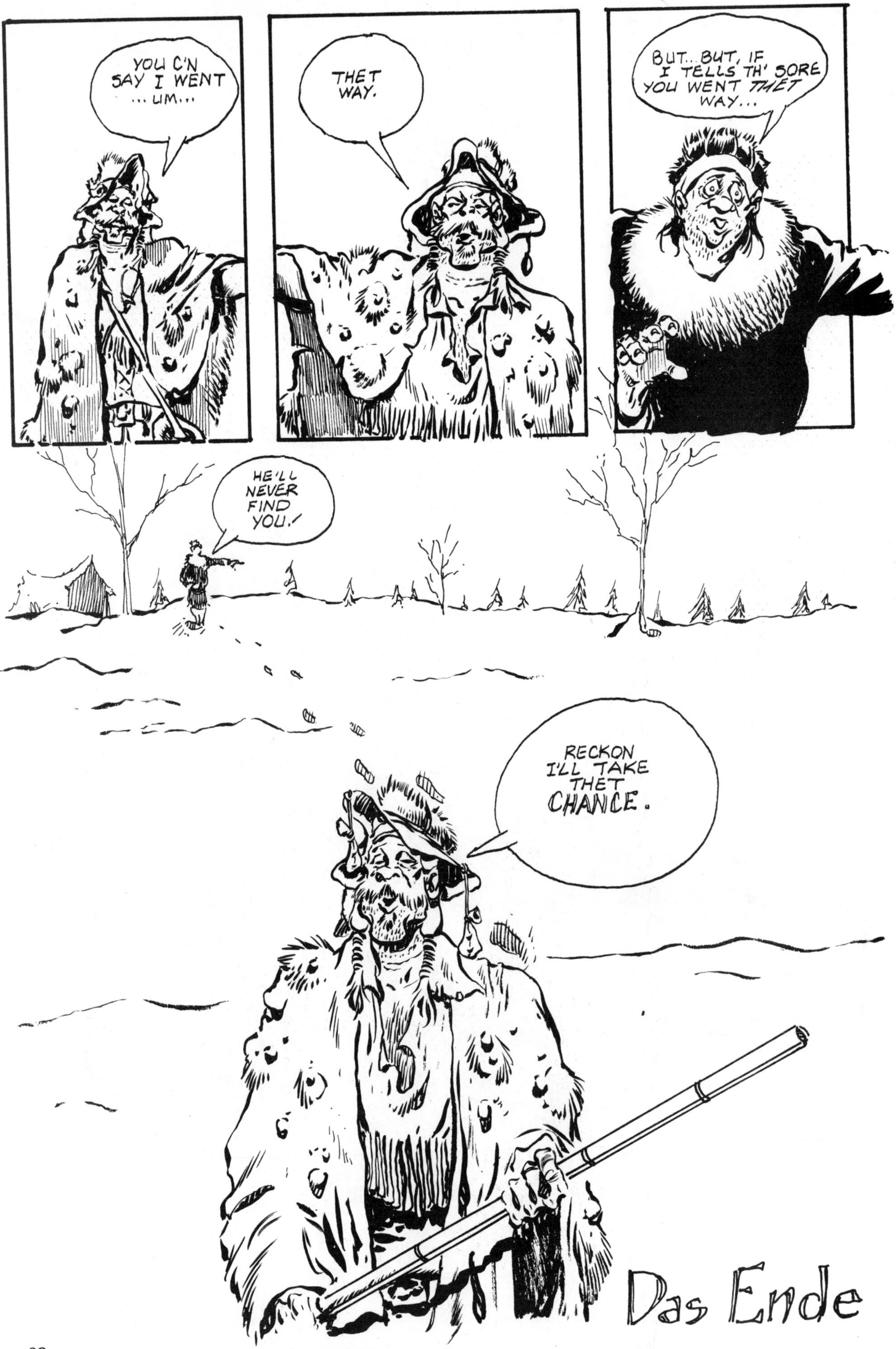
YOU C'N SAY I WENT ...UM...
THET WAY.
BUT... BUT, IF I TELLS TH' SORE YOU WENT THET WAY...
HE'LL NEVER FIND YOU!
RECKON I'LL TAKE THET CHANCE.
Das Ende